Roads to Rome: Being Personal Records of Some of the More Recent Converts to the Catholic Faith

John Godfrey Raupert

BIBLIOLIFE

ROADS TO ROME

BEING

PERSONAL RECORDS OF SOME OF THE MORE RECENT CONVERTS TO THE CATHOLIC FAITH

WITH AN INTRODUCTION

BY

HIS EMINENCE CARDINAL VAUGHAN

ARCHBISHOP OF WESTMINSTER

COMPILED AND EDITED

BY

THE AUTHOR OF "TEN YEARS IN ANGLICAN ORDERS"

LONGMANS, GREEN, AND CO.
39 PATERNOSTER ROW, LONDON
NEW YORK AND BOMBAY
1901

INTRODUCTION

THIS unpretending volume is full of interest and personal incident. Both psychologically and religiously the accounts, written independently by sixty-five men and women of education, of their return to the Catholic Church, will naturally excite attention, as they will certainly call forth many and diverse reflections.

The fact of the existence of any religious conviction, capable of creating in men's minds, one after another, and quite independently of each other, a revolution involving the greatest losses in the natural order and oftentimes the most acute personal agony, challenges the attention of the most languid as it does of the worldly. It is a practical declaration that there are people who really live upon a belief and a hope in the invisible, and who count all as dross to win Christ.

Then there are hundreds of thousands all round us, lay and clerical, men and women, who feel that the foundations of Protestantism have broken down under them ; who are secretly asking themselves whether there be any solid and divinely inspired religion ; who are half and more than half convinced of the claim of the old Church to their submission. Many of these will eagerly peruse and examine a book full of such personal experiences, in the expectation of obtaining useful and instructive information.

There will also be others who will make it their business to throw discredit on everything that points towards Rome. It is easy to foresee many of the criticisms they will level against a book like this. But the answer is : The book must not be taken to be what it is not, and what it does not profess to be.

First, it is not a full and exhaustive consecutive narrative or argument. It is rather a collection of indications, suggestions, reminiscences, and facts. It is a miscellany of episodes, of phases of thought, all ending in the same conclusion. It is a book of sketches of many minds in their search after Divine truth.

It stands to reason that a perfect and adequate history of the individual lives of nearly seventy persons, widely differing in character and antecedents, could not be compassed within a small volume of 350 pages.

To take such a step as that of becoming a Catholic may seem to be a very simple process ; and so it is, if by this is meant merely the last step, the last act of reception into the Church. But, before a person reaches this last step, he has spent perhaps a lifetime, sensibly or insensibly, alternately advancing and standing still, balancing, doubting, inquiring. His moral nature and his intellectual, his prejudices and his instincts, his whole life and character, have been subjected, perhaps imperceptibly, to the gentle action of a long period of growth.

He may, indeed, have been affected and driven by a single argument, by a single line of thought, so strongly and visibly, that in any brief record he may have to pen, this comes uppermost and stands out alone. But he cannot publicly take into account, he cannot portray, all the subtle growth of his intellectual, moral, and spiritual life. The conviction and the last step come as the formal conclusion to much that no man can accurately and fully describe. Hence there must always be many forces and arguments that are absent and wanting to such narratives as those contained in this book. And many a man will say, after he has perused the ablest of them, " I am not satisfied by So-and-so's account of himself—that is, it does not convince me." Of course it does not, for he was unable to tell you all ; there is a long, a deep, a minute history that is lacking, simply because space and time and ability do not admit of the reproduction of a soul's inner life, which is the real field upon which the grace of God has been secretly working for years.

Lord Brampton, who is perhaps the most widely known contributor to this book, seems to illustrate what I am saying in the few lines he has written. So careful and judicial a mind as his, with his long experience and facility in summing up, dismisses the question, " Why I became a Catholic?" in a dozen lines. To reason out such a matter in a manner thoroughly satisfactory to himself would require, he says, much more time and care and space than were at his immediate command. A particular argument might be easily stated, but the accumulative argument, made up of a thousand converging experiences and convictions, which carries the whole soul with it, is not to be set forth within a few pages, even by the ablest of Judges. He, therefore, with characteristic directness, contents himself with saying, " I have unwavering satisfaction in the conclusion at which I have arrived, and my conscience tells me it is right."

Finally, some persons may expect to find the gift of Faith within the covers of this volume. They will be disappointed. They will not find it within any volume, not even within the volume of the Gospels. Divine Faith is a supernatural gift. It is as direct a gift of God as the created human soul. The latter is never created until certain definite antecedent conditions have been laid by man ; and the former is never bestowed until man has fulfilled the conditions required for the reception of the gift of Faith. These conditions are ordinarily : correspondence with God's light and invitation, prayer, humility, and self-denial. " If any man will come after Me, *abneget semetipsum.*"

The present volume is an unconscious record of the fulfilment of such conditions.

HERBERT, CARDINAL VAUGHAN,
Archbishop of Westminster.

LIST OF CONTRIBUTORS

The Rev. GEORGE ANGUS, M.A.,

St. Edmund Hall, Oxford; formerly Lieutenant H.M. Indian Army and Curate of Prestbury, Gloucestershire; Catholic Church, St. Andrews, N.B.

In becoming a Catholic, I was not troubled with the difficulties which I believe stood in the way of others who are, like myself, converts. I mean such matters as—Mass in Latin; the veneration given to Mary and the Saints and Servants of God; Anglican Orders; Indulgences; Popular Devotions, and some other things. All these I put away as side-issues. I addressed myself to one point : What, and Where, is the Church of God ?

What ? Now, the way was so far easy, as both High Anglicans and Catholics were, and are, quite agreed that the Church is a Visible Body. " A city set on an hill that cannot be hid."

Three things, then, might be asserted concerning this Visible Body.

(1) This Visible Body has a Visible Head—the Pope.

(2) This Visible Body has no Visible Head.

(3) This Visible Body has several Visible Heads—the Bishops ; the Universal Episcopate.

Now take (2) and (3). The Visible Body has no Visible Head. Then it is an abortion or a corpse.

Or, This Visible Body has several heads. Then it is hydra-headed, and is—a monster.

I really could not have anything to do with (2) or (3), so had to fall back upon (1), a Visible Body with a Visible Head. This brought me to, Where?

Was there any society claiming to be the Visible Body with its Visible Head? If so—where? The Church of England? No. She claims to be *a* Church, but not *the* Church. The Greek Church? No, again. For if she claims to be *the* Church, she neglects her obvious duty of trying to persuade all men to belong to her. In a word, she does not "go and make disciples of all nations," nor does she even attempt to preach the gospel to all men.

There remained, then, the Roman Church—using popular language. About *her* position there could be no doubt. She is a Visible Body with a Visible Head. She claims to be the One Universal Church. She tries to make disciples from all nations. She endeavours to preach the gospel to all mankind. She knows no limits of nationality or geography. Judgment, I think, goes by default. There is no other claimant.

After this, there was no course open but to submit to her claims, as those of the One Divine Teacher, commissioned to guide men into all truth. So I submitted, and was received.

Was it pleasant? Not at all. It was going out, like Abraham—"not knowing where he went." It was a break-up. It was "the parting of friends." It was beginning all over again. And after? Well, for the first three or four days, there was a sense of bewilderment and confusion. "I am really now a Roman Catholic—is it possible?"

This was a Sunday, nearly twenty-eight years ago. Then, on the Thursday, I was confirmed by Cardinal Manning, and, on that day, there came upon me the "sensible sweetness" which, amid all the changes and chances of this mortal life, has never left me. It was, realized, the "joy and peace of believing."

Do I like everything in the Catholic religion now ? By no means. As the Church has her human element, as she is composed of men and women, of course I do not like everything—or, for that matter, everybody—with which, or with whom, I come in contact. But these things are matters of taste.

In the Catholic religion there is an amount of freedom found nowhere else. We believe whatever the Church teaches, simply because she *is* the Church, and, in all else, she allows her children a wide liberty. I do not say that she authorizes, or even approves, every popular devotion, practice, habit, or custom to be found here or there. But, as a loving mother, she tolerates what she may not approve, and would not authorize. To tolerate is one thing ; to approve, or authorize, is another.

Have I ever repented the step I took in becoming a Catholic? Never. I am in communion with the See of Peter. I have part and lot with that See—its past, its present, its future. I find it "as the shadow of a great rock in a weary land." I say, with Lady Georgiana Fullerton—

> " ' Oh that thy creed were sound ! ' I cried,
>   Until I felt its power ;
> And almost prayed to find it false,
>   In that last solemn hour.

Great was the struggle, fierce the strife,
  But wonderful the gain ;
And not one trial, not one pang,
  Was sent, or felt, in vain."

I say with St. Teresa, "Well, after all, I am a Catholic."

Ne quæras quis hoc dixit?   Sed, quid dicatur, attende.

W. D. A.

As a schoolboy I was tutored in the tenets of the English Establishment. Subsequently I imbibed the agnostic views prevailing in the Cambridge science schools, where my education was continued. In the medical schools of London I had no inclination to ponder over metaphysics, and indeed little time for it.

Many years afterwards the following questions suggested themselves to me:—

(1) Is there a revealed religion?

(2) If so, is that religion Christianity?

To both these I found an affirmative answer. Moreover, on its own showing, Christianity involved a Catholic and Apostolic Church, if it involved anything.

Where was this to be found? Not in Protestantism, which appeared to me already moribund. Was it to be found in that section of the Anglican community which repudiated the name "Protestant"? "We are catholic and apostolic," they said. Whether they were or were not, this at least was obvious, namely, that they were falsifying history to assert their claims, and insanely aping Roman Catholic ritual to support them.

I turned then to the Church which, at any rate, did not

5

deny the facts of yesterday, nor attempt to bolster itself
up by adopting beliefs and practices which it had only
just ceased to condemn. To this Church, the Roman and
Catholic, I eventually submitted, convinced that it was She
who had received the original commission. In Her fold,
thank God, I have ever found shelter and rest.

Sir HENRY BELLINGHAM, Bart.,

Of Castle Bellingham, Co. Louth, Ireland.

THE chief thing that attracted me to the Church was its universality, as opposed to the insularity of Episcopalianism, in which form of Christianity I was brought up. And I felt this very strongly during my first visit to the Continent. Detail had never much difficulty for me, for when once I had grasped the notion of a Teaching Church, all followed as a matter of course.

My first impressions of Catholicism were amongst the poor in Ireland, where I was born. Brought up myself in a school of extreme Low Churchism of a deeply religious character, but surrounded by masses of practical good-living Catholics, I was struck by the little impression the educated Protestant classes made on their poorer brethren, and was very favourably impressed with the simple devotion and faith of these latter.

As years went by, and I mixed with Catholics of position and education, I found the same devotion and faith amongst them that I had admired amongst the poor.

Previous to this, my education at Oxford had thrown me more or less under the influence of the High Church party, and I drifted thenceforward almost insensibly into

7

the bosom of the Church, and had ceased to believe in Protestant Episcopacy or any other form of Protestantism some time before taking the final step.

But the personal example and simple faith of the Irish poor were the first things that impressed me. I compared it favourably with the class of Protestants in Ireland amongst whom I mixed, and whose doctrines consisted more in hatred of Rome than in any definite belief. The language they used first irritated and then disgusted me, and predisposed me to make inquiries. At Oxford I was still further impressed by the conversion of many of my acquaintances, especially of the late Fr. Clarke, S.J., then a Protestant minister and fellow of St. John's College, who lost his fellowship and sacrificed his career for his faith. He put things before me in an altogether new way, and I always consider that my conversion was largely owing to him.

EDWARD BERDOE, Esq., M.R.C.S., ETC.,

TYNEMOUTH HOUSE, VICTORIA PARK GATE, N.E.

I WAS bred in the Nonconformist ranks and educated amongst men of science. Always of a religious turn of mind, with strong leanings to mental analysis and logical deduction, I turned to the study of Anglicanism and the Catholic Faith out of a desire for knowledge, and especially to gratify my taste for the study of comparative religions. At last, and after many years of anxious thought, I found the claims of the Catholic Religion on every ground to be irresistible. I embraced it. It satisfies my reason and solaces my heart, stirs my emotions and convinces my intellect.

It has often been said that there is no logical standpoint between Agnosticism and the Catholic Faith. Were I not a Catholic, I should be a Buddhist. I cannot be an Agnostic, because I consider Jesus Christ the greatest Fact in human history. He was either what He claimed to be, or the greatest of impostors. But He was more than man, and the Catholic Church knew Him, spoke with Him, and she speaks now with an authority no other Church claims or dares to usurp. This compels my obedience. All else is shifting sand.

9

The Rev. ROBERT BRACEY,

PRIEST OF THE ORDER OF ST. DOMINIC, HOLY CROSS PRIORY, LEICESTER.

WHEN I seek to give an account of the manner in which I found my way into the Catholic Church, I have no complicated process of thought or painful grappling with difficult intellectual problems to record. Faith (if one may dare so to couple the great and heroic with the very little) came to me as it came to St. Paul, by means of a sudden illumination, without struggle or effort on my own part.

As a small boy, I lived in an atmosphere of ecclesiasticism of a decidedly Low Church type. Those members of my family under whose influence I chiefly fell, were immersed in Church and parochial work. My uncle was the Evangelically-minded vicar of the parish, my grandfather the still more Evangelical churchwarden. Sermons, conversations, books, all alike breathed a hatred of Popery and Ritualism, and shaped and moulded my character to such an extent that, before I was twelve, the mere sight of a priest or a crucifix excited my contemptuous horror, and I spent my pocket-money with the utmost willingness in subscribing to the funds of the "Church Association," and my time in attending its meetings, and in the delightful perusal of the "*Rock.*" Of

the Catholic Church I had heard and read nothing but
evil ; my conception of it was pure caricature, and I thought
all Catholics must be either dupes or rogues. In church-
going and church affairs generally I took a thorough
delight ; and yet I doubt if I ever really believed anything,
or if my fervour in the cause of Evangelicalism and the
Established Church was anything more than a mere attachment to a party, and the outcome of an hereditary tendency
to fall down and worship existing institutions. Certainly
from a very early age I never said any prayers, and experienced no sense of responsibility to a higher Power.
I think this was the result of a conversation I once over-
heard on the impersonal nature of God and the Devil.

One unforgotten day, being then in my sixteenth year,
I went to the Oratory at Edgbaston to High Mass. I had
been once or twice before, chiefly out of a desire to see
Newman, and had not been at all impressed. And, on
this occasion, I remember well my contempt for all I saw,
and my complete ignorance of the meaning of everything.
The sermon that morning happened to be a very poor one
indeed, and the preacher floundered about sadly. And
yet it was in the midst of that very sermon that Faith
came to me. I suddenly found—how, I know not—that
I *believed* in this religion of which I knew so little, and
that (to my own utter dismay, for I foresaw the troubles
and difficulties such a change would involve) I was a
Catholic. I went out of that church with my brain in a
whirl, but as certain of the truth of Catholicism as I am
to-day, and quite prepared to give up everything for its
sake. That night, for the first time since I was eight
years old, I said my prayers, and on the morrow bought

some Catholic books and began to study them with great earnestness.

The more I read, the more satisfied I was ; very soon · I felt able to give reasons for the faith that was in me ; but the firm conviction was there before ever the reading began. Yet, terribly afraid lest I might be under an hallucination, it was some time before I had the courage and assurance to give outward expression to the alteration in my mind ; and, when I did, there were the inevitable arguments, letters, and entreaties to answer and to withstand. Among books sent to me at this time was one which was an especial help, and took away the very last lingering doubt—Littledale's " Plain Reasons." I compared it with Father Ryder's reply, and it had upon me an effect hardly intended by its author.

In eighteen months from that memorable Sunday, I was received into the Catholic Church. That which I think seemed to attract me most in her was her claim to infallibility. I saw clearly the uselessness of revelation without a key, of the Bible without an interpreter. Every page of the Gospel bore upon it an indication of our Lord's own provision of such a key and such an interpreter ; and the fact that only one claimant for this absolutely necessary position of infallible guide existed, seemed to leave me no power of choice save that between Catholicism and an unreasoning scepticism.

THE RIGHT HON. LORD BRAMPTON
(SIR HENRY HAWKINS),

FORMERLY JUDGE OF THE QUEEN'S BENCH.

5, Tilney Street, Park Lane, May 9, 1901.

MY DEAR SIR,

It is not very easy to write a definite reply to the question—Why I became a Catholic? I will not therefore make the attempt. To reason the matter out would require much more time than I have at my command, and I would not undertake the task unless I felt that I could accomplish it thoroughly and with satisfaction to myself. To undertake a work and fail to perform it would distress me. Those, therefore, who look for my reasons for taking the important step I took so late in life, cannot have their expectations satisfied by me. It must suffice them to know that it was the result of my deliberate conviction that the truth—which was all I sought—lay within the Catholic Church. I thought the matter out for myself, anxiously and seriously, uninfluenced by any human being, and I have unwavering satisfaction in the conclusion at which I arrived, and my conscience tells me it is right.

Believe me, truly yours,

(Signed)   BRAMPTON.

13

The Rev. JAMES CRAWFORD BREDIN,

PRIEST OF THE BIRMINGHAM DIOCESE, AND PROFESSOR OF SCIENCE AT
ST. MARY'S COLLEGE, OSCOTT.

MY reasons for leaving the Church of England were not,
I think, theological. I knew little or no theology till many
years after I had become a Catholic. The unscrupulous
mendacity of the average Anglican controversialist, or
"Church Defence" lecturer ; the crawling subserviency of
the Anglican clergy to the State—speaking of them, of
course, as a class, and allowing for exceptions ; the utter
impossibility of pinning the Anglican body down to any
definite statement ;—these were the reasons that forced me
to seek rest elsewhere.

I know these are hard words, but I must be honest if
this statement is to be of any use. Dr. Littledale's
"Plain Reasons" is a book gangrened with falsehood.
These falsehoods have been exposed over and over
again by Catholic writers, and yet the book is sown
broadcast by clergymen. I had a copy given me fifteen
years ago after Dr. Ryder's "Answer" had been
published. I have heard clergymen since say they
considered it a most useful book. I think I have always
thought such conduct entirely without excuse.

The "Church Defence" lecturer was beginning his

career in my day. I need not insist on the reckless un-
veracity of his statements. Yet educated clergymen, who
have read their history, employ him and never think of
correcting or of modifying what he says.

A third feature of controversial literature which struck
me was the occasional wanton attacks on the Catholic
body. Without any provocation, without any reason
that one could discover, a pamphlet on " Roman Misquotations " or " Italian Inaccuracies " would appear—fully
as untrustworthy as Dr. Littledale.

As to the second point the conduct of the Anglican
High Church body in regard to the Jerusalem bishopric
in 1888 may serve as an example. " The State," say they,
" is going to commit an act of schism "—" We hope we are
misinformed." By-and-by the intentions of the Government are unmistakable. " We won't endure it ; we shall
all be involved in the guilt of schism if we stay ; " and some
are heard to threaten that they will " go over to Rome."
The Government calmly proceeds on its way, and the blow
falls. The Anglican bishop is appointed in Jerusalem,
and then every one discovers that things are not so bad
after all, and the " Church " is more beautiful and more
Catholic than ever after her last trial. One is inclined to
ask : will the worm never turn ?　·

It would be superfluous to insist here on the third
point. The Gorham decision—to which the Church of
England is bound—will serve as an example.

The late Dr. Rivington, I believe, defined a Ritualist
as a person without a sense of humour. Their obvious
imitation of Catholic practices, even down to having colour-
able imitations of our religious Orders and Congregations,

as F.J. (Fraternity of Jesus) for S.J., O.H.R. for C.S.S.R. ;
their perpetual insistence on the titles of " Father,"
" Priest," and the like, did much to disgust me with them,
long before I had any clear idea of the nature of the
Catholic priesthood. I knew they were imitation priests,
though I did not know what the reality was like.

I have many dear friends still in the Anglican body—
one or two clergymen. How they stay there, I cannot
think ; but I hope that one day their eyes may be opened
and they may see the true character of the body to which
they belong. There may be heresies more fundamental
than Anglicanism ; there are few so contemptible.

JAMES BRITTEN, Esq., K.S.G.,

OF THE NATURAL HISTORY MUSEUM, SOUTH KENSINGTON.

FROM my earliest days, I was brought up at St. Barnabas', Pimlico—one of the churches most intimately associated with the growth of High Church views in London.

My memory dates, I suppose, from somewhere about 1856. The two great waves of conversion to the Catholic Church which followed the secession of Newman in 1845, and Manning in 1851, had passed; and in spite of occasional Protestant outbursts, the efforts of Protestant lecturers, and the adverse judgments of Privy Councils and other bodies, the High Church movement was steadily and everywhere gaining ground.

Here I was taught that our Lord founded a Church, which He had built upon the foundation of his Apostles, He Himself being the chief corner-stone; that He had conferred on His Apostles certain powers by which they were enabled to carry on His work; that the Apostles had the power of forgiving sin, of consecrating the Eucharist, and of transmitting to their successors the supernatural power which they had themselves received;

that the Apostles and those whom they consecrated were
the rulers of the Christian Church ; that this Church had
power to define what was to be believed, and that it
could not err, because of the promise of Christ that He
would be with it, even to the end of the world ; that the
Church, moreover, was divinely guided in a very special
manner by the Holy Ghost, and that its definitions to
the end of time were inspired by the Holy Ghost, of
whom Christ had said, " When He, the Spirit of Truth, is
come, He shall lead you into all truth ;" that the Church
and not the Bible was God's appointed teacher ; that the
traditions of the Church were of equal authority with the
Bible ; and that the Church was its only authorized
interpreter.

I was further taught that the grace of God was con-
veyed to the soul principally by means of the Sacraments,
and that by Baptism the stain of original sin was removed.
With regard to the Real Presence of our Lord in the
Holy Communion, I can best explain the teaching I
received by saying that, when I became a Catholic, I was
never conscious of any change of belief. The books
which I used as an Anglican I could use equally well as
a Catholic ; they were compiled almost exclusively from
Catholic sources, and, before I had ever entered a Catholic
church or read a Catholic book, I was familiar with the
wonderful Eucharistic hymns of St. Thomas, and the
other doctrinal hymns, modern as well as ancient, of
the Catholic Church.

With regard to the Church, I was taught that there
were three branches—the Anglican, the Greek, and the
Roman—and that of these three the Catholic Church was

made up : that in this country the Church of England represented the Catholic Church, and that the Roman branch had no business here—yet, I am thankful to say, that I cannot remember ever having heard at St. Barnabas' a single sermon against Roman Catholics, or an uncharitable word regarding them.

I remember one sermon on the honour due to the Blessed Virgin, in which the Roman devotion to her was spoken of as excessive ; and another on St. Peter, in which his primacy, as distinct from his supremacy, was acknowledged : but, until I was seventeen, I never heard the Protestant side of the Church of England advanced from the pulpit, although then, as now, the itinerant Protestant lecturer presented to those who were credulous enough to accept his statements, a caricature of the Catholic Church.

I never attended a Roman Catholic service, and had only once entered a Catholic church. This was the old Oratory, into which I went one winter afternoon on my way to the South Kensington Museum. One of the few things I knew about what I considered the Roman branch of the Church was that the Blessed Sacrament was reserved on its altars, and I remember kneeling in the dark, flat-roofed Oratory, with its lamp burning before the altar, in adoration of the Presence which I felt to be there.

This was my position until, at about the age of eighteen, I went down to High Wycombe to study medicine. I shall never forget my first Sunday there. There was a magnificent old parish church, with deep chancel and broad aisles, choked up with pews of the most obstructive design. A small table with a shabby red cloth stood away under the picture which concealed the east window; a choir of a handful of men and boys, unsurpliced and untidy, sang the slender allowance of music; a parish clerk responded for the congregation;— these were the objects that met my eyes and ears that first Sunday of my exile. But that was not all. We had a sermon, delivered by a preacher in a black gown on behalf of the Sunday schools. That sermon I shall always remember. In the course of it, the preacher enumerated the things they did *not* teach the children in the schools: they did *not* teach them they were born again in baptism, they did *not* teach that the clergy were descended from the Apostles, they did *not* teach that they had power to forgive sins, they did *not* teach a real presence in the Communion—"Real *presence!*" I heard a parson say in that church; "*I* believe in a real *absence!*" —they did *not* teach the doctrine of good works. I began to wonder what was left to be taught, until the preacher explained that predestination and salvation by faith alone were inculcated upon the children. On the next Sunday the Holy Communion was administered—*how*, I can hardly describe, except by saying that it was manifest that no belief in its supernatural aspect was maintained. I can see now the parish clerk, at the end of the service, walking up the chancel, and the minister coming towards him with the paten in one hand and the chalice in the other, waiting while he, standing, ate and drank the contents of each.

My first feeling was that these clergy had no right or place in the Church of England. There was a moderately "high" church five miles off, and whenever I could, I found my way there. But it became unpleasantly plain that the Church of England, which I had regarded as an infallible guide, spoke with two voices :—I began to realize that even on vital matters two diametrically opposed opinions not only *could be*, but *were*, held and preached. I knew my Book of Common Prayer, and its rubrics, as well as I knew my Bible ; but to one part of it my attention had never been called, as it now was Sunday by Sunday. I had known without realizing all that it implied, that the Queen was, in some way, the Head of the Church—or rather, of two Churches, one in England and one in Scotland ; but I now found that she declared herself to be "Supreme Governor of the Church of England, and, by God's ordinance, Defender of the Faith :" that General Councils, which I had been taught to believe infallible, could not be held "without the commandment and will of princes," and not only might err, but had erred, in things pertaining to God ; that Confirmation, Penance, and the like, were not Sacraments of the Gospel ; that the benefits of Baptism were confined to "they that receive it rightly ;" that the reception of the body of Christ in the Holy Communion is dependent on the faith of the recipient; and that "the sacrifices of Masses . . . were blasphemous fables and dangerous deceits." This last was indeed a trial to me. It is true that twenty-five years ago the word "Mass" was not in common use among Anglicans as it is now, and I do not think an Anglican clergyman would have been found to say in public, as one said the other day, that "he would not stay a minute in a Church where the Mass was

before, that the first mark of God's Church was Unity—a mark which no one can pretend to find in the Church of England ; and, after a period of anxiety such as none can know who have not experienced it, I was received into that Unity, on May 26, 1867.

The Rev. HENRY BROWNE, M.A.,

New College, Oxford; Priest of the Society of Jesus; University College, Dublin.

BEFORE having to face the question of the claims of the Roman Church, I had previously, as an Anglican, made up my mind on another momentous controversy: the question of the Real Presence of Christ in the Eucharist. As my process of thought was identical in the two cases, and, in fact, the latter decision depended on the former, I will here briefly explain both and their connection.

As to the Eucharistic question, having read a good deal about it, having discussed it with others, and having pondered and prayed over it with much earnestness, I felt bewildered by the arguments, metaphysical, scriptural, and historical, which were used on both sides of the controversy. What finally led me to a conclusion, to an acquiescence in the doctrine of the Real Presence (the question of Transubstantiation I did not enter into), was the following train of thought. I do not know how it came first into my mind, but I felt with more and more certainty that if Christ was God, and therefore foresaw the course of events, He must have known that, as a matter of fact, the enormous bulk of His followers would take (as, indeed, they have taken) His words in the most literal sense—in

a sense which, if false, has led and leads them into practices which are really, though unconsciously, idolatrous.
Now, I convinced myself, gradually but more and more
clearly, that Christ, foreseeing this effect following from
His words, and foreseeing, on the one hand, that the
effect would be most widespread, and, on the other, that
it came from a too simple and too literal interpretation of
His own words, would have been bound, as the God of
Truth, to take some effective means towards guarding His
followers against such a pernicious and (at least to take
a thousand years) universal error. Now, so far from this,
He had used expressions which, even though we leave
their hidden meaning an open question, yet certainly give
a very good *primâ facie* ground for the belief in question.
Consequently, I felt with more and more certainty that
the belief in the Real Presence is bound up with and
included in belief in the Divinity of Christ. I held then,
long before I had any doubt as to Anglicanism in general,
to the belief that the process of reasoning I have indicated
is perfectly unanswerable and perfectly sound, and I hold
to it still.

At a later date, when I came to consider the validity
of the Roman claims, I saw that the position which I had
previously accepted as to the Real Presence could be, and
ought to be, applied to the question of the Papal Supremacy as of Divine origin. For it rests on words of Christ
which, however they may be discussed and tortured by
controversialists, are in reality as direct and simple, as
naturally understood in the Roman sense, as are the words
of institution of the Eucharist: "Thou art Peter . . . to
thee I give the keys of the Kingdom of Heaven."

THE RT. REV. W. R. BROWNLOW, D.D., M.A.,

TRINITY COLLEGE, CAMBRIDGE.

LORD BISHOP OF CLIFTON.

St. Edmund's College, Old Hall, Ware, March 6, 1900.

MY DEAR SIR,

Your letter reached me here, where I am staying until Thursday.

If you are in the library of the British Museum, and care to look at a little pamphlet I published in 1864, " How and Why I became a Catholic," you are at liberty to make any use of it that you like. I have no copies of it left, or I would send you one. There were so many different matters which all pointed me in the direction of Rome that I could not put them into a short paragraph. It was history that more than anything else brought me into the Church. And among Christian writers, St. Irenæus and St. Vincent of Lerins influenced me more than any others. Then the history of the English Reformation— the violent break of continuity under Elizabeth, etc., etc. ; the utter inability of the Anglican Bishops to defend any Catholic Doctrine : Baptism, the Holy Eucharist, Absolution, Inspiration of Scripture, and the Eternity of Heaven and Hell ;—all this traceable to the surrender to the Crown of the Keys of the Kingdom of Heaven, and contrasted with the attitude and action of the Pope in every page of the history of the past eighteen hundred years. Evils, scandals, abuse of power, and all these sort of things, did not affect me in the least, but rather showed that the institution that could survive all these abuses must be Divine.

Yours sincerely,
(Signed) W. R. BROWNLOW,
Bishop of Clifton.

THE REV. BEDE CAMM, B.A.,

(2ND CLASS THEOL., 1887), KEBLE COLLEGE, OXFORD; FORMERLY
CURATE OF ST. AGNES', KENNINGTON PARK, LONDON, S.E.; PRIEST
OF THE ORDER OF ST. BENEDICT; ST. THOMAS' ABBEY, ERDINGTON,
BIRMINGHAM.

IT is very difficult indeed to set down concisely in black
and white the reasons which led one to submit to the
Catholic Church. Or I would rather say it is impossible.
The introit for the Mass for the Third Sunday after Pentecost, the day when at last I found the light so long sought
for, seemed to me then, as now, to express the whole truth.
"*Factus est Dominus protector meus et eduxit me in latitudinem, salvum me fecit quoniam voluit me.*" The Lord
had become my Saviour; it was all His doing, none of
mine. He had led me out of the confined prison of heresy
in latitudinem "into a broad place," even into the liberty
of the sons of God. He had set my weary feet upon the
Rock, and ordered my goings. And the reason? Ah!
that was His secret. "*Salvum me fecit, quoniam voluit me.*"
He saved me because He wanted me. Why He should
want one so useless, one so worthless,—that was His secret;
a mystery of His predestinating love, which I can only
wonder at and adore.

I had been long tossed about with doubt, weary of controversy, sick of strife. Over and over again I had flung

aside the whole subject, disgusted and wearied. All I
read seemed only to confuse me more.

I had been brought up to love the Church of England,
to believe in her with all my heart. The figment of her
"continuity" had been so ingrained into my very being,
that it seemed as if I could as soon doubt my own identity.
For years I had not a doubt. All my Oxford time was
cloudless. When, however, I went to Cuddesdon, doubts
began to spring up thick and fast. They were partly
suggested by companions, partly by my environment,
principally, I think, by the official lectures on the Thirty-
nine Articles and on Church History. I conscientiously
tried to fight these doubts as temptations. Yet, once
aroused, they could never be stilled, or at least for more
than a short time. When I was ordained deacon and
began work in a London parish, these doubts grew stronger
till they held me by the throat. The whole system was
such a miserable *fiasco*. Here was a Church that had had,
for three hundred years and more, full power, enormous influence, over the whole land. She claimed to be Catholic,
a branch of the Church of God. Yet the people knew
nothing of this, nothing of the faith—were practically
pagans, in fact. They had lost all idea of sin (the Church
had practically abolished the Sacrament of Penance); they
did not know how to make an act of contrition; the com-
monest Catholic duties, such as the obligation to hear
Mass on Sundays, to receive Holy Communion at Easter,
were utterly unknown. Next door to us was a Church of
the extreme Protestant type, where all we held most sacred
was denounced unsparingly every Sunday. There was no
unity of belief anywhere, because there was no unity of

teaching. Even among my colleagues, who were of the extreme High Church party, there was no agreement on such vital points as Schism, Transubstantiation, the necessity of the Sacrament of Penance for those in mortal sin, even Eternal Punishment. I felt more and more that the Church of England was a failure, and, considering her claims, a ghastly failure. But were not these claims a delusion? Were they not, indeed, of recent date? I saw that the Bishops were, to a man, heretical on one or other point of the Catholic Faith; that heresy among the clergy was not only tolerated but approved; that the people had lost all sensitiveness as to it, all horror for it. I felt more and more that the arguments which were urged against the Roman Church, and in defence of our abnormal position, were such as all heretics had urged from the beginning. I thought, "If I could see it from the outside, should I not see clearly then that all these pleas were mere specious delusions?" I went about with a sorrow at my heart that was real physical pain. For I could not be sure, and I was afraid, so afraid, to take an irrevocable step in the dark—a step which might be, and which I was told would be, an act of apostasy, of wilful schism. And then I read three books which helped me more than any others— Newman's "Development," Manning's "Temporal Mission of the Holy Ghost," and Faber's "Life and Letters." I also read Allnatt's "Cathedra Petri," and the catena of Fathers there quoted made an immense impression on my mind. I began to see that communion with the See of Peter was of old the essential test of orthodoxy, the *signum stantis vel cadentis ecclesiæ;* and if so, why should it not be so still? St. Augustine's words haunted me: "*Extra*

Ecclesiam Catholicam totum potest præter salutem. Potest habere honorem, potest habere sacramentum, potest cantare Alleluia, potest respondere Amen, potest Evangelium tenere, potest in nomine Petris et Filii et Spiritus Sancti fidem et habere et prædicare, sed nusquam nisi in Ecclesia Catholica salutem poterit invenire " (Serm. ad Cæs. Eccles. plebem, No. 6). And when I turned to Rome, and saw her so firm, so invincible, so serene, so unfaltering in her teaching, so uncompromising with heretics, so sure of her own rights, so immovable throughout the ages, I fancied that to her, and to her alone, could apply those other words of the Saint : " *Ipsa est Ecclesia sancta,* Ecclesia una, Ecclesia Catholica, contra omnes hæreses pugnans ; pugnare potest, expugnari tamen non potest. Hæreses omnes de illa exierunt, tanquam sarmenta inutilia de vite præcisa: ipsa autem manet in radice sua, in vite sua, in caritate sua. Portæ inferi non vincerit eam " (De Symbolo Sermo ad Catech.). But still I was tormented with fears and anxieties, still I did not see clearly. At last I went abroad for a holiday, and there, kneeling one day in a monastic church, I heard the brethren chant those words of the *Credo:* " *Et unam sanctam Catholicam et Apostolicam Ecclesiam."* And as they sang them the clouds rolled away from off my soul, and the light of faith shone on it once for all. I saw then, in a way which I cannot describe, but, like the blind man of old, " *One thing I know, that whereas I was blind, now I see."* I saw that all this time I had *not* been believing in *One* Church. I saw what the unity of the Church really was, and seeing, I rejoiced and thanked God.

A conversion, then, is, and must always be, the work of God. No amount of reading, no amount of controversy, will ever bring to a soul the Divine light of faith.   It is dark till God illuminate it.   Nevertheless, to the soul who humbly seeks it and earnestly prays for it, surely He will never deny this grace.

> " O gift of gifts, the gift of faith !
>   My God, how can it be,
>   That Thou Who art discerning Love
>   Should'st give this gift to me ? "

For that gift I thank Him, and shall thank Him for all time and eternity.

Misericordias Domini in æternum cantabo.

D

The Rev. W. R. Carson,

Of Trinity College, Dublin.

CARDINAL NEWMAN was, under God, the chief factor in my conversion. Not that I was acquainted with any Catholic, clerical or lay: until the day of my reception I had scarcely even spoken to one. I became of my own accord painfully alive—how could it be otherwise?—to the babel of discord that the Church of England had substituted for the sweet harmony of the city of peace—the Jerusalem whose Maker was God. Everywhere I was confronted with a different doctrine, a different interpretation. No two authorized representatives of the religious body in which I found myself agreed together—except to differ.[1] I could not disguise from myself that the very note of comprehensiveness, which is the life and soul of Anglicanism—although it had its attractions for the natural man—differed *toto cœlo*, not merely from the characteristics of

---

[1] My frame of mind was very similar to that of a "learned Tractarian writer," quoted by Dr. F. G. Lee in his recent instructive *brochure*, "The Ecclesiastical Situation in 1899," as writing to him: "I do not at all want to know the faith or opinions of any bishop—Ryle or King, Carpenter or Creighton; but I am anxious to learn what doctrines our Church teaches, and what it forbids" (p. 14, *note*). He continues: "I have been referred to a book, but the book never speaks; and to a vellum document, but the document owns neither mind nor mouth" (ibid.).

the two largest portions of Christendom to-day—the Eastern and the Western ; not merely from the uncompromising hatred of indefiniteness in belief, and communion *in sacris* with heretics, that sent Athanasius into exile[1] and made the Apostle of Love refuse to hold even social intercourse with a disciple who had denied an article of faith ; but plainly and unmistakably from the salient features delineated in Holy Scripture of a " Church" which, if a man neglect to " hear," he is placed inexorably with the " heathen and the publican "[2] outside the Palace and the Feast.

All this I felt keenly,—the diversity of doctrine ; the inability of any one—be he bishop, priest, or layman—to tell me what *was* the teaching of the Church of England, and, more important still, the teaching of " the whole Catholic Church of Christ ;" the universally condoned fellowship with unbelievers, condemned as it was by the Apostle ; the lack, except in favoured quarters[3] where the atmosphere was exotic and Catholic, of *supernatural* religion, as distinct from mere sentimental pietism ; above all, the practical denial of three of the latter articles of the Creed—" the Holy Ghost, the Holy Catholic Church, the Communion of Saints."

[1] Cf. Newman, " Essay on Development:" "Can any one who has but heard his name . . . doubt for one instant how . . . the people of England, ' we, our princes, our priests, and our prophets ' . . . would deal with Athanasius,—Athanasius who spent his long years in fighting against sovereigns for a theological term ? " (ed. 1878, p. 98).

Cf. St. Irenæus' account to the heretic Florinus of St. Polycarp's hatred of heresy (Euseb., H. E., iv. 14).

[2] St. Matt. xviii. 17.

[3] I should be the last to deny the devoted work done in such parishes as St. Peter's, London Docks, by devoted and apostolic men like the Rev. L. S. Wainwright, or the reality of the religious life practised at Cowley and elsewhere.

But I also saw as clearly that antagonism to one religious system was no valid reason for embracing another. Why could I not be content to stay where I was? A leap in the dark is always dangerous ; it may land one in worse places than one has quitted. He who takes it "may chance to alight upon his feet, . . . or, on the contrary, be dashed to pieces " (Balzac).

The Church of England was in possession ; I was her son, bound to her by many ties ; my grandfather was one of her bishops, my father died her faithful presbyter ; and I belonged to her communion through no act of my own. Unless I could be convinced that her rival's claims on my allegiance were absolutely and imperatively sound, I did not see that I was justified in leaving her. But my mind was still perplexed and uneasy. I became a prey to doubts on point after point of the Christian Creed. I had no sheet-anchor for my faith. If the individual judgment was at liberty to decide for itself as to what was or was not an essential matter of belief—to reject Transubstantia- tion and to hold fast the doctrine of the Trinity—I could not see how any one could be sure that he personally had not made a mistake in choosing the dross for the gold.

I made a careful study of Newman's works ; and at last one day there came to me, with all the clearness and peremptoriness of a distinct call, that passage in one of his Catholic sermons (which seems to me still to give the key to his change of faith, and the position from which, in spite of misunderstanding, trouble, and manifold trial, he never afterwards swerved by a hair's breadth) where he shows there can be no logical alternative between a Divine Teacher and the uncertain guidance of one's own fickle judgment and changeable mind—between Agnosticism, on the one hand, with all its painful indecision, and the safe haven of Catholicism, on the other. "The question," he says, "lies between the Church and no Divine Messenger at all. There is no Divine revelation given us, unless she is the organ of it, for where else is there a prophet to be found?" [1]

These words rang in my ears like the "Tolle: lege" that allured the great introspective doctor of the West from the sensual charms of Manichænism to the pure doctrine of Ambrose; or like the "securus judicat orbis terrarum" that led the latter-day Augustine home. The whole question at issue seemed to me to be summed up in this short phrase. What had puzzled me for so long— the impossibility of being certain that the overwhelming claims of Rome were true—received a satisfactory and a final solution.

Either God had revealed Himself to us in a way so plain that he who runs may read; or His revelation was useless—nay, no revelation at all, for each man would take his own different subjective meaning out of it. A message implies a messenger; a revelation, an interpreter and a guide. Unless God intended men to make havoc of His Truth—to rend it piecemeal, to mistake the tares for the wheat—He must have instituted on earth a means by which they could know infallibly and surely, without danger of mistake, what He actually taught, and what they must believe if they would inherit eternal life. A Revelation, a manifestation of the Divine Will, *implies* an exponent of it—possessed with like authority, capable of

[1] "Discourses," p. 278.

teaching it to the individual, independently altogether of
his natural predilection or judgment. That need for a
Divine Teacher, telling me in the name of God His
authentic doctrine, I saw to be satisfied by the Catholic
and Roman Church, and by her alone.[1] She claims to
be the one Oracle of Truth, the sole Depository and
Unfolder of the Christian revelation *as a whole.* He
who rejects one part of her message because it is unpala-
table to him personally, has no logical reason for not
rejecting the rest. If he once ignores her authority, he
has none other to substitute for it but his own. Ultimately,
the issue lies between a Teacher sent from God, and the
clouded guidance of the natural unaided reason. " Revelation is not discovery, or rather revelation is the discovery
of Himself by God to man, not by man for himself. It
is not the activity of the human reason which discovers
the truths of revelation. It is God's discovery or withdrawing the veil from His own intelligence, and casting
the light of it upon us." [2] " There can be no intermediate
between the Divine Mind declaring itself through an organ
of its own creation, or the human mind judging for itself
upon the . . contents of revelation. There is or there is
not a perpetual Divine Teacher in the midst of us. The

[1] Cf. Fr. G. Tyrrel, S.J. : "[Rome's] exclusiveness and dogmatism is at
once conspicuous and altogether distinctive. It is to us the mark or characteristic of Christ, to others of anti-Christ. But all alike allow that it is notorious
and peculiar to Rome alone. Other bodies claim to have the true interpretation
of Christianity ; . . . but there is some modesty in their claim ; they do not
pretend to be infallibly right ; they are open to conviction ; they allow outsiders
a right to their opinion. But Rome alone claims living infallibility, to be
not only true, but certainly true, and alone true " (*Hard Sayings,* ed. 1,
p. 443).

[2] Manning, "Temporal Mission of the Holy Ghost," p. 91.

human reason must be either the disciple or the critic of revelation." [1]

When I came to examine attentively the method chosen by Christ to propagate His doctrine, I found the fact of the institution of a definite teaching office in the Church as plainly taught in the Scriptures as the fact of a Divine Revelation itself. Christ spoke with authority the message of the Kingdom, and He commissioned His Apostles in no different way to go out among men to teach them the authentic doctrines which He taught. " As the Father hath sent Me, I also send you." The claim, the authority, the commission, are the same. " Go ye," He says to His Apostles on the eve of His Ascension, " into the whole world, and preach the gospel to every creature." [2]

He appointed, therefore, a messenger—the Holy Catholic Church, the Bride of His love—to carry in His name, with the voice of His authority, His revelation to the ends of the earth. He left behind Him a way by which men could know certainly and infallibly His pure doctrine, as it flowed unsullied from His lips, when He committed to an organized society the task of continuing His office of Teacher.

He gives, moreover, to His representative a promise and a guarantee of infallibility and indefectibility. For He makes this solemn promise, twice spoken : " I will ask the Father, and He shall give you another Paraclete, that He may abide with you *for ever*, the Spirit of Truth, . . . He will teach you all things ; . . . He will lead you

[1] Manning, *op. cit.*, pp. 71, 72.
[2] St. Mark xvi. 16 ; cf. St. Matt. xxviii. 19.

into all Truth." [1]   Again, "Lo, I am with you *all days*, even unto the consummation of the world." [2]   Our Lord thereby showed quite plainly that this method of bringing home His Truth to individual souls was not temporary and transient, confined to the Apostolic age, or ending with the fourth, fifth, or seventh Œcumenical Council.   " I am with you *all days;* . . . the Paraclete shall abide with you *for ever*," is His distinct promise.   The gospel was to be promulgated throughout the "whole world."   "All nations" were to be "taught."   This the Apostles did not do.   Their short day was soon cut short by sword, cross, and flame; it was left to their successors in the government of the Church, and especially to him in whom was centred the fulness of the Apostolic power [3]—the heir from age to age of Peter's supreme and infallible authority—to carry on their mission, to teach through all time the very doctrine that Christ taught on earth.

Such a Teacher I found in the world to-day.   The Roman Catholic Church alone laid claim to be one and the same with the Church of Pentecost, possessed of its

---

[1] St. John xiv. 16, 26; xvi. 12.

[2] St. Matt. xxviii. 19.

[3] A point often lost sight of, which, however, came home to me very forcibly before my conversion, is that, on the Anglican theory, the Apostolate has to all intents and purposes ceased to be.   *Bishops* are not *Apostles;* they have neither universality of jurisdiction nor, taken singly, official infallibility; and, if there is no Apostolic See in which is concentrated the peculiar powers of the Twelve, one is compelled to admit that the Apostolate, given to the Church at a time when heresies had scarcely arisen, and the aroma of the Lord's visible Presence was an abiding reality, died out at the very moment when there was most need for it.   The Catholic Church has preserved in Peter's successor the office, not merely of the chief Apostle—the "first" (πρῶτος) of them, as St. Matthew (x. 2) calls him—but of the whole Apostolic Band for the precise end for which it was instituted, the preservation of unity of faith and government.

authority, commissioned uniquely to guard and teach the revelation of God given in His only-begotten Son.

The fact of the existence amongst us of a Guardian and an Expounder of Truth, bearing the authentic authority of the Redeemer, professing to teach every soul in His name the doctrines of salvation, carried with it to my mind a corresponding obligation of obedience.[1] If Christ really spoke to me through a Society identified with Himself—His Body and His Bride; if the Church spread throughout the world, united to Peter (the rock-bed of its solidity), of whom St. Ambrose in the fifth century could say, "Where Peter is, there is the Church; where the Church, there no death but life eternal;"[2] "Upon whom," in St. Cyprian's words, "Christ built the Church,"[3] "from whose chair [which he calls in the same epistle the root and womb (*radix et matrix*) of the Catholic Church] the unity of the Priesthood took its rise,"[4] where "faithlessness can have no access;"[5] if that Church to-day, alone among the religious bodies surrounding it, claimed to represent that Society and to possess its authority; I saw that nothing was left for me but unquestioning obedience to its rule. Christ's words were solemn, searching, unmis-

---

[1] Cf. Fr. Tyrrel, S.J. : "We have to seek a body that claims to carry on the work of Him Who came to teach not the few, but the millions; not the learned, but the rude; not the science of earth or the philosophy of man, but the wisdom of God and the mysteries of heaven; and Who, therefore, taught, not as the scribes by reasonings and discussion, but *with authority as God, claiming the obedience of the mind, not its patronage; the assent of faith, not the critical approval of reason*" (*Op. antea cit.*, p. 443).

[2] In Ps. xl. n. 30.

[3] Ep. lxxiii. ad Jubaian.

[4] Ep. lv. ad Cornel.

[5] Ibid. The reference is to the "Roman Church," which is called in the same letter the "ruling" or "principal" Church (*ecclesia principalis*).

takably plain : "If any man hear not the Church, let
him be . . . as a heathen and a publican."[1] "Go ye,"
My successors in teaching, "go ye" in My Name, with
My authority, "into the whole world "—into England as
much as into Asia Minor—"and preach the gospel to
every creature. . . . He that believeth . . . shall be saved ;
. . . he that believeth not shall be condemned."[2] I saw
with St. Jerome that I must "speak with the successor of
the Fisherman" and be " in communion with the See of
Peter" ("that rock," I knew, "on which the Church was
built "), if I would escape being numbered with the
"profane" who attempt to "eat the Lamb outside the
House,"[3] which is " the Church of the living God, the pillar
and ground (ἱδράίωμα) of the Truth."[4]

Other arguments shone upon my soul—especially the
marvellous coherence and unity of dogmatic truth, one
part connected with another (as limb with limb in a living
organism) by the joints and bands of vital membership,
forming a definite homogeneous whole ; and the orderly
harmonious development, age after age, of each separate
doctrine, from the protoplasmic germ in the almost form-
less embryo, to the highly specialized structure of well-
defined and articulated formulæ in creeds, canons, and
conciliar decrees. But to develop this line of thought
would lengthen unduly the present paper. I have treated
it with some fulness in a recent article in the *Weekly
Register*,[5] to which I would refer those readers who are
interested in the subject.

[1] St. Matt. xviii. 17.   [2] St. Mark xvi. 15, 16.
[3] In Ep. ad Damasum, written in the fourth century.
[4] 1 Tim. iii. 15.
[5] On " The Evolution of Catholicism," *Weekly Register*, December 30, 1899.

As soon as I realized, in all its significance, that there was a Church on earth, *i.e.* a Depository of Truth, a Teacher sent from God, having Divine sanctions for the fulfilment of its office, possessing an equal authority with the doctrine committed to its care, that idea (which Manning has acutely declared to have died out of the English mind) expanded within me; its bearings became clearly marked out, its consequences unmistakable. Newman's voice spoke to me imperatively through the closing lines, full of infinite pathos, of his "Essay on Development:" "Time is short, eternity is long. Put not from you what you have here found; regard it not as mere matter of present controversy; set not out resolved to refute it; . . . seduce not yourself with the imagination that it comes of disappointment, or disgust, or restlessness, or wounded feeling, or undue sensibility, or other weakness. Wrap not yourself round in the associations of years past; nor determine that to be truth which you wish to be so, nor make an idol of cherished imaginations. Time is short, eternity is long." [1]

[1] *Ed. cit.*, p. 443. Cf. the beautiful appeal in his "Discourses to Mixed Congregations:" "Oh! long sought after, tardily found, desire of the eyes, joy of the heart, the truth after many shadows, the fulness after many foretastes, the home after many storms, . . . how can ye doubt that she (the Catholic and Roman Church) is the messenger for whom ye seek? . . . Come to her, poor wanderers, come to her, for she it is, and she alone, who can unfold to you the meaning of your being and the secret of your destiny" (p. 281).

A CATHOLIC LAWYER,

A DOCTOR OF LAWS,

GIVES an account of his conversion to the Catholic faith in these words :—

What led me to embrace the Catholic faith, when a law-student of twenty-two, was the many and serious differences of belief prevailing in the different Protestant sects, and even within the Church of England itself; and yet all these disputants appealed to the Sacred Scriptures as their one standard of truth, interpreted, however, by each individual for himself and upon his own responsibility.

I was brought up by a pious widowed mother in the so-called Evangelical school of the Church of England, as modified by John Wesley. I received regular religious instruction, which consisted of the Church of England Catechism and Scripture history, and I learnt by heart every day at least two texts of Scripture. I also had pecuniary rewards occasionally given to me for learning by heart certain entire chapters in the Bible, and a special "tip" (I think half a crown) for committing to memory the whole of Dr. Watts's "Divine and Moral Songs." My mother's views were, in fact, a mixture of Calvinism and Arminianism, though, like Wesley, she scouted the *name* of Calvinism as dangerous heresy. I was taught that man was justified by faith alone without good works—which, however, must be done after justification; that when he put his trust in Christ as his own individual Saviour, he was at once converted and justified, the righteousness of Christ was imputed to him, and he felt within himself the infallible assurance of pardon. But, on the other hand, she taught me, in opposition to the strict Calvinists, that we had free will, were accountable for our actions, and were not sure of final perseverance, but might, after conversion, become backsliders and be eventually lost. I was, of course, also taught that the Pope was antichrist. It may seem strange that such comparatively abstruse theology should be taught to children under twelve years of age, but my dear mother thought that religious truth could not be taught too early or too often; and in my case the result was that, at the age of sixteen, I had developed an acquaintance with the differences prevailing between the different Protestant sects, and with some of the distinctive doctrines of the Catholic Church, that might be expected from a theological student rather than from a schoolboy.

At about the age of fifteen I was prepared for confirmation by an "Evangelical" clergyman. His views were, like my mother's, virtually a modified Calvinism, but shorn of such of its doctrines as are most dangerous in practice.

Up to this point I had learned the Catechism of the Church of England by heart, but I was not taught clearly or emphatically that the sacraments were channels of grace to the soul; on the contrary, it was tacitly assumed that Baptism was merely a formal admission into the visible

Church, and that the Eucharist was a mere commemorative rite to recall to our memories the Passion of our Lord. I was, of course, also told that we as Protestants only recognized two sacraments, while the Catholics claimed seven. I doubt whether I was validly baptized in my infancy, for the clergyman who performed the ceremony probably did not believe in baptismal regeneration, and would therefore not be careful that the essentials of baptism were duly performed.

Although I was brought up in the Church of England, my mother occasionally took me to the Nonconformists to hear popular preachers; amongst others, to the Wesleyan Methodists, Congregationalists, and the Baptists.

Mr. Spurgeon made a great impression on me by his controversy with the Evangelical Church party. He pointed out that baptismal regeneration was clearly taught in the Church of England Prayer-book, and that no one could honestly remain in the Church who did not believe in that doctrine.

At about the age of sixteen I used occasionally to go to High Anglican churches. I was at this time studying logic, so I did not take much interest in the details of ritual, but I took a keen and even precocious interest in doctrine. At these churches I did not hear anything about justification by faith alone, or about imputed right-eousness, but I heard a great deal about grace and salvation to be obtained by the right use of the sacra-ments, of regeneration by baptism, of the real presence of our Lord in the Eucharist, of the power given by Christ to his Apostles (and the clergy as their successors) to give absolution to penitent sinners. In other words, I heard, for the first time in my life, the sacramental system and the Apostolical Succession expounded by their advocates instead of their adversaries, who had always told me before, that the High Church party put the sacraments in the place of Christ, and Apostolical Succession in the place of the inward conversion of the heart. I now learned that the High Churchmen had been entirely misrepresented.

About the same time a public discussion took place in London between two clergymen (one a Ritualist and the other an Evangelical) on Catholic doctrine generally, and the sacrifice of the Mass in particular. I carefully weighed and considered the arguments on both sides, and took especial pains to look up the texts of Scripture relied on by both disputants. After prayer and careful deliberation, I came to the conclusion that the High Church view was the scriptural one, and in accordance with the teaching of the primitive Church, and I renounced for ever such of the doctrines of Calvin and Wesley as were opposed to that view. From that time I attended a church where High Church doctrines were taught; but the ritual was not very advanced, and I read with pleasure Keble's "Christian Year" as containing the true and sound Anglican doctrine.

Some time after this Dr. Pusey's "Eirenicon" came under my notice, and made a great impression upon my mind. This book urged that the Roman, Anglican, and Greek Churches should sink their differences, meet on the common ground of their Apostolical Succession, and again become the one and undivided Catholic and Apostolic Church. The refusal of the Catholic Church to accept this invitation roused my indignation, and seemed to

resuscitate my old Protestant prejudices against the
Catholic Church.

It did not, however, shake my belief in the High
Church doctrines, but rather intensified and extended it.

When I was about twenty-two I made the acquaintance
of a law-student who had been brought up as a rigid,
uncompromising, supralapsarian Calvinist; he had, however, been induced to examine the claims of the Catholic
Church, and after research, deliberation, and prayer, had
become a Catholic. He challenged me to investigate the
teaching of the Catholic Church, boldly predicting that, if
I did this carefully and impartially, I should certainly
become a Catholic. I ridiculed the idea of such a result,
saying that I was satisfied that the Church of England
had the true sacraments and the Apostolical Succession,
and that I was contented with her ministrations; but I
said that I always acted on the principle *audi alteram
partem*, and I would therefore read the best books on
both sides of the controversy. I began by praying for
light, making the resolution, with the help of God, to live
a higher life, and begging the saints to pray for me. I
then commenced my reading. On the Catholic side of
the question I read Milner's "End of Controversy,"
Marshall's "Comedy of Convocation in the English
Church," Cardinal Wiseman's sermons, Cardinal Manning's
"Grounds of Faith," and Abbot Sweeny's sermons. On
the Protestant side I read Chillingworth's "Religion of
Protestants," Dr. Cumming's "Hammersmith Discussion,"
Isaac Barrow's sermons, Stillingfleet's sermons, and various
histories of the Reformation on both sides. I also found
my intimate acquaintance with the text of Scripture taught

me by my mother of immense service ; and I may add that I did not take Bishop's Milner's authorities on trust, but verified many of his references to the works of the Fathers for myself, because many Protestant controversialists had said that Catholic quotations were often garbled, misinterpreted, or misapplied. I also made other laborious researches.

This long and anxious inquiry occupied six months. My eyes were now opened to the fact that the Catholic Church had been shamefully slandered by her enemies, who had, for three hundred years, used all the arts of falsehood, with painfully successful results ; that Anglicanism had been founded and propagated by cruelty, injustice, crooked statecraft, and even murder ; that I had not believed all the Catholic faith, but only part of it ; that although I believed a great mass of Catholic doctrine, as taught by High Anglicans, I accepted it only on the Protestant principle of private judgment and interpretation, whereas our Lord had taught us that we must believe His truth on the authority of one universal Church divinely guaranteed by Him against the possibility of error. This naturally led to the inquiry, " *Which* is this Church ? " I then examined the notes of the true Church as indicated in the Bible, and was forced to the conclusion that, if I sought for the true Church, I must look for the Chair of St. Peter—*ubi Petrus ibi ecclesia.*

My reason was now convinced of the Divine authority of the Catholic Church, but I shrank from cutting myself off from all intercommunion with my High Anglican and even Evangelical friends, and I realized for the first time in my life that one can have intellectual conviction without

E

faith. I prayed for light, and a holy religious prayed too, and offered the Holy Sacrifice on my behalf. The result was that in a few days he had the happiness of receiving me into the *one* Holy Catholic Apostolic and Roman Church.

That is many years ago. Since then I have had no more doubts on religious questions, though I am a doubter of doubters in matters outside religious truth, such as politics, law, history, etc. I have been happily married to a Catholic wife, herself the granddaughter of a Scotch officer, a convert from Presbyterianism. My son is a science student at a German University, surrounded by unbelievers ; but his faith is clear and strong, he is regular in attending to his religious duties, under the direction of a good German Dominican friar, and he sees nothing in science or nature to contradict God's holy revelation.

I can truly say with the Apostle, but in all humility, [*Deus*] *inquirentibus se remunerator* (Heb. xi. 6).

The Rev. JOHN CHAPMAN, B.A.,

(1ST CLASS LIT. HUM., 2ND CLASS THEOL., 1887), CHRIST CHURCH, OXFORD ; PRIEST OF THE ORDER OF ST. BENEDICT ; SUB-PRIOR, ERDINGTON ABBEY, BIRMINGHAM.

IT was not till about the time I took my degree at Oxford that I had any thought of taking Orders. Brought up at home, and in clerical society, and quite familiar with bishops, deans, and canons, I had no particular veneration for the eminence of their vocation, nor did it strike me to think of "going into the Church" as anything but a profession. But it so happened that a large number of my friends at Oxford were High Church, and intended to become clergymen. They had a serious view of their call, and one or other of them even went to confession. I was easily persuaded to go with them, a few times, on Sunday evenings to St. Barnabas'. I was so far pious that I had been accustomed never to miss my early Sunday Communion ; and now I began to wonder whether the expressions about the love of God in the "Imitation of Christ" meant anything real. In a vague way I felt some sort of a call to God. I have now not the least doubt that it was the beginning of a gracious call from God to the religious life.

I went to Cuddesdon eventually, and there began my gradual movement towards the true Church, which lasted some two years and a half.

I wanted, in the first place, to learn what I could of the spiritual life. I saw plainly that the ordinary teaching of the Anglican Church ignored the spiritual life altogther, and went in for respectability and propriety, and nothing further. The Evangelical school I admired, but I thought it logically led to the Salvation Army, and had no historical basis. But the Catholic devotional literature, which I now began to use, opened to me a new world ; and I could not go back, I could only go forward. I began to laugh at adaptations, and to use Catholic books as they stood ; and also to say part of the Breviary in English. I did not care for ritual ; I might almost say I disliked it, except as the ancient and historical custom of the Catholic Church.

This was only one side of the movement of my whole self. The other, and far the more important, was the dogmatic side. I had to study doctrine and Church history, and soon came to see in the Reformation the uprooting of all that I was just beginning to love and venerate. For the purpose of elucidating some points in the Thirty-nine Articles, I began to examine the Scholastic theologians, and many later ones. I went to the Bodleian, and consulted Scotus and Aleusis, Vasquez and Soto and Stapylton, and such-like. Aristotelian training had made St. Thomas easy to me. I have still a hundred pages of analysis of a volume of Suarez. The amount altogether was not very great ; but I learned for the first time that Anglicans, whether present or past, knew no theology in the strict sense. I lost all confidence in them as guides, just as I gained my first love of what little I knew of Catholic ascetics.

After a year at Cuddesdon, I had not a single *practical temptation* to leave the Anglican communion, here and now. But I looked upon the idea as one that would probably develop some day.

I went as a deacon to a parish where the clergy were as extreme in their views as they were moderate in their practice, "for fear of the Jews." In fact, to my great distress, I had to wait some months before even a daily Communion was instituted.

Now began my troubles in earnest. I had to teach. I asked myself on what authority. Not the bishop's. Not that of the Articles, which I hated; nor that of the Prayer-book, which we all laughed at. Not of the present Catholic Church; for East and West agreed only in holding me to be a heretic. As to antiquity, if I took in the fourth and fifth centuries, why not the sixteenth or nineteenth? If I stopped at the first, should I agree with Lightfoot, and lose religion as I understood it, or with Harnack, and give up Christianity? It seemed to me that Christianity must be continuous, and the Church infallible. But, if Rome was right, I must be wrong. My friends told me I wanted to be too logical. I merely urged that they were illogical, and enjoyed it; but that I was not made like that. I had not been brought up to High Church views. I would not take them from my friends without authority, and they had none to allege.

I hated parish work, because I felt I was doing no good with such uncertainty. I used to wish to go, but my vicar would not let me; and I used to find also that the work itself was somehow wound round my heart—the slums, and the choir-boys, and so on. I used to rush away and pray in open—and empty—churches (Reservation, now claimed by Anglicans as a part of their "Catholic heritage," was unknown to London churches, with one exception, in 1889). I sometimes talked or wrote to a friend, a curate at the other end of London, who was in the same difficulties as myself; and I prayed that he might be the first to go. I was much nearer the Church than he was; but he was a Ritualist, and I was not. I read controversy, when I had time, and sometimes the Fathers.

After nearly a year, I went up to Oxford in Lent to study, for ten days. I talked to Gore and Bright, who were kind. They told me history made it impossible to become a Romanist. I had already tried, and failed, to convince myself of the fact, and there was nothing else to keep me back. I remember reading all the acts of the Council of Chalcedon in Mansi, with Hefele to help me, at the Bodleian, and studying St. Basil's letters in the quiet Pusey library.

I returned, and told my sympathetic friend that I could find no difficulties in history, which disappointed him somewhat. But I added that there seemed to be grace in the English Church, and that I was not ready to move yet—I ought to wait.

We both made the novena of the Holy Ghost from Ascension Day till Whit-Sunday. That day was the last on which I preached in an Anglican Church, and it was the last on which he worshipped in one. On the feast of Corpus Christi, he was converted in Belgium, and I first felt I was not sure of Anglican Orders.

Directly I heard of his conversion, I left my parish for a holiday, and from home wrote to my vicar, explaining that I could not conscientiously return; and this time he saw it was useless to resist.

But I could decide nothing. I was afraid to go to a Catholic priest, knowing too well that I should make up my mind at once. I stayed six months at home, in uncertainty. I had to go on Sundays to the village church. I used to rub my eyes, and say to myself, "Is that man a Catholic priest," as the grey-bearded parson read "Dearly beloved" in a sing-song, or sprawled over the north end of the Communion table. I could not stay away from Communion on Sundays; yet I thought it almost certain that I made only a spiritual Communion.

And yet I did not move. The truth of the Catholic position was so absolutely clear to my mind, that I could not see how good and clever and learned men could deny it. And this made a new difficulty. The case was *so* clear to me, that perhaps somehow I was wrong. I intended to go away, and make a sort of retreat alone, to pray and think. But I knew what would be the result. I waited, and waited, to satisfy my father, and to give myself the chance of getting over the fever of internal impatience and anxiety that held me. But at the same time I was conscious that the worldly and idle life I was leading was bad for me, and that I was praying less often and less well. At last, on one of the last days of November, I summoned courage to tell my father I must settle matters. I went to a small seaside place, and took a lonely lodging, and read and thought and prayed. I remember writing a list of controversial books for my father, all of which I had studied. It would prove, not that I had studied deeply, but that I could not have overlooked any important difficulty. I again read through Gore's "Roman Catholic Claims" and Canon Carter's "The Roman Question," and I found that there was nothing in them to which I could not give a sufficiently satisfactory answer. There was only one Church possible, and that must be the Church of Rome. There must be authority and a living voice to decide controversies, and there must be supernatural sanctity and religious orders, and miracles and signs and wonders.

I was sure that I had a vocation to the religious life, and this increased my anxiety to join the true Church. But I had never spoken to any Catholic, still less to a priest, on the subject.

I went up to London, took the underground to South Kensington, and, leaving my portmanteau at the station, I went with trembling heart to ring the bell of the Oratory and to ask "for one of the Fathers." A good Father duly appeared in a parlour. "I have come," I said rather feebly, "because I have been for a long time troubled about the claims of the Roman Church. Will you give me some advice?" I was relieved when he laughed: "Well, if you want my advice, of course I advise you to join it!" After this I laughed too, and we were at once excellent friends. The next day (St. Nicholas') I was reconciled, and the day following I made my first Communion. The happiness with which I was flooded is unspeakable. I have had plenty of trials since then, but a doubt about the true Faith, never.

H. C. CORRANCE, Esq., B.A.,

CHRIST CHURCH, OXFORD; FORMERLY RECTOR OF WEST
BERGHOLT, ESSEX.

I DO not suppose that my path to the Catholic Church differs very greatly from that which many others have trod of recent years. But, as I have been asked to contribute to this volume some account of the reasons which convinced me of the truth of the Church's claims, I will endeavour to present as briefly as possible the main line of thought by which I reached that conclusion. I say advisedly "the main line," as it is of course impossible, within the necessary limits of such a contribution as this, to even touch upon all the causes and influences which co-operated to the final result.

Brought up in the old-fashioned school of High Church Anglicanism, I was early convinced from the reading of the New Testament Scriptures that Christ founded a Visible and Universal Church, and also of the reasonableness of such an idea on *a priori* grounds. This outline was gradually filled in, partly by study, and partly by the influences of the so-called Ritualistic movement, which was making itself felt at Oxford while I was there.

Naturally, at first, I accepted the idea that the body to which I belonged formed part of that Church, though for many years I was neither offered, nor did I form for myself, any definite theory of its relation to the existing whole. Apostolic succession was the only principle which in my mind distinguished the Church from the sects. Questions of government and jurisdiction had not yet presented themselves to me. This vagueness of view as to what constitutes the Church continued, along with steady growth in Catholic ideas and practices, throughout my theological studies at Oxford, and until after my ordination in the Church of England. It was not till soon after this that I became acquainted with the theory, through a tract that I had chanced to buy, that the Roman, Greek, and Anglican are three branches of one Catholic Church. This theory was then in its first beginnings, but has since become popularized among High Church Anglicans.

Later on, when I had come to hold nearly all the distinctive doctrines of Catholicism, I met with another theory invented by the extremest section of the Ritualistic party to account for and to justify their position. This was, in brief, that the two Anglican provinces of Canterbury and York form an integral part of Western Christendom, though communion has been unhappily suspended for a time between the severed portion and the main body. I may say that I was present at the birth of this theory, when first propounded in an address given by a well-known Anglican clergyman to some of his fellows. Since then this theory, like the former one, has left the esoteric stage, and has been steadily winning its way to acceptance by the extremest wing of the High Church party. The former, however, is still the favourite, as it accommodates itself better to the vagueness of moderate High Churchmanship.

To the "Two-Province theory" (as I may call it), its very definiteness is its danger, as the safety of the "Three-Branch" theory lies in its vagueness. The former, indeed, supplies a more plausible explanation of the position of Anglicanism in England in relation to "the rest of the Church," but it does not attempt to meet the insuperable difficulties presented by foreign jurisdictions. Consequently, I cannot say that I ever made the theory my own. I can see now that its very definiteness rendered clearer the inconsistencies of my then position, though I could not at once realize the consequences, being held by so many sentimental ties to the Church of England.

So for a time I left theory alone, and continued my work as a parochial clergyman. But the changes of mental attitude in the advanced party to which I belonged had produced in me a certain state of unrest, and their formulating of new theories in the place of old was preparing the way for my acceptance of one more in accordance with facts. At length I made up my mind to study the whole subject, with the result that I became convinced of the essential nature of the Church's unity in all time. This "theory," if I may call it so, had great advantages over the other in its simplicity and harmony with the past and present states of Christendom. Having thus been brought to recognize that a Visible and Catholic Church must have an actual, and not merely a theoretical, unity; that it must be subject to one system of government, be international, and be able to speak with a living and authoritative voice, I could see none possessing these marks except that of which the Pope is the head. The theory of the development of doctrine enabled me to understand that the Papacy, my one-time crux, had attained its present prominence, in common with other matters of government and doctrine, through a steady and orderly process of growth which was natural and inevitable. In this theory of development lies the reconciliation between the Church's past and present, and it illuminates the progressive continuity of the Catholic system, a continuity which Anglicanism does not possess.

On the one side was the Church's actual and magnificent unity; on the other, the modern, conflicting and changing theories of Anglicanism, each one accepted by but a portion of the whole body, and, for the most part, totally at variance with the existing conditions of their Church. Their plea of continuity in doctrine and government had no foundation in history, and the same was true of their claim that conditions parallel to their own existed in the early Church which justified their present position. On the contrary, the position of Anglicanism in almost every respect is unique in the history of Christendom. The genius and spirit of that body, which is avowedly "comprehensive," is neither that of the early Church nor early schisms, of the present Eastern Churches, or of the Catholic Church. The claim, therefore, that these form part of one whole, possessing, *de jure* if not *de facto*, the same faith and discipline, seemed wholly unreal.

But if the question had been simply an historical one, I should have been left in uncertainty. I have no wish to decry the appeal to history. But so many controversial writers of equal learning and ability have been able to make it yield the conclusions they desire, that every one must either follow the lead of some school or form his own theories. I realized that the surest guide to the past is the present state of Christendom. The opposite (Anglican) method of interpreting the present by the past is to substitute opinion for fact, the contradictory conclusions of biased scholars for the direct appeal to existing evidence. And present-day facts are against the Anglican theory of Christendom. When I had reached this point there were only two courses open to me—either to renounce for ever the possibility of forming a rational theory of my position, or to secede. I chose the latter.

Those points which I have mentioned as seeming to me fatal to the pretensions of High Anglicans are referred to by some of them as " difficulties," which should no more induce a man to secede than the difficulties of Theism justify the surrender of the belief in God. But the two cases are not parallel. The difficulties of Theism are inherent in the nature of the subject which lies on the spiritual and transcendental plane, and is therefore mysterious. But the " Sacramentum Unitatis " is quite different. It was designed by Christ, according to His own statement which Anglicans accept, as a witness of His mission to the world, and is therefore on the plane of phenomena. It is chiefly a matter of external evidence. To ignore this important aspect of the question, and to deny that the argument from " simplicity " is valid in such a case, seems to me to misunderstand and confuse the whole question by postulating an ideal Church which has no concrete existence, and is therefore not " Visible " in any sense of the word.

The Rev. MATTHEW CULLEY,

OF COUPLAND CASTLE, NORTHUMBERLAND, PRIEST OF ALL SAINTS, THROPTON, NORTHUMBERLAND, AND J.P. FOR THE SAME COUNTY.

I WAS born in 1860, in Northumberland, the eldest son of the late Matthew T. Culley, of Coupland Castle in that county, of an old northern family that certainly remained true to the Catholic faith (in some of its members, at least) for some time after the change of religion in England, but apparently fell away in the latter part of the sixteenth century or early in the seventeenth. Like most Northumbrian families, we could count Catholics among our kith and kin not very far back. My great-grandmother had many Catholic relatives—amongst them a Dominican Father who, as I always heard, was found dead in the attitude of prayer before the altar, early in the last century. Then, again, Northumbrian-like, we had Catholic neighbours and friends ; for Northumberland, like Lancashire, is pretty full of Catholics.

My father and mother both belonged to the Established Church (so-called) of England. My father, though his tendencies were High Church, could hardly be called a High Churchman ; on the other hand, my mother was a

pronounced High Church woman, of the old Tractarian
type, and belonged to a very High Church family (of
Jacobite traditions), who were to a great extent the
pioneers of High Anglicanism in Northumberland. I
lost my mother when in my twelfth year. Her example
and teaching had left a deep impression on my mind.
Within two years after her death I began to pray, of my
own accord, before a picture of Our Lady and the Holy
Child that my mother had given me some years previously,
and which always hung in my room. At the same time,
having strung some beads together, I taught myself to
say the Rosary, learning it from a book I found in the
library at Coupland. I ought to mention that our parish
church, the last in England in that direction—for the parish
was bounded for many miles by Scotland—was of a most
Evangelical type, and the prevailing atmosphere of the
whole district was, and still is, Protestant and Presbyterian.
Whenever I had the opportunity, in London and elsewhere, I attended advanced High Church places of worship, and, of my own initiative, I went to confession to
a clergyman at St. Cyprian's, Dorset Square, when seventeen years of age. Owing to very delicate health, I was
educated for some years at home, but, just after my
eighteenth birthday, was sent to a tutor at Oxford to
prepare for the University. At Oxford I was a regular
attendant at a very advanced church, and sometimes went
to the Jesuit Church in the evenings. I recollect being
more and more dissatisfied with the inconsistent teaching
of the High Church party ; I heard some of their leading
men preach at this time. My chief difficulty with regard
to Rome was that I failed to understand or to see the

reason for the doctrine of Papal Supremacy and of the infallibility of the Holy Father. I think I believed everything else taught by the Catholic Church, at least as far as I knew at this time. Fortunately for me, during the autumn of that year (1878), a distinguished Catholic preacher and controversialist came to Oxford and gave a course of sermons on Sunday evenings in the Jesuit Church on the very subject that had been a difficulty to me. He put the whole question of the Pope's supremacy and the universality of the Roman Church in a light in which I had never seen it before. I had no conversation with the preacher, nor indeed with any other priest, but his sermons helped me immensely, and by degrees the way became quite easy before me. On the 21st of the following April, 1879, being eighteen years of age, I was received into the Church. Until I went to the priest—the late Mgr. Canon Clarke, V.G., of Clifton (R.I.P.)—to ask to be received, I had never spoken to a Catholic priest, nor had I had any consultation with Catholics on the step I then took.

The Rev. AUGUSTIN DANIELS, B.A.,

King's College, Cambridge; Priest of the Order of St. Benedict.

In the early days of my undergraduate life at King's College, Cambridge, I entertained hopes of one day becoming an Anglican clergyman. I was at that time much attracted to the teaching of the late F. D. Maurice, Charles Kingsley, and other members of what is called the Broad Church School. For two or three terms I even attended some Divinity Lectures. Gradually, however, a change took place in my religious opinions. Beginning with doubts as to the historical truth of the principal events recorded in the Gospels, I drifted away from positive Christianity and fell under the influence of Spinoza's philosophy. By the time I took my degree in 1885, my views had developed further, and in matters of religion and philosophy, I had adopted a very anti-metaphysical Agnosticism. My ethical ideal at that time was that of modern Humanism. A life devoted to the pursuit of science and the solution of social problems seemed to me the only one worth living. From time to time, in the course of the next few years, I came into occasional contact with Catholicism, and this mighty Creed under whose

F

shadow I had fallen, produced no small influence upon
me. The tendencies to which such impressions gave rise
seemed to me to be emotional and consequently anti-
social, and so I repressed them and continued along the
old path. At the date of which I am speaking I had
already spent some time as a student at the University of
Heidelberg. Here I became sceptical as to the fundamental principles of my Agnosticism. My theory of the
universe seemed to me to be based upon fallacies and
false hypotheses. I was driven to admit, not only the
possibility, but also the reasonableness of a revelation. It
was obvious to my mind that no actual antagonism could
exist between any well-established or even reasonably
probable result of science and the Christian revelation as
far as I understood it. This speculative revolution was
followed a little later on by a practical change. I was dis-
atisfied with my ethical ideals, and Darwinism no longer
sufficed to account for the phenomena of conscience. The
words of the poet were ringing perpetually in my ears,
and gave utterance to the most intense convictions of
my soul—

> "... aliudque cupido,
> Mens aliud suadet. Video meliora proboque,
> Deteriora sequor."

I recognized clearly that the only sufficient explanation
of the inward voice of conscience was the existence of
One without, Whose Voice it is. I had become a Theist
again. I found, however, that the knowledge of God
which my conscience was able to supply was insufficient
to satisfy my needs. How was the sense of sin to be
removed? I began to pray, and, in answer, heard the

voice of One saying, "Come unto Me, all ye that labour and are heavy laden, . . . and ye shall find rest for your souls." The wish to believe was already present, and I yearned to respond to this invitation. I began to re-examine the evidences for the Divine authority and supernatural origin of Christianity.

The truth of the Resurrection was the principal question to which I turned my attention. Amongst my German friends I had a number of Rationalistic theologians, who also admitted the fact which must strike every reader of the New Testament. I mean the prominence assigned by the Apostles to the doctrine that their Lord had really risen from the dead. My friends, however, would not admit what seemed to me to be the only reasonable explanation of this fact, viz. the historical reality of Christ's resurrection. They essayed to explain away the supernatural element, and I found their attempt unsatis-factory. The causes assigned were inadequate to account for the effects which were to be explained. The existence of Christianity and the growth of the Christian Church are facts so weighty that they cannot be reasonably sup-posed to have their origin in the ecstatic illusions or spiritualistic fancies of the first disciples and followers of Jesus. Such an assumption would involve such an enor-mous number of difficulties, that common sense and reason both prefer to accept the simple statement of the Evange-lists as historical fact.

Further inquiries led to the confirmation of my belief in the genuineness of the New Testament as a whole. I found that a false assumption, expressed or implied, invari-ably underlay all the arguments of the negative critics, viz.

the impossibility of miracles. This supposition, however, seemed to me to be entirely untenable, and indeed philosophically absurd. Thus I was led by the grace of God to accept the Christian revelation as contained in the New Testament.

Like many others, I soon found in this collection of books many "things which are hard to be understood"— things capable of various, even apparently contradictory, explanations. Which of these was I to accept? Certainly the one suggested by that Spirit Whom Christ had promised to send to lead His disciples into all truth. The question then arose in my mind, Where is this Holy Spirit now to be found? I knew that the Roman Church claimed to be the sole heir of this promise, and, as I have already hinted, I had a certain predisposition of mind towards Catholicism. The wondrous unity of its doctrine, the unsurpassed beauty of its liturgy, and the glorious traditions of its past, had often combined to impress me in the course of my studies. The step of entering into its communion was, however, one of far-reaching consequences, and for a time I shrank back. I knew that many Anglicans professed their Church to be the legitimate heir of Christ's promise in England. They predicated of the Church "established in these realms" the notes of unity, sanctity, catholicity, and apostolicity. I therefore began to examine the Anglican claims. The result, however, was that at the end of my investigation I found myself nearer to Rome. My first impression had been favourable to the presence of a valid priesthood in the Anglican Establishment. It seemed to me at least very probable that the material and formal apostolical succession had not been broken on Parker's elevation to the see of Canterbury. I was, however, afraid that, owing to the defective intention of so many bishops, the number of true priests amongst the ranks of the English clergy could not be very large.

On proceeding to an examination of the apostolicity of the Anglican teaching, I soon found myself in great difficulties. The Book of Common Prayer contained much that easily bore a Catholic interpretation, whereas the Articles, according to their plain and literal sense, were opposed to the historical practice of the Church and the explicit teaching of the Councils and Fathers. I wanted to know the doctrine of the Anglican Church. Its own authoritative formulæ and liturgy were inconsistent with one another. Naturally, I turned to the official exponents of the system, and found the bishops in hopeless disagreement as to some of the most vital points of the Christian revelation. I found, too, that episcopal utterances on matters of faith seemed not to be binding either upon clergy or laity. My question as to what to believe in order to be saved must remain unanswered in the Anglican Church, and my only consolation was the advice of a learned and earnest theologian to wait for the re-union of Christendom and the next General Council for a settlement of all my difficulties. I could not, however, afford to wait so long. I had a soul to save, and was perfectly certain that our Lord could not have failed to fulfil His promise, and that if I were only to find my way into the true Church, I should attain certainty as to what to believe. I began to see that the Church of England could be no part of Christ's visible kingdom on

J. DUFFUS-HARRIS, Esq.,

QUEEN ANNE'S MANSIONS, ST. JAMES'S PARK, LONDON.

I HAVE for a long time thought that if the ordinary man of the world who has been happy enough to arrive at a definite and settled religious faith were to relate the processes by which that goal was reached, more good would result to doubters and inquirers than is likely to be effected by volumes of professional theology. I consider it necessary, therefore, to explain that I am a man of good social position and of fair means, and that I have been leading the life of hundreds who are situated in London similarly to myself. I was for several years engaged in an active financial business in New York, which occupation was arrested by a breakdown of health, ending in a long and tedious illness, during which—I wish this to be specially noted—I cannot recollect having given a moment's thought to religious matters. I cannot, therefore, admit that my conversion to the Catholic Church was in any way brought about by mental depression or by my condition of physical weakness. Indeed, I did not begin to occupy myself with religious inquiries until my health was sufficiently re-established to enable me to resume what is known as "enjoying life." I had for nearly twenty years given up all practice of religion. I had silently accepted the usual agnostic position, although I confess to a secret feeling of repugnance which I experienced when open attacks were being made upon that very orthodox belief which I had long ceased to hold myself. Although my faith appeared to me to be irretrievably lost, I mourned that loss sincerely. Up to my twelfth year I had been educated in the principles of the Church of Scotland, and that education had been of a most uncompromising character. My family regarded even the revising of the Authorized Version of the Bible as a device inspired by Satan. There was, however, no austerity connected with our form of religion. We had a cheerful and luxurious home. Our Sundays began with attendance at church, followed, as far as I was concerned, by Bible and Catechism ; but it invariably ended in our receiving visitors at our house. We had many Catholic friends, and I cannot remember to have heard in my childhood much of that vituperation of the Catholic Church which is generally so marked amongst Protestants, and of which I have had more than enough since my conversion. From the age of twelve to past twenty, I was at various educational establishments in England, and the services of the Scotch Church being generally inaccessible at these places, my family allowed me to join in the Anglican form of worship. By my twenty-second year I had made up my mind that the Anglican Church was a Church of mere forms and shadows, and that if any one inquired what these meant, he was sure to receive an answer which was both vague and unsatisfactory.

Subsequent to this I entered upon that long period of doubt and agnosticism to which I have already referred. During this time I examined some of the many philosophical systems which have all had their day and their influence, but which appeared to me to prove nothing. They had all passed out of fashion, much as fiction and other literature is apt to do. Emerson attracted me at first, but he seemed to me to have no definite hold upon any fundamental religious principle, and so he wearied me at length, and I ceased to read his works. Then there came the time when the possibility of the Catholic Church first presented itself to my mind. I had already proved the truth of the saying that "a little study leads to doubt, but that further and more accurate study leads to belief." I read and thought a good deal, and had an opportunity of observing human life, both in business and in society, in different parts of the world, and, after a time, became not only firmly convinced of the existence of God, but began once more to read the Gospels. A peculiar unaccountable something, which was so strong that it quite angered me, made me feel sure that the essential doctrines of the Gospels were true. My next step was belief in the reality of sin, and in the debt which we owed God as a consequence. This conviction came upon me more by intuition than by reasoning. I felt that the reasons which can be adduced in favour of our Lord's Divinity were more powerful than the objections which were urged against it, and, in the course of time, the difficulties of my mind yielded to faith. I had therefore now reached a point at which I felt that my convictions would have to be supported by some definite and regular practice corresponding with them.

Circumstances naturally pointed to the Anglican Church ; but, on confronting it afresh, all my early objections seemed to return with tenfold strength. There was, in the first place, the disagreement amongst her clergy as to fundamental doctrine, and her adoption of certain forms and ritual which were the cause of endless controversy. Then there was the stress which was laid upon her Nationalism, as though God had made contrary and different revelations to different peoples. There was, finally, the circumstance that, in spiritual and theological disputes, the court of final appeal was Parliament, a lay body among whose members there might be Hebrews and Atheists, possessed of the right to pronounce binding opinions upon matters of Christian faith and practice. It seemed to me that the Anglican Church as a body had actually lost the faith, that she taught nothing definite, that she was a mere quicksand to a mind in distress. At that very time struggles were going on about such trivialities as lights and incense, while some of her highest dignitaries were allowed to cast doubts upon parts of the Gospels which were clearly essential to the very being of Christianity. Even bishops sneered at great principles, and one of the most prominent of these had only just proclaimed himself an Englishman first and a Churchman afterwards, and had said in public that the right thing to discover was what the British wanted in matters of religion. To discover the commands of our Lord seemed the last thing that this eminent prelate was thinking of. The sermons which were being preached in great churches seemed to me to be either ethical essays or glorifications of national pride. The Great Preacher of the mountain seemed to

be either forgotten or to be treated to a mere perfunctory
and formal salute.

The various books which were appearing, with a view to
establishing the continuity and Catholicism of the Anglican
Church, caused me to reject this position more and more.
They might suit those people to whom nationalism was
of more importance than Christ's teaching; their very
premises, it was clear, were rejected with derision by all
impartial thinkers outside of England, and their reasoning seemed sometimes absolutely puerile. I shall never
forget how, one day, when thinking of these matters, the
word "Rome" suddenly thrust itself upon me, flashing
through my brain like a piercing sword. I had, of course,
during my life been present at Catholic services; but my
attitude had always been a purely impersonal one, such
as I would have maintained in a Buddhist temple or a
Mohammedan mosque. When, however, the possibility of
Catholicism being applicable to myself came home to me,
I was seized with an agitation the like of which I had
never experienced before. But in spite of an inner feeling
of revolt and repulsion, not unmixed with a feeling of
attraction, it very soon became my imperative duty to
give the Roman Church a hearing. The first time I went
to Mass it was as an interested spectator only, but I
thoroughly realized the truth of Thackeray's passage in
which he says, that he is always conscious of a kind of
vague dread in Catholic churches—of a sort of holy and at
the same time uncanny feeling.

A course of lectures was at this time being given in
the Farm Street Church which I attended. It soon became
clear to me that, instead of trying to grapple with this or

that doctrine, perhaps specially obnoxious to Protestants, the following were really the questions which would have to be answered :—

"Do I believe in our Lord's charge to Peter?

"Do I believe that He founded an indestructible Church on earth?

"Is the Roman Church that Church, or is it not?"

The books which helped me most in the attempt to answer these questions were De Maistre on "The Pope," Cardinal Gibbon's "Faith of our Fathers," Pascal's "Divinity of our Lord," and, of course, Cardinal Newman's writings. But I think I was more helped by his sermons than by his controversial works, as I had already by thought and reflection arrived at many of his conclusions—in a much-clumsier manner, of course. Some unbiassed non-Catholics, however, aided me more, I think, than any purely Catholic writer, and I would strongly advise all inquirers to examine the writings of such men as Leibnitz, and to study carefully Macaulay's Essay on "Von Ranke's History of the Popes." Another thing which influenced me greatly was the circumstance that I was constantly meeting with scientific men of mark from celebrated American Universities, such as Harvard and Pennsylvania, who were without any definite religious convictions, but who seemed to take it for granted that if our spiritual knowledge justified acceptance of any definite Creed and Church, no other Church but that of Rome was worth considering. One of the most prominent Biblical critics of Harvard, Professor Toy, has lately given a course of lectures at that university, in which he has demonstrated that every Catholic doctrine to which Protestants most strenuously object, such as that of Purgatory and Indulgences, is an inevitable consequence of the teaching of the Gospels provided ordinary methods of reasoning be employed. Thus obstacle after obstacle disappeared, until I found myself convinced intellectually that to refuse to become a Catholic was to refuse to obey the conclusions of my own reasoning and to quarrel with my destiny. I was accordingly received into the Church at Farm Street by the Reverend Father Rickaby on May 7, 1898, being then forty-three years old. I suppose that few people have found their way into the Church with as little human aid as I have. I trod most of my " Road to Damascus " alone, and consulted priests for the purpose of verification rather than for that of receiving instruction. Delicacy and tact I found everywhere. No priest ever called upon me in London, though it was known to two or three that I was studying Catholicism. My Catholic friends in England and in France never approached the subject of religion, although I discovered afterwards that my French friends had formed a little league of prayer for me.

I have heard it said of many thoughtful men that, but for the solemn and awe-inspiring general confession, they would become Catholics. I adopted a more logical course than this ; nevertheless, I must confess that the prospect of a general confession filled me with dismay. I was forty-three years old, had lived but little or no better than my neighbours, and I had a painfully accurate memory which extended back to my eighth or ninth year. I made up my mind that I would choose a confessor whom I would never be likely to see again. Circumstances at the last moment caused me to go to the very priest whom I knew best of all. He was patience, kindness, and encouragement personified, and, instead of experiencing a kind of degradation according to the conventional view of the matter, I felt a sense of relief and happiness such as I cannot describe. When I see my confessor now—he has left London—we talk on every subject quite naturally and without restraint, and I quite forget at the time that he was the witness of a moral cleansing which had been waiting its accomplishment for thirty-eight years. I do not go often enough to confession ; but I consider it one of the most inestimable blessings which God has conferred upon man. Little more remains to be told. Would that what I have written would go to encourage others, and show them where an inward happiness, such as they do not dream of, is to be found! The Church has widened my sympathies, it has cast down many prejudices, it has provided me with a spiritual support such as outsiders can have no possible idea of. My intellect is satisfied, and if there be trials and discouraging moments in life, the Church has innumerable remedies to cure them: they all proceed from and return to the one point— the manger of Bethlehem. Let no one say that submission is an act of servility. Submission of our individual opinions to the Vicar of Christ is no more servility than is an inferior officer's submission to his superior. He may not be able to see the situation in all its bearings, but he obeys because he believes that his superior represents his country and his Sovereign. In like manner, when the Vicar of Christ speaks to define a disputed question of faith, or to give a moral counsel, or to warn the world of certain dangers, the Catholic humbly and

cheerfully obeys, because he believes that God is true to
His promises, and that He is teaching truth by the mouth
of His Vicar on earth.

NOTE.—I have omitted to state that I consider "Christianity or Agnosticism," by the Abbé Picard (an excellent
translation of which can be found at the libraries), perhaps
the clearest, most convincing, and most readable book on
this subject which I have ever seen. I would strongly
urge all inquirers to study this work.

REGINALD B. FELLOWS, Esq., M.A.,

TRINITY COLLEGE, CAMBRIDGE; BARRISTER-AT-LAW.

SOME years ago I became convinced that the doctrine of
the Real Presence was of the essence of Christ's teaching,
that it had been taught by the Apostles and insisted on by
the primitive Church, and that the same doctrine had been
taught as essential by the Church of England down to the
time of the Reformation. At that period, however, it
appeared that a belief in the doctrine of the Real Presence
ceased to be any longer necessary for membership in the
Established Church. It seemed to me that strong and
cumulative evidence of this change—this protest against the
ancient faith—was found in the incidental notices which we
have, *e.g.*, in Churchwardens' Accounts, both of the pay-
ments which were made for the removal of altar stones and
for the demolition of altars, and also of the sales of those
sacred vessels and vestments which had for centuries formed
part of a ritual which had been the expression of a belief
in the doctrine of Christ's Presence on the Altar. It
further appeared to me that, although a certain number of
the members of the Anglican Church believed in the

Catholic doctrine of the Real Presence, the Church as such had ceased to consider it to be of the essence of Christianity ; that a belief in the doctrine was at the best merely allowable, and that for a very considerable period in the history of the Anglican Church after the Reformation, *any* belief in the doctrine was most exceptional.

But if the doctrine of the Real Presence is really an essential part of Christ's teaching, it must also (I argued) form an essential part of the Christianity of this or of any other age. Now, it appeared to me that there actually existed in England a body corporate claiming to be the Church of Christ, and also to be the legitimate descendant of the Pre-Reformation Church and teaching ; moreover, that a belief in the Real Presence was absolutely essential for Church membership. The conclusion at which I arrived was that this body, the Catholic and Roman Church, was *primâ facie* the true Church of Christ. Since, then, a strong presumption was raised in favour of the claims of this Church to be the true Church, I felt that it was incumbent upon me to ascertain, to the best of my ability, if there was anything in her general teaching to rebut that presumption. Although I found that there were difficulties in accepting the teaching of the Catholic Church, I found that these difficulties were not insuperable, and that they were not greater than those which exist in accepting any form of dogmatic Christianity.

Further evidence in favour of submitting to the Catholic Church was found in the fact that Protestantism tended to reject, or at least to minimize, those precepts of Christ which are difficult to obey and irksome to human nature : *e.g.*

abstinence and fasting ; confession ; voluntary poverty and the other counsels of perfection. A strong presumption appeared to me to be raised by this consideration alone against the claim of any Protestant Church to be the true Church of Christ.

The Rev. JOHN H. FILMER,

King's College, London ; formerly Curate of St. Margaret, Roath, Cardiff ; now a Student at the Collegio Beda in Rome.

I AM afraid that I cannot say anything very interesting or helpful with regard to my conversion, for its history can be set forth in the few words that God gave me grace to see His light and then to walk in it.

To set down in any helpful way the arguments by which He led me, or the motives with which He prompted me, would need a treatise such as I have not time at present to write.

But since I am asked for some account, however short, I may say that, broadly speaking, I regard my conversion as the result of the Holy Spirit's gradual education in the truth of God, and my submission to the Church as the logical consequence of principles which I learnt to hold while still a member of the English Church. For I had learnt, step by step, to believe the whole body (with one exception) of Catholic Doctrine, from the Church as a teaching body, through the whole list of distinctively Catholic tenets, such as the Seven Sacraments, Invocation of Saints, Purgatory, finding each in turn (to my surprise, for I had at one time held them in abhorrence) bear the tests of Scripture and of Reason. And I remained a member of the Church of England, and for five years was one of her ministers, merely because I believed her to be a true part of God's One Church, and that therefore her formularies must be, and honestly could be, interpreted in the Catholic sense ; while their mistiness, together with the difficulties encountered by any Catholic-minded person within her Communion, were simply the natural result of the sins of our forefathers who at the Reformation compromised themselves and their Church with foreign Protestantism. This was my position when it dawned upon me that I had built up this superstructure of Catholicity upon two foundations, the truth of which I had taken for granted, viz. that the Church of England was a true part of the One Catholic Church, in spite of appearances to the contrary, and that the claim of the first bishop in Christendom to be infallible was a new and a false claim.

Then asking myself, Why do I believe Infallibility alone of all other Catholic doctrines to be false ? I found I only rejected it (not knowing anything about it) because I was prejudiced against it, and because to accept it meant to give up the whole Anglican position. I had accepted all other truths which at one time in my ignorance I rejected, simply because I had learnt more about them. I now knew what they meant. I saw they were scripturally and reasonably sound ; might it not be the same with this one ? So I felt bound to learn more about it, and, applying the same tests of Scripture and Reason, I was convinced first of its necessity, then of its reasonableness, last of its scriptural authority. But I remained long in doubt because of the maze I got into with the historical evidences on both sides—historians, apparently of equal renown, absolutely contradicting one another—until I saw that those historians who had the plain meaning of Scripture, together with the plain common sense of Reason on their side, must be right ; then, by the grace of God, I was convinced of its Divine institution.

Having thus destroyed the foundation of my faith in the Church of England, I saw the rest crumble away, and understood why that Church is never able to teach definitely what is of Faith, why its formulas are capable of two opposite meanings, why it is so comprehensive as to allow all shades of thought to be believed and taught within her, and saw the true answer to a question I could never solve before, viz. why England alone should have received a special revelation of a pure gospel, while all other enlightened nations were still steeped in the superstitions of Popery.

So, God helping me, I made my submission to His Vicar on earth, and found the Catholic Church not, as I had been led to expect, a community of uneducated clergy and of an irreverent, superstitious, priest-ridden laity, the whole in the last stages of discontent and decay, but a living, thriving Church, with enlightened minds and devoted, holy lives among priests and people, lived in an atmosphere of religious freedom, such as Anglicans, Protestant and Catholic-minded alike, never dream of.

The Rev. PHILIP FLETCHER, M.A.,

EXETER COLLEGE, OXFORD; MASTER AND FOUNDER OF THE
GUILD OF RANSOM.

QUOMODO?

THAT, in one word, is the question I am asked to answer.
Quomodo? "How?" How did you become a Catholic?
What were the grounds and leading motives which
prompted you to abandon your former religious position,
and to submit to the authority and claims of the Catholic
Church? Let me look back once more and trace the way
by which I came.

I was brought up by a saintly mother in what she
believed to be the principles of the Church of England, to
which she was sincerely attached. During this period of
"home influence," which lasted till I was sixteen and a half
years old, and which was supplemented by four or five
years of sojourn at two quiet Church of England schools,
my religious knowledge was chiefly composed of the text
of the Catechism, of the Collects, and of the Christian
Year, Old Testament history, and a few parables, weak
health hindering me from going to a public school. I
studied from about fourteen and a half years to seventeen

and a half years at home, going afterwards to tutors, and
finally, for four years, to Oxford. The home part of this
period increased my acquaintance with the text of Holy
Scripture, both Old and New Testaments, for it was the
custom at home to read the Psalms and Lessons every
day. Yet, in spite of this head knowledge, and in spite
of the "good home," I had, up till sixteen and a half years
old, the vaguest ideas of God, scarcely any of the Blessed
Trinity, or of the Incarnation. Sunday was tedious to me,
and prayer a form. Confirmation and Communion were
not thought suitable until after sixteen. Still, I owe this
to the home training: an intimate acquaintance with the
English and the subject-matter of the Bible. Reading for
Honours in the Theological School at Oxford made me
further familiar, not only with the English, but, in the
New Testament, with the Greek text, and I became, I
may say, so drenched with Holy Scripture, that it ran off
me at my very fingers' ends. At sixteen and a half an
entirely new light broke in upon me, and in it I was able
to see that the Bible had a soul as well as a body, and,
after that date, I added to a knowledge of the text, a deep
appreciation of the mind of Holy Scripture.

About this time I reached a turning in the way, which
took me out of the gloom in which I was walking and
showed me a new country. It was called "Religion," but
was quite different to the country which I had hitherto
thought was "Religion," and which I had voted dreary
and uninteresting. This new view, now spreading before
me, was, on the contrary, bright and fascinating. The
"wicket-gate" by which I entered it was "St. Michael's,
Brighton," where the services, though out of the same

Prayer-book as we had at "St. John the Baptist's," were yet
as different as a fine day is from a wet one. I became
converted at once. Yes, it was a case of instantaneous
conversion. I was introduced to Mr. Beanlands, the
Incumbent of St. Michael's, at the house of the Rev. John
Purchas, whither a friend took me for an evening party.
I took to Mr. Beanlands and he to me. I went to his
church, and from that day until I became attached to St.
Bartholomew's, I loved that little church with a passionate
devotion, being never happy away from it. I became
detached from my home in a degree which would not be
commended to a Catholic, and spent every spare moment
at St. Michael's. Its friends became mine ; its religion
mine. There I made my first Communion on a Maundy
Thursday, having been prepared for it and for Confirmation
by Mr. Beanlands. My view of Religion, now that I had
turned that corner and had passed through the wicket-gate,
was quite changed. It became my one absorbing subject ;
not merely feasting my eyes with bright ritual, nor my
ears with beautiful hymns and "Mass"-music, but really
changing my heart, turning it to and throwing it upon
One Whom hitherto I had only known by name—Jesus
Christ, Son of God, Saviour. The influence of St. Michael's
upon me was good, very good, at the time, and for the
future. Undoubtedly, it led to my future being a Catholic
one.

As my home training had grounded me well in knowledge of the Bible, so the St. Michael's training introduced
me to the idea of a Church, and particularly to a delight
in Liturgical services. At first, my knowledge of these
was limited to the Matins and Evensong of the Prayer-book.

Evensong became my *beau-ideal* of a Liturgical service, and I still think it by far the best thing the Church of England has got, and a very beautiful thing in itself. Here, too, I got my first ideas of "Mass," and these ideas were very richly clothed at St. Michael's, so that a beginner was easily deceived into supposing that the Anglican Communion service, dressed as it was at St. Michael's, was really the Mass. In those days, however, the word "Mass" was not so well known to me as it became afterwards at St. Bartholomew's. The whole idea of the Real Presence was new to me, and I was taken up with that, without looking much into details.

During my four years at Oxford my love for St. Michael's never waned, and in the vacations I was always there. Whilst in residence I was assiduous in attendance at chapel (Exeter College), and was in the choir. I easily dropped into a quiet set, and my friends were T. B. Dover, George Dover (afterwards a Catholic), Sidney Little (afterwards a Catholic), W. Lovell (afterwards a Catholic), Egerton Harding (afterwards a Catholic), the two Adyes, the two Moores (sons of the Rev. Daniel Moore), George Druitt, and J. M. Davenport. The last named and I were great friends, and it was he who brought me into contact with the Cowley Fathers, whom I got to know very well. He and I at one time used to start off every morning (often in the dark) down the "High," over Magdalen Bridge, and along the Iffley Road to the "Monastery," and there join with the Fathers in "Prime," coming back in time for College Chapel at eight. At first my favourite "outside" church was St. Philip and St. James', but later I went to St. Barnabas'. I had a district in Holy Trinity parish, though the vicar there, Mr. Linton, was "low;" but Edmund Garnet, a deacon, was attached there, and he and I became great friends until he "went over." Happily we were able afterwards to renew and increase our friendship in the bosom of the Catholic Church, when I found him as Father Garnet of the Oratory.

The most important event of my spiritual life, during my sojourn at Oxford, probably was my introduction to the principal of Cuddesdon College, Dr. King. To him I was persuaded to pay a visit and to make my first confession. I went full of trepidation and came back full of joy. From that time till my conversion, Dr. King's influence was strong with me. I saw much of him and of Cuddesdon during my sojourn at Garsington, close by, where I spent the last "Long" reading for Honours. After taking my degree, I went to Cuddesdon (January, 1872) and read "Theology" there, till my ordination as Deacon in May. I became a fervent disciple of the "Principal" along with most of my companions. The influences of Oxford and Cuddesdon were to make me loyally Anglican. I had once at Oxford had a Roman fit when Monsignor Capel made a raid and captured George Dover and others. But it passed away, J. M. Davenport being very Anglican and at that time my chief friend.

The last period I have to deal with is my time at St. Bartholomew's, Brighton, to the curacy of which I was appointed in 1872. My time of hard reading was now over for six years, and I plunged into work among the poor with great eagerness. Though a convinced Anglican, I was extreme in spite of the influence of Dr. King. Leanings to Rome had begun, though I cannot remember how. But I know that the Bishop of Chichester had thought it necessary to have a quiet talk with me after my examination for either Deacon's or Priest's Orders, because, in one paper, I had given it as my opinion that Transubstantiation was a possible explanation of "This is My Body."

I was at St. Bartholomew's for six years all but two or three months, and my time, interests, head and heart were absorbed in the services, schools, confraternities, clubs, entertainments, etc., of the parish. Yet through all the happy hubbub of children's voices, bright evenings, processionals and recessionals, High Celebrations, school-treats, choir breakfasts, concerts and entertainments, there was a word which rang ever and louder in my ears, and that word was ROME.

Somehow it seemed to me to rhyme with "Home" (as, indeed, it did). When I come to search for the influence which drew me to Rome, it seems to me that it was something external to myself. Rome pulled me to herself. It was the hand of my mother which would not let me go. There were hundreds pulling at me to prevent my going: my mother who bore me and brought me up, and who loved me even more than I loved her (if that were possible); my family, my flock. "I am so fast in prison that I cannot get forth." Chains bound me tightly to the Church of England: every convert knows how it hurts to wrench one's self away from these chains. Yet, all the while, something was pulling, pulling *away* from the Church of England. Was there anything push-ing as well as pulling? Well, yes, the state of the Church of England, its divisions, its want of discipline, the arguments which a Catholic can bring against it. All these, no doubt, pushed. But I think I was pulled rather than pushed. A voice was calling me, a grace was drawing me which, in spite of the many voices begging me to stay where I was, obliged me at length to break away. It was not, I think, so much disgust with the Church of England as love for the Church of Rome. I became, during my time at St. Bartholomew's, better acquainted with the devotions and the teaching of the Catholic Church. At my ordination, the chaplain of Cuddesdon College had given me as a present the "Paradisus Animæ Christianæ." This thenceforth became my daily companion instead of the "Treasury of Devotion." I am sure that the prayers of that "Paradisus" helped me as much as anything. I bought also a "Vade Mecum" and used that much. I purchased a Missal and a Breviary, and began saying the Day Hours in Latin every day. I also at this time read the Lives of St. Dominic (by Lacordaire), of St. Francis of Sales, the Curé d'Ars. All these gradually imbued me with the spirit of the Catholic Church, and made me long in my heart for it as an exile from home. Only the journey was difficult, and had I the courage to make it?

I dreaded the journey, and tried to find excuses. "So-and-so, so-and-so, so-and-so; therefore I cannot come." Fortunately I could not say, "I have married a wife, and therefore——" I only had myself to look after, which immensely simplified the problem. To the married clergyman and even lay-person, how terribly is the trial aggravated! I must bolster myself up. Let me look around for stuff (the word sounds satirical in this connection!) to put into my bolster. The Branch theory, will that do?

Dead leaves. I had been taught it, of course. I had seen it flourishing like a green bay tree. But now, "I went by, and lo! it was gone. I sought it, but its place could nowhere be found." Once I sang the song, "Woodman, spare that tree!" Since then my common sense had become the woodman, and the tree had come down. I had become convinced that Rome was the real centre of the real Christendom. We in the Church of England were cut off—at least were outside the circle. But where I was, I was not by my choice. I was where, apparently, God had put me. Ought I not to remain? But could I remain and yet be a Catholic? Well, could I not imagine that God had work for me to do where I was? Was He limited to that circle around Rome? Did He not wish all to be drawn in, and might not I, and others of like ideas, help to draw the Church of England, or at least a part of it, into that circle? We could reach where Rome could not. We could work for Rome from outside. How dishonest! Traitors within the camp! So, many said. But wait a minute. Were there not such things as Uniat Churches? Why not an English Uniat Church? The Pope might arrange it—for us advanced Anglicans, at all events. He might allow priests already married to remain married; a vernacular Liturgy for those who preferred it, and some such concessions. Anything short of the pain of complete separation from our old ties and associations. And were there not signs that the Holy Spirit was working in the Church of England? How otherwise account for the wonderful movement upward which we had witnessed, in which we had taken some part? Had we not *felt* grace in our confessions, our communions? Had we not seen

that virtue had gone out of us in our confessionals?
Surely we could work for God and the Catholic Church
where we were, at least for a time—even though Rome
was the centre. And lastly, in spite of the many clerical
witnesses against us, were we not priests—*sacerdotes?* The
Pope had never distinctly condemned Anglican Orders. I
could not give up my Orders, but if I "went over" I should
have to; I should be reckoned a mere layman.

Up to the last day of my ministry in the Church of
England, I believed in my Orders. It was the last rope
to which I clung. That did not snap till the final day;
and then? The rolling, tossing sea; the blackness of
storm; the danger of being lost; until, through the mercy
of God, He set my feet upon the rock and ordered my
goings. But the shipwreck came before the last rope
snapped. The ship in which I had been sailing for well-
nigh thirty years, in which I had been comfortably happy,
where I had found work and comrades equally congenial,
where I had a comfortable cabin, and in which I had hoped
to reach the last port without changing,—this ship broke up
under me. The storm burst midway in the reading of the
"Apologia." When the last page was reached—indeed
before, I was a castaway. I could not resist the logic of
the great thinker, the great convert. He held out as long
as he could, but *had* to let go. So must I. It was painful
holding on by that one rope; but I did for more than a
year. Other ropes, too, were tugging hard—"the cords of
a man;" my love for my family and my people. They
pulled at my heart. My mind still clung to the hope that
I was a priest. Meantime, Rome was drawing, drawing
still. Who was that in the October of my last year,

drawing so gently, yet so strongly—in the month of his
Feast, too, though I knew it not ? Ah ! it was St. Francis
of Assisi. In my last retreat at Cowley I took in with me
the Life of St. Francis by St. Bonaventura and read it—
a new Saint to me. He won me to himself completely.
And when one of the Cowley Fathers, whose name I will
not mention, spoke disparagingly to me of this Saint, of
whom my heart was now full, I was indignant, and there and
then said within myself, " I will never come into this house
(Cowley) again." And I never did. His was the influence
—his, St. Francis'—which I am sure, under God, drew me
at length to the shore. Four months afterwards, Pope Pius
IX. died. I read with intense eagerness every detail about
that last illness and death, and was impressed with the
world-wide interest displayed in the Pope. On the
Monday, or Monday week, afterwards, the senior curate of
St. Bartholomew's, my dear friend, expressed the thought
that he must go away to think things over. He doubted
if he could hold out. He and I, I should say, had walked
together in the same direction for a long time, and I doubt
not that he helped me immensely in my own journey.
But my duty is only to speak of my own. The next
morning, Tuesday, after celebrating the Communion, and
whilst coming down the steps, I seemed to hear a voice,
at least with the ears of my mind, saying, " You are not a
priest, you are not a priest "—perhaps only the echo of my
own fears. All day long the same voice persisted, and in
the evening I came to the conclusion that I too would
go away with my friend and think it all out—away from
the distractions of work. We left Brighton on the Satur-
day, remained together quietly with some friends until

Ash Wednesday, when we went to Manresa Roehampton. There we made a little retreat, and on the Eve of St. Gregory, 1878, Father George Porter (God rest his soul!) received us into the Church.

Looking back upon the road which led to this happy portal, I find that it may be divided into four stages: (1) Home, (2) St. Michael's, (3) Oxford and Cuddesdon, (4) St. Bartholomew's. Each stage was a step forward and higher, and I may perhaps give the steps these names: (1) The Bible, (2) Evensong, (3) Anglicanism, (4) Romeward. And then *Civitas Dei*.

W. D. GAINSFORD, Esq., J.P.,

OF SKENDLEBY HALL, SPILSBY.

I AM not, strictly speaking, a convert; since I belong to a family always Catholic, and was myself baptized and educated a Catholic. But as I lived for many years as a Protestant, professed myself an Anglican, and honestly thought I was one, perhaps my experience may be not less useful than that of a convert properly so called. Anyhow, to tell it will be a small penance.

The outcome of twenty-eight years' honest trial of Anglicanism is the conviction that its *fons et origo mali* is far more serious and far more deeply rooted than Catholics usually suppose. When remorselessly probed to the bottom, I found it to be nothing less than a positive (though unconscious) disbelief in a *present* supernatural.

I mean that Anglicans do not believe in any supernatural existence *hic et nunc*.

They believe there *was* a supernatural creation and a supernatural Incarnation, and that *in days long ago* physics and miracles were mixed up in a very perplexing manner; and, moreover, they believe that a similar condition of things will again arise at the Last Day.

But, *hic et nunc*, all is understandable enough. Both God and the devil, no doubt, exist somewhere, but they don't interfere with the decent order of things here below nowadays.

Of course, no Anglican would admit that to be his belief; he would most strenuously deny it. But such is really his unconscious conviction—the real belief on which his life and conduct are based.

That such is so is apparent in many outward indications; *e.g.* by his contemptuous rejection of all latter-day miracles—though he readily admits the principle of miracle formerly; by his disbelief in the intercession of saints—which really means that he does not believe the saints to be now actually existing in Heaven; by his disbelief in prayer for the dead, and the general doubt of any conscious existence between death and the Last Judgment (*i.e.* no supernatural state *now*); and lastly, by his utter repudiation of all notion of sacerdotalism (by which I mean the administration of supernatural power through human beings and the existence of supernatural function in a material object).

For a long time I held these rationalistic prejudices, without realizing that it is upon an exclusively materialistic basis alone that such can be held consistently.

I believe that the great majority of educated Anglicans hold similar views in utter unconsciousness of the principles thereby necessarily implied, and that they are denying all supernatural existence, were they but consistent.

Educated Anglicans, for the most part, take too little interest in such matters to analyze their concrete opinions, and to arrive at the principles on which they are founded.

But there are a few who do so, and some of these leading Anglican thinkers I have had the advantage of conversing and of corresponding with.

I find that these eventually fall without an exception into two classes (*i.e.* when they do not join the Church). Either—

1. They become actual agnostics, or even positive disbelievers, regarding religion as no more than a popular fancy, useful in promoting morality and humanitarianism ; prayer, for instance, held to have no objective validity, but to be an excellent exercise for inducing subjectively a moral frame of mind ; and Christian dogma being legendary folk-lore, more valuable in the government and guidance of the uneducated. Or—

2. If their faith be strong enough to hold out against what they conceive to be their reason, they give up the question in despair, saying, "Well, our religion is not satisfactory. I can make out nothing clear or straightforward. But it's the best I know, and I must believe something."

For my own part, I took the first line. The supernatural seemed to me to contradict reason, and since God had given me reason, He could not intend me to act in defiance of it.

In a lucky moment I read Kant's "Critique of the Pure Reason," and when I could understand what he meant (which took two years), I saw that reason was limited, and moreover that beyond its scope there was still an existence, or at least the possibility of such.

So that, after all, there was not, nor could there ever be, any contradiction between reason and revelation.

So the difficulty vanished, and I was able to be a Catholic again.

What all really thoughtful Anglicans have found out, or are finding out, is that *Protestantism is positively irrational,* but that there is existing a supernatural system which is *not irrational, but is ultra-rational.*

Such is the pith of my story.

The Rev. W. T. GORMAN, B.A.,

ROYAL UNIVERSITY OF IRELAND, QUEEN'S COLLEGE, BELFAST; FORMERLY
CURATE OF ST. LUKE'S, CAMBRIDGE, AND NOVICE S.S.J.E., COWLEY,
OXFORD; ST. MARY'S, KINNOUL, PERTH, N.B.

IT is obviously impossible, in a short space, to do more
than briefly indicate the leading consideration which the
Holy Spirit used to bring one into His true fold : to do
more would need a volume, and the analytical pen of a
Newman. The religious position in which I was for many
years was that which is most conveniently described as
that of the most "extreme" school of the Church of
England. I had grasped early in life the Catholic principle
of the authority of the Church (*congregata vel dispersa*) as
the only basis on which a secure belief could rest, and I held
and taught the Infallibility of the Universal Church as a
necessary consequence of our Lord's promises. So in every
part of theology but one I employed Catholic methods, and
followed, as best I could, approved Catholic writers. There
was no Catholic doctrine or practice which I did not strive
to teach, as far as was possible, to those whom I had
opportunity to influence, except Indulgences, which could
have no practical place in any tenable Anglican theory
of jurisdiction. The part of my theology, however, where,

unconsciously, I abandoned Catholic methods, and took to the ways of the most thoroughgoing Protestantism, was in that fundamental and important part, viz. the definition of the true Church. Under the influence of prejudice and early teaching, I looked upon the Catholic view of the Church and the claims of the Holy See as a question very little more open to discussion than the revolution of the earth round the sun. The Anglican and the Eastern Churches were as surely parts of the Catholic Church as was the Roman Church, and it was to the consentient teaching of all three parts that I looked for my authority in faith and morals. The proof of this theory of the Church was chiefly negative, and drawn from Anglican books of controversy, but I contented myself with a more or less superficial study of the question, on the perfectly reasonable plea that my duties in large and poor parishes did not leave me sufficient leisure, even had I the ability, for a careful investigation at first hand. My only answer to Anglicans who had doubts as to their position was: "The whole question is so difficult and involved that we ordinary and busy people must leave large tracts of it to experts. We have got the Apostolic ministry, and valid Sacraments, and the submission to the Holy See is far too serious a step to take on a mere doubt." So far was I from seeing the real issues involved, and the inherent absurdities of my position. It came to pass, in the good providence of God, that several people of ordinary education, and of the most conspicuous singleness of purpose, came to consult me early in 1900 on doubts that they had as to their safety in the English Church. I was thinking one day how strange it was that such souls should be troubled about the very foundation of their faith, and was casting about for some legitimate ground of justification for telling them to put their doubts away as a temptation, when the Holy Spirit brought to my recollection Isaiah's prophecy of the Church (ch. xxxv.), with its promise that "the wayfaring man, though a fool, shall not err therein." Well as I had known the words before, it was then for the first time that I saw their force, and that they contained the answer to my perplexity. The finding of the true Church of God (and the consequent certainty about revealed truth) was not really a matter for learned investigation at all, otherwise there could be no responsibility to find it resting on almost any one, and the only alternative was the ultra-Protestant dogma, "One Church is as good as another." God had promised by His prophet that the "fool"—the ordinary unlearned person—should be able (at the very least) to find the Catholic Church, and so with certainty to avoid error. So the actual facts of the realization gained a new meaning—"To the poor the gospel is preached;" "How hardly shall they that have riches *enter* the Kingdom of Heaven!" "Except ye be converted, *and become as little children*, ye shall in no wise *enter* the Kingdom of Heaven." The marks or signs which God had given by which to distinguish the true Church from all false religions must absolutely be of such a character that they would appeal to, and be discernible by, "the fool," "the poor," "the little children," and all other considerations were simply beside the point. So that it was quite certain that whatever difficulties might be raised (and one must expect many), there must be a satisfactory answer to them, and one was not merely entitled, but bound, to trust Almighty God about them.

I therefore had to look, in a candid and simple way, for the body which obviously and clearly presented those characteristics which God had appointed to be the signs or marks of His Church—Unity, Sanctity, Catholicity, and Apostolicity. Any body which failed in any one of these points might be dismissed at once, and, unless Christ's promises had failed utterly, there must be a Church which showed them unmistakably. They must be, moreover, signs or marks of such an evident character as to be real guides to unlearned people of ordinary common sense, and not merely spiritual properties, necessitating proof from other considerations ; for this would be to reverse the Divine method under the dispensation of the Incarnation, and to make them something quite different from marks or notes.

So, still more or less under the influence of my old habits of thought, and with every desire to justify the Church of England, I began slowly and laboriously to apply this test to her. I could hardly bring myself to believe that Christ's gospel was so simple, and so I tried to turn the matter over in every possible way, endeavouring to find some weak spot in the argument, or to make the English Church fit in with it. But it could not be done. Not merely in one, but in all of the four notes of the Church, she broke down. Obviously she was not *one*, either by herself, or even still more obviously, with that which her keenest advocates acknowledged to be the " rest of the Catholic Church," in any such sense that could appeal to those to whom the appeal lay, so that the plain evidence of one's senses had to say, when the fact was

pointed out, "Yes! the English Church and the Roman
Church and the Greek Church obviously form one external
body." It was only by a logical *hysteron-proteron* that the
many good people to whom I went for help, could meet
my difficulty: "We have the Sacraments, therefore we
are united to Christ the Head, therefore we are one
with all Catholics." But the Sacraments are guaranteed
by the Unity, and not *vice versâ* (not to dwell on the fact
that the argument included equally well all Protestant
sects, and also assumed that a bishop *could* not fall into
schism). Moreover, the Anglican theory of unity involved
one in all sorts of absurdities as to jurisdiction (*e.g.* as was
pointed out to me by a dear and revered friend, very
obviously in the diocese of Montreal), and reduced matters
of faith to a question of geography.

Again, the note of Sanctity was not clearly shown by
the Anglican Church ; for even admitting all that could be
said about the possession of valid Sacraments, and the
ordinary type of sanctity in her people (which experience
would not let me admit), there was not even an attempt to
assert the heroic sanctity of any of the children of her
"miscarrying womb and dry breasts," ever since the time
when the rest of Catholic Christendom asserted her schismatic position. While all the time the Catholic Church
had been bringing forth her eminent saints, whom every
one acknowledged, in great numbers, as St. Teresa, St.
Alphonsus, St. Philip Neri, St. Vincent de Paul, St. Francis
Xavier ; and even in England, that which it was fashionable to call the "Italian Schism" had borne its ripe and
perfect fruits of a Blessed John Fisher, Thomas More, and
countless others.

And likewise with the note of Apostolicity. Here it was that most of all I departed from the simplicity of the Divine method, and involved myself in reading and collateral questions. The Primacy of Peter—was it of Divine right, and such as the present occupant of the Throne of the Fisherman asserted ? After the failure of the English Church to exhibit Unity and Sanctity, it was not really necessary to examine this point, for the present teaching of God's Church must, by virtue of His promises, be in accordance with her teaching from the beginning. However, one does not always see everything very clearly while in the actual grip of a great question ; and so, that I might leave nothing undone to gain still clearer grounds for the action that seemed inevitable, I waded again through the maze of the controversy as well as one who was very far indeed from being competent for the task could do. But to argument after argument I had to reply either *nihil ad rem*, or "How could it ever have imposed upon me ?" The absolute irrelevancy, even where they were fair, of such books as "The Primitive Saints and the See of Rome ;" the special pleading and astonishing misrepresentation of Regius Professors when they tried to explain away as "fulsome adulation" the utterances of Œcumenical Councils ; the sheer unabashed Protestantism of such controversialists as Canon Gore ;—all became, step by step, in God's mercy, clear to me. The one fact that stood out as the sun in a cloudless sky was that, in order to overthrow the claims of Leo XIII. to my submission and allegiance, I should have to admit methods of argument in the interpretation of Holy Scripture, of the Fathers, and of tradition, which would tell with infinitely greater weight against every Catholic doctrine which I held dear, and would bring me with irresistible force to a sheer agnosticism. With what relief and gratitude one kept listening to the words of the good priest who later on received me into the Church: "Remember, our Lord really did say, ' *Tu es Petrus.*' "

[1] Of course the matter was then ended ; for the positive side, the recognition of all the notes of the Church, clearly, evidently, and indisputably in the Holy Roman Church had proceeded *pari passu* with the perception of their absence in the Anglican body. No one who accepted Catholic principles made any serious attempt to deny her possession of them ; that she was One, Holy, Catholic, Apostolic, was obvious to the man in the street, once the terms were explained to him and the fact pointed out. Plain hard fact as to the actual belief even of those who rejected the Catholic idea of the Church abundantly proved this.

Such, then, is the outline map of the way by which God led me into the Fold of the Good Shepherd. I should have liked to mark on it some of the pitfalls and bypaths which He showed me, and enabled me to avoid ; and to expose some of the counterfeit maps which well-meaning friends, much more fit than I was to make the journey, tried to put into my hands, for they deceive many ; but the limits assigned me forbid.

The two chief things that the process of my conversion has impressed on me are—that faith is the gift of God,

---

[1] For the sake of brevity I have omitted to speak of the note of Catholicity ; more particularly as it was only the assumption that she was in the Unity of the Church, and therefore must be Catholic, that had enabled me to explain away the clear evidence to the contrary, and to teach and act as a Catholic in the English Church.

given according to the inscrutable mysteries of the Divine Vocation ; and that the means to obtain it are in the hands of every one who perseveringly prays, and has recourse to the unfailing patronage of our Blessed Lady, *Sedes Sapientiæ.* "Thou hast hid these things from the wise and prudent, and hast revealed them unto babes." Fundamental truths, indeed, and simple ; but, alas ! put quite out of sight, from the necessities of their position, by Anglican controversialists.

HARTWELL DE LA GARDE
GRISSELL, Esq., M.A.,

BRASENOSE COLLEGE, OXFORD; CAMERIERE D'ONORE DI NUMERO DI
SUA SANTITÀ.

IT is difficult to touch, however briefly, on such a subject as I am asked to write about, without appearing unduly egotistical; and I only do so in the hope that this slight record of my experiences may be of use to others.

When an undergraduate at Brasenose College, Oxford, in the early sixties, I became much interested in the High Church Movement, and fell under the influence of Dr. Liddon and other well-known leaders of the party. I joined the English Church Union, and was a Secretary of the Association for the Promotion of the Unity of Christendom. I was admitted by Dr. Liddon into the Brotherhood of the Holy Trinity, which was a society of which he was Master, and which had been established for the promotion of High Church principles within the University. I was in the habit of attending compline every evening in a private oratory which certain undergraduates used for devotional purposes. In due course I, in company with a friend, opened a private oratory on our own account, and several Oxford clergymen were in the habit not only of taking part in the services, but of celebrating the Holy Communion there. In the year 1865 I was requested by Dr. Wilberforce, the then Bishop of the Diocese, to discontinue these celebrations, and I at once obeyed his directions. About this period I published a book on ceremonial, called "Ritual Inaccuracies, or Errors commonly made in the Celebration of the Holy Eucharist." This was drawn up in the humble belief that it would prove a means of insuring greater ritual accuracy, and of teaching ritual to those who otherwise might find the subject dry or difficult. It was taken almost entirely from Roman sources, and intended to help my friends in their difficult endeavour to bring the rubrics of the Protestant Communion Service into line with those of the Roman Missal. This brought me into correspondence with several Catholic priests whom I had consulted on certain details of ceremonial; and they very naturally did their best to show me my illogical position. I soon came to the conclusion myself that this exhumation of scraps and snatches of an ancient rite, and the profane distortion (as a Catholic friend had the courage of his convictions to call it) of the rubrics of the Roman Missal for the disguise of Protestant worship was little better than an imposture. At the same time, my love for liturgical studies, so far from leading me to become a Catholic, had the very opposite effect, and I well remember, when at last I made up my mind to join the Church, the regret I felt in the thought that I should no longer be able to take part in the Church of England services to which I was still so greatly attached.

At the suggestion of the Rev. Father Edward Caswall of the Birmingham Oratory, I commenced reading Catholic books, both historical and dogmatic, among them being

a vindication of the Primacy of the Apostolic See by Dr.
Kenrick, Archbishop of Baltimore ; and I came, after careful study of the question, to the conclusion that the Church
of England, being a purely national church, could hardly
be considered Catholic and universal, in the sense of its
being the Divine teacher of all nations, and that it was in
schism.   I believed nevertheless firmly in the priesthood of
the Anglican Church, and was sensible that I received grace
from her ordinances ; although, as I know now, such graces
derive their efficacy rather from the dispositions of the recipient than from the ordinances themselves.   At the same
time, I felt that even if her Orders were absolutely undoubted, it would be still my duty to get out of schism, just
as it is a man's duty to get out of any other wicked state.
The Catholic Church I knew from our Lord's promise was
one, and could not be divided, although it could be diminished
in size.   I began to see that at the Reformation it was not
divided but only diminished, and that there were still many
old Catholic families in England who had never ceased to
belong to the pre-Reformation Church and had kept the
faith, though the majority of the English people had fallen
away from it.   I saw that its unity still remained, after this
loss, the same as before.   I also learnt that the Catholic
Church is not so exclusive as is sometimes supposed, and
that while remaining one and undivided by reason of her
Divine institution, she includes within her borders very
many more than those belonging to her visible communion.
For a while I hoped that I myself was but in invincible
ignorance, and might belong at least to the soul of the
Church, although not actually united to her corporate body.
St. Augustine says there are many wolves within the fold

and many sheep without, and I felt satisfied, as I still am, that many of my Protestant friends and relations were living in union with God and in a state of grace. I felt, on the other hand, that any bodies which formally separated themselves from union with Rome, ceased to be in the visible Church, which would still remain one, in spite of their departure, though numerically smaller. I at last seriously asked myself: Am I in that good faith which would allow me to be reckoned as invisibly united with the One Visible Church? Am I ready to obey those promptings which invite me to abandon my present sectarian position, or is there some secret influence at work which prevents me from listening to them? Prayer at length obtained for me the inestimable happiness of submitting myself to the Church, and of obtaining thereby the full certitude of my possessing undoubted and valid sacraments, and the enjoyment of that peace on earth which the true old faith can alone assure.

I should like to say, in reference to one's attitude towards those outside the Church, that I have always felt that argument and controversy more often provokes than does good. We should endeavour, it seems to me, to show our separated brethren that we Catholics love truth for the truth's sake, and that we sympathize with the struggles of those who are groping their way towards the light. I feel persuaded that merely controversial victories and smart sayings in many cases repel rather than attract. Men are convinced not so much by reasoning as by a clear conception of positive truth. As Cardinal Newman so justly remarks, false ideas may be *refuted* by argument, but only by true ideas can we hope to *expel* them.

I

The Rev. H. F. HALL,

OF THE PRO-CATHEDRAL, KENSINGTON, W.

I AM bound to regard myself as belonging to the
category of the least worthy of those who have come
home to the Church from the ranks of Protestantism ; for
inclination, with me, preceded grace.

My childhood's training was not such as directly to
encourage a Catholic bent except in two particulars. My
father sometimes took me to the Children's Benediction at
St. Joseph's Old Church, Highgate, and there I received my
first impressions—and a very impressionable mind I always
had—of Catholic worship. Later on, during annual visits
to Brighton, we used to visit High Churches upon Sunday.
This always seemed to me a very agreeable but rather
naughty proceeding, as became, perhaps, the relaxation of
holiday-time. Apart from these things, I was nurtured on
such food as is to be found in the *Sunday at Home*
and Scriptural picture-books. At all times " Pilgrim's
Progress " and the Bible were a delight to me. Perhaps
as the natural result of all this, and although my father
was a devout Churchman, I seemed to grow up with an
instinctive feeling that Dissenters were somehow or other

really the best kind of Christians, but that Church was much nicer; while with regard to the Catholic Church, my childish judgment was, I think, in a state of suspense altogether, being always strangely attracted by a feeling of its warmth and reality, yet tinged somewhat and repelled by a lurid fire of seeming corruption and past tyranny.

I remember the relish with which I recited the clause in the Nicene Creed, " I believe in one Holy Catholic and Apostolic Church," in which in some confused way I thought we professed a sort of attachment to the Roman Catholic Church; and the same indefinite charm belonged to the " Te Deum Laudamus," especially in the verses " The glorious company of the Apostles praise Thee. . . . The noble army of Martyrs praise Thee. . . . The Holy Church throughout all the world doth acknowledge Thee.' All these things brought to my mind pictures of majestic beauty which I could not have expressed, but which I after- wards saw reflected in the conceptions of Fra Angelico. Between, I think, my tenth and thirteenth year I was a choir-boy in the church of the parish. This was to me at the time the summit of my ambition. A Mission held, I believe, in the year 1883 at this church by a very zealous country clergyman whose name I forget, but who was, I know, of the strictly Evangelical type, gave me, I think, my first real sense of spiritual responsibility, and at about this time I was baptized. Strangely enough, during these years I had been attending the Baptist Sunday school, and there too I do not forget, even at this distance of time, my indebtedness to a still respected inhabitant of the district for his earnest and manly teaching and his own personal goodness. Even more was I indebted, in after-years, to a Churchman in the parish, who on Sunday afternoons held a Bible-class for young men in his own house, to which work he sacrificed a large portion of his only holiday—for he was a busy city man.

My indebtedness to my parents for the personal example of their lives, and their real loving affection for our Divine Saviour and the characters of Bible history— among whom the holy name of Mary was held in honour, in spite of Protestant prejudice—I can never properly know or appreciate in this world.

At sixteen or seventeen years of age, my voice having broken, I was free to attend some other church, and it was then the subtle attraction for ornate service that drew me off to a neighbouring High Church Mission : there I entered with zest upon the work connected with the worship of the Church, and there I was enlightened for the first time as to what is called the Anglo-Catholic position. Yet, while growing day by day to love more and believe intensely the doctrines of the Real Presence, of the Teaching Church, etc., I do not think I ever sincerely accepted the High Church branch theory. I passed through that phase in the space of two years or thereabouts, but my nineteenth year found me a Catholic, and I was only kept back so long by the influence of a friend, whom I hope I am not wrong in believing to be sincerely good, but who could never give me a satisfactory answer to the radical difficulty—the absence of definite, living teaching, and God-representing· authority. After the departure of my friend from England, I was not long in taking the inevitable step. Some few things stand out conspicuously as giving me a helping hand in that direction. The first was the action of a Wesleyan friend with whom I became acquainted during a visit to Folkestone. Going with me to the High Celebration at midday at the parish church—both of us having comfortably breakfasted—he to my indignant amazement walked up to the Altar rails and received the Communion. Think of that to a High Churchman ! A Wesleyan, to him a schismatic and heretic, receiving the Sacred Mysteries at midday on a well-filled stomach !

This incident was enough to revive all my perplexities with a vengeance. I now began to read Roman Catholic sermons ; and one sermon in particular by, I think, Bishop Bagshawe, on the Unity of the Church, affected me very deeply. For some long time, too, I had recited the "Ave Maria" daily ; in fact, I took to Our Lady like a child to its mother very soon after my High Church experience began.

The greatest factor, however, of my preparation for the Church was a visitation made by Cardinal Manning to the church of the neighbouring Roman Catholic Mission. I attended the High Mass, and with the man's history and his ever-present personality in my mind, his ascetic and emaciated form and features ; the princely and yet tender pastoral bearing—the glory of his pontifical dress making him look like one of the old stained-glass figures which I loved so much ;—the beautiful simplicity of his homily on the Gospel of the day : all these things drew me like a magnet ever nearer and nearer. Inclination was all towards the Church. The will moved by grace—as I firmly believe and know—was not long behind. I spoke to the priest : it was the first time to my knowledge that I had ever spoken to a *real* Catholic. I thought in my simplicity he would receive me into the Church the next morning. Instead of that he said, "This is a grave step, my boy, and requires prayer and preparation. I will lend you a book to read." Though it mortified and humbled me, there could not have been an attitude more calculated to confirm me in my resolution if confirmation were wanted. It was my first experience of the thorough genuineness and reality of Catholicism, and was fraught with influence for good. After a time of careful instruction I had the happiness of becoming a Catholic. There is no need to speak at length of the intense joy and freshness of one's neophyte days. The buoyancy, the light-hearted Christian gaiety of that time, is common, I suppose, to most converts; but it is a time to look back to with gratitude to Almighty God, and it ought to be a constant source of strength and confidence in the future.

It was some few years afterwards that I received the unspeakable additional grace of vocation to the priest-hood.

P.S.—Perhaps I ought to add that the most astonishing thing in my conversion to my parents and friends was, I believe, my perseverance in it; for I had always been fond of "some new thing," and oftener than not I wearied of any undertaking directly use or reflection had sobered my first enthusiasm.

MRS. C. H.,

TERTIARY OF THE ORDER OF ST. DOMINIC.

I WAS brought up under strictly Evangelical influences, and looked upon religion as an affair to be confined to Sundays, and to perhaps a few week-day services in Lent. I was glad to escape from it at other times as a dreary bore indeed. But at length I chanced to stray, on a certain Ash Wednesday, into a Ritualistic church—one of the first to introduce ornate services and to teach some measure of Catholic doctrine in the American city in which I then resided. I was bewildered and fascinated at the same time. Could this be the service I had been listening to all my life? How different the pretty altar, with its cross and candles, and the clergymen in their purple vestments, to the "three-decker" pulpit and reading-desk combined, of good old St. M.'s, to the parson in his Geneva gown and bands, and, ye gods! *black silk gloves!* The gilt rays over the tables of commandments, supposed to represent a glory but strongly suggesting an arrangement of brass stair-rods; Jackson's "Te Deum;" "Greenland's icy mountains," and the like;—how different these from the sweet harmonies of the vested choir, which, to my enraptured eyes, might have been the very white-robed army of martyrs itself. Then the, to me, mysterious decorations and pictures of St. A.'s—stations and the like, as I soon after discovered them to be,—what a revelation they were! For the first time in my life it struck me that there might be something interesting in religion, and I determined to frequent for the future the free seats of St. A.'s— another delightful contrast to the locked-up pews I had been used to. It was not, however, till some two years later that I became acquainted with the Rector of St. A.'s, and that I made some dear and intimate friends in the altar and other societies. It was to one of these friends that I owed my acquaintance with Catholic writings, and my earliest doubts as to the truth and reality of " Anglo-Catholicism."

The "Introduction to the Devout Life" was the first Catholic work I had ever seen, and, while reading it, the thought came home to me: "If this good bishop (St. Francis) were now living, and I were to tell him how much I was impressed by his book, I think he would say to me: 'If you like my book so much, why don't you belong to my Church?'" Shortly after, however, asking the Rector of St. A.'s to explain to me just what was the Catholic Church, and in what way he and I were members of it, I was told of the "branch theory," which, for the time, satisfied me. But there came a disturbing incident. Attending another Episcopal church, and making a genu-flexion to the altar, as I had been taught to do at St. A.'s, I heard it said afterwards that there had been a *crazy lady* at service last Sunday, who must have thought she was in a Catholic church! Then came the famous "Gorham decision," and again I was troubled to the utmost. Could this be the true Church, with authority to teach, wherein every teaching, from the Real Presence to the non-essentiality of Baptism, could flourish side by side? For the first time I read over the Thirty-nine Articles, and saw at once how completely they were at variance with the tenets of the Rector of St. A.'s, and thought: Can a man be honest who has subscribed all this, and yet preaches the doctrines he does? But now God in His great mercy prepared the way for me still further by means of a series of most eloquent sermons—I do not remember the author's name—on the parable of the Prodigal Son. While reading these one evening, all at once a powerful conviction came over me that I had never known what it was to have real contrition, that I had never realized that I was a sinner, who had need to draw near to God in deepest humility to implore His pardon, and that I did not even know how this coming to Him must be accomplished. I felt I must have help and counsel; and the following day I hastened to pour my trouble into the ear of the Rector of St. A.'s. He advised me to come to him for confession. I hope and trust the poor man sincerely believed that he had a right to receive such a confession, and that he could truly impart absolution. Certainly *I* was too ignorant even to wonder where, and from whom, he had got his faculties. The remedy was tried, and I tasted a partial peace; but the more I thought and read, the more my mind misgave me. At last, in a crisis of anxiety, and of even positive terror as to my spiritual state, I took a desperate resolve. I would go to a *real* Catholic priest and make my confession. Little did I dream that what I

thought of doing would be hardly less than a sacrilege!
I bought a Catholic Prayer-book—it was "The Catholic's
Vade Mecum," I remember—and carefully read over the
"confiteor" and "examen of conscience;" then I slipped
one afternoon into the nearest Catholic church, having given
notice at the presbytery that I wished to go to confession.
Thank God! the priest must have suspected that something
was wrong, for, after hearing what I had to say, he replied,
"I cannot give you absolution; you must go away now,
and return another time." I went home bewildered, and
almost in despair, when it dawned upon me what I had
done—that I had attempted to *steal a Sacrament*, so to
speak. There remained but one logical conclusion to the
matter:—I must seek admission to the Catholic Church,
if I was ever again to know peace of mind. I knew no
priest personally, but I had heard of the late Father Hecker
and his community, and I thought: He is a convert; he
would be more likely to understand a convert's difficulties
than a born Catholic. A letter addressed to this holy
priest elicited the reply, that he was himself too ill just
then to receive me, but that if I would ask at the convent
for Father A. or Father H., either would gladly give me
all the information I desired. I at once hastened to avail
myself of this permission.

The first thing that struck me, on entering the Paulist
house, was the look of poverty and austerity that pervaded
it. I was shown from a bare entry into a carpetless room,
furnished only with a table, two wooden chairs, and a
cheap crucifix against the wall. What a contrast to the
luxurious drawing-room of the Rector of St. A.'s! Father
H. entered the room, wearing his biretta. I thought: How

strange, and how very rude, that he does not remove his
hat in presence of a lady! However, I said, "Father, I
am thinking of being received into your Church. I am
already well instructed, but there are *some* little points of
your faith I feel I don't *quite* understand."

"Yes, my child, we will begin with the *Creed*, if you
please!"

I *was* taken by surprise! To be told I did not so
much as understand the Creed! There seemed nothing
for it but to attend to the instructions of this masterful
man, who spoke "as one having authority." But not
quite prepared as yet for unconditional surrender, I soon
recovered sufficiently to ply him with questions, many and
various. Purgatory—that was a sad stumbling-block;
did it not seem to set at nought our Lord's atonement?
St. Joseph—who was he in particular? and why did the
Church make so much of him? (God and St. Joseph
forgive me!) Then relics. Did he, an educated gentleman, a graduate of Oxford (I soon found he was an
Englishman), mean to tell me that *he* really attributed
any virtue to a parcel of old bones? And as to the
Rosary—no, indeed! I would never use *that*. That was
only for the old women who couldn't read! But still I
continued to visit the good Father at frequent intervals,
and, one by one, found my objections melting away, and
my convictions of the truth deepening. At last I said:
"Father, I ought to tell you that I have been going to
confession to the Rector of St. A.'s, and, before I go any
further with you, I think it would be only fair to let him
know that I have nearly decided on leaving the Anglican
Church." To this Father H. courteously agreed, and the

next day I called, for the last time, at the beautiful rectory, and frankly told my story. But oh, what a tempest I stirred up! The rector raged; he stamped about the room; he used such intemperate language against the Church that I could not but think: Is this the conduct of a humble, charitable Christian? Finally, as a crowning argument, he exclaimed, "You are going from a *clean* Church into a *dirty* one; there are so many *poor, dirty* people attending Romish churches"!

This was a touch too much. "Sir," I said, rising, "I read in *my* Bible that one of the proofs Christ gave of His mission was, that 'to the *poor* the gospel is preached.' I am very glad to know there *is* a church to which the poor are welcome. I wish you good morning." And I beat a retreat, the rector shouting after me the pleasing information that I was going straight to the devil. So much for the "Branch theory!"

Again I was seated in the poor little room at the convent, telling all this to my new-found friend, Father H. —for by this time I had come to feel that he was the first real friend I had ever had—and after a short conversation—

"Well," said he, "are you ready to be baptized?"

"Oh, I can't tell!" I cried, much agitated and almost in tears. "It seems such a tremendous, almost terrible, change, now I am really come to the point."

"Oh, you be baptized, and the faith will *soak in!*" he answered, in a quaint, comical way he had, which turned my tears into cheery laughter.

Just at that moment a message was brought—"a poor woman wanted to see him." He went into the adjoining

room, and, as I sat awaiting his return, the following
thought came into my head—"Now, this good Father has
been very kind to you, but perhaps it was because he
thought he had secured a rich convert ; perhaps he is
short and disagreeable enough with this poor woman."
The doubt was overwhelming. I felt that everything
depended upon my knowing the truth, and I did a most
unladylike thing—I stole to the half-open door of the other
room, and listened ! But when I heard the pleasant, sympathetic tones of Father H., when I found that he was just
as kind and patient towards the poor woman as he had
been to me, I said in my heart, as I returned to my chair :
" Well, *that* man is a *real* Christian, and his Church is the
true one." And on Father H.'s return I said at once, " It
is all right now, Father ; I beg you to give me baptism as
soon as possible." So, in a few days more, I made my
general confession, and was reconciled to holy Mother
Church. I pass over the domestic storms in consequence
of my action—a light trial, indeed, compared with the
great grace I had received. Twenty-two years have passed
since then. Father H. still continues my fast friend, and
two of my dear children have consecrated themselves to
the service of God—the one in the cloister, the other at the
altar. *Deo gratias, et Maria semper Virgine !*

The Rev. ERIC D. HANSON, M.A.,

CHRIST CHURCH, OXFORD; PRIEST OF THE SOCIETY OF JESUS;
ANCIENNE ABBAYE, BELGIUM.

I HAVE been asked to describe the principal reasons which led me, fourteen years ago, to embrace the Catholic religion. The task is not a congenial one to me. No importance whatever, except to myself, attaches to my conversion. I was never in any sense before the public, as, for instance, an Anglican clergyman is. If my narrative is an unprovoked display of egotism, I must leave the responsibility with the editor of this volume, but for whose representations I should never have contemplated writing anything of the kind. I am well aware that I can hardly fail to offend many of my readers. Catholics will be displeased on account of the intolerable slowness with which at length I succeeded in arriving at a conclusion which to them has always been as clear as day. Many Protestants will take offence at the unpleasant things which, to my sincere regret, I cannot avoid saying. And the wholly undenominational and indescribable person, who is superior to any kind of religious conviction, often has reasons of his own for impartially disliking all people who, by a deliberate change of faith, purely for conscience' sake, seem to imply

that it is seriously worth a man's while to seek first the
kingdom of God and His justice, and that there is a right
and a wrong way in the service of Almighty God as in
most other matters. With all due apology to the reader,
therefore, I will begin my story, which shall be as plain
and honest as I can make it.

My home was in Protestant Clapham. The presiding
genius of the "Clapham Sect" or of its heirs and assigns,
guarded or rather haunted my childhood, and an un-
speakably gloomy and dismal tutelage was the result.
But at the age of fourteen I was rescued, religiously, by
a kind Providence, and brought under High Church
influences. After a prodigious amount of Bible-reading
and other studies, not commonly pursued by a public
schoolboy, I surrendered in course of time to the new
doctrines, and became, as I grew up, increasingly attached
to the High Church party, and really devoted to the practice and spread of what I believed to be the Catholic
religion. When I was seventeen I began going to confession, a practice which was continued with exactness till
close upon my becoming a Roman Catholic at the age of
twenty-six—that is, long after I had ceased to believe in
Anglicanism, as will be seen in the sequel. At the least
it was a means of my making a good act of contrition, and,
until my mind had arrived at a positive and definite conclusion, I was unwilling to break with religious observance
externally. But this is anticipating. I became a member
of the "English Church Union," and an associate of the
"Confraternity of the Blessed Sacrament." It was a time
of many legal prosecutions for Ritualism, and I accepted
without question the theory maintained by the Ritualist

party of the canonically illegal constitution of the tribunals
before which these ecclesiastical matters came for trial.
The Courts were incompetent because they were secular.
The Reformation Settlement had in no way compromised
the spiritual freedom of the Church of England. The
Judicial Committee of the Privy Council was secular in
origin, in authority, and in its members; the Church,
whether by Convocation or otherwise, had never sanctioned
or recognized such a tribunal. Similar objections attached
to the Court presided over by Lord Penzance under the
P.W.R. Act.

Now, it was the "discovery" (in the sense in which a
short-sighted man, or a man in a London fog, may be
said to "discover" the sun) of the historical absurdity
underlying this contention which was the first conscious
blow to my belief in Anglicanism. It gave me intense
pain. The discovery was merely the result of studying
patiently the Reformation period of our history. I found
that at no time since the breach with Rome was the final
Court of Appeal one whit less secular in its source and
authority than at present; in short, I saw for the first time
that the Reformation Settlement was in this and many
other respects a rendering to Cæsar of the things of God.
A forcible pamphlet by Mr. Dibdin (an expert authority
on the ecclesiastical Courts) chanced then to fall into my
hands. He criticized the E.C.U. thesis from the Erastian
standpoint, and quoted a passage from a charge of Archdeacon Palmer (the brother of the late Lord Selborne)
somewhat to this effect: "I am not aware that, at any
time since the separation from Rome, when ecclesiastical
Courts have been created or remodelled, Convocation has

ever been consulted by the Crown or been allowed any voice in the matter."

I submitted that sentence, which gave authority to my own conclusions, to the late Archdeacon Denison, to the Hon. C. L. Wood (now Viscount Halifax), and to several other prominent persons, asking them whether they were willing to admit the truth of the statement. Further, I urged that the whole of our case, based on the supposed illegal character of the Courts, was rotten, so long as we continued to appeal to the Reformation Settlement; in honesty we were bound to avow that the Reformation was against us, that it placed the Church in a condition of shameful subjection to the State in things spiritual, and especially in regard to legislative and judicial functions; we ought to admit frankly that we wanted a new Settlement, a new Reformation.

Archdeacon Denison sent me two immensely long letters, mainly concerned with his own personal history, and leaving my plain question unanswered. Mr. Wood also was misty and evasive. Two things became clear to me: (1) That the Tudor Settlement of religion left the spiritual independence of the Church at zero point; and (2) that a frank admission of this, an avowed policy of "undoing the Reformation," would be fatal to the position of the E.C.U. Hence it did not surprise me that I received evasive answers to my question. The conclusions at which I had arrived did not necessarily point to Rome. But I had come to see that I professed a State-made religion; I was a member of a Church made by the State and controlled by the State. And a conviction of that sort in the mind of a young and ardent High Churchman

K

is disturbing. It was the first blow, but it did not mean Rome yet.

The second blow came from a book; it was a book written by one of the deepest and clearest thinkers of our age—a man whose secession to Rome was only second in significance to that of John Henry Newman. Archdeacon Wilberforce's " Principles of Church Authority ; or, Reasons for withdrawing my Subscription to the Thirty-nine Articles," which by a strange providence I found and read at this time, has long been out of print. The book might be republished most advantageously with annotations by a Catholic theologian. It would be unreasonable to expect from an Anglican, however learned, a faultless treatment of the theme which the first title indicates. Yet the value of the book is immense. I remember its quiet dignity, its calm theological tone, the scientific orderliness of the argument, the patristic learning, the insistence on the Church's living *magisterium*, and on her essential and inviolable unity in communion with and dependence upon the Apostolic See of Rome ; and lastly, in his chapters on the Royal Supremacy, the unanswerable demonstration that the Reformation in England was mere State-craft, that at every stage it was marked by the surrender of inalienable spiritual prerogatives to Cæsar, that it was heretical and schismatical in the most exact sense of those words as used by the Fathers ; in short, that it was an apostasy. And to these qualities of the book one must add the personal element arising from the author's great name and position, and from one's consciousness of the immense sacrifice made to the sacred cause of truth by this truly courageous confession of his faith.

It has often been to me a melancholy reflection that
I could not see my way at this stage to beg for admission
into Christ's One Fold. But I felt alarmed at so great
a step. And I was alone, with none to guide me. Much
pressure was brought to bear on me by persons to whom
I owed great consideration. I resolved at length to enter
upon a course of protracted inquiry into all the principal
charges brought against Roman Catholicism by Anglican
writers. Above all, I would do nothing in a hurry. However, the long persistence of these inquiries and the inde-
terminate character of my religious position exposed me
to much danger from the prevalent religious scepticism
with which I came into contact at Oxford. Externally I
continued to practise my religion as an Anglican, but to
one or two intimate friends I spoke in this way: " These
religious problems are insoluble. I think I have no real
faith. I see no means of attaining to the certainty which
faith implies. No, I have only hope." The possession of
hope without faith may be difficult theologically, but the
meaning of the remark is sufficiently clear. Throughout
those four years at Oxford, a time for me so troubled religiously, a time of interior darkness suspected by few who
knew me, I found comfort especially in two prayers which I
think I said every evening. One was the *Salve Regina;* it
exactly expressed my trouble and my longings: . . . *et Jesum
. . . nobis post hoc exilium ostende!* The other was the
hundred and forty-second psalm (Vulg.). I clung to the conviction that before long the clouds would lift. *Auditam fac
mihi mane misericordiam tuam, quia in te speravi. Notam
fac mihi viam in qua ambulem . . . doce me facere voluntatem
tuam. . . . Spiritus tuus bonus deducet me in terram rectam.*

The book which helped me most in my conflict with the philosophical difficulties brought against both natural and revealed religion was Mansel's Bampton Lectures on "The Limits of Religious Thought." And I still think that no apologetic is secure, especially in these days, which does not include somewhere in its foundations a really active appreciation of the principles emphasized by Mansel. I say the principles which he emphasized, for, on the one hand, these principles were well known to the Schoolmen, and are in no sense new or a concession to the modern mind; and, on the other hand, in his development of those principles Mansel cannot everywhere be safely followed. The affinity between the minds of Mansel and Newman needs no demonstration here. Any careful reader of Newman's "Apologia" and of the "Arians," not to mention certain significant sayings in his sermons, and the touching epitaph he wrote for his gravestone, will understand in what light Newman viewed the Mansel-Maurice controversy. But I am reluctant to speak here more particularly of Mansel's teaching. To one class of readers it would be superfluous, and to another possibly open to misunderstanding. Not every science, not even every doctrine, can be securely packed into a single sentence.

Now, this work of rebuilding my faith from what is called in the Epistle to the Hebrews the *inchoationis Christi sermo* had one unexpected result. It gave me a fresher appreciation of Christian doctrine. Somebody once said that if only it was possible to discard all the old words and adopt new ones to describe the articles of our Faith, many people would be helped to exchange a merely notional for a *real* assent to those truths. We talk so

easily of the Incarnation! Convention and usage dull the
edge of words which otherwise would cut so deep! They
do not get into our understandings. They are sounds
rather than words, or they are symbols of ideas rather
than of things. Professor Seeley's "Ecce Homo" impressed
men because of its freshness, its manifest sincerity, the
absence of nearly all *præjudicia.* I read this book with
singular delight during this time of doubt. By degrees
I came to see in some measure what was the extent of
the marvel which I was asked to credit. I forced myself
to look with new eyes, as it were, upon the Christ as
portrayed to us by His contemporaries. Like a flash at
length this thought burnt me : Suppose that this Wonder
ended here, ended where the story ends, *would it be
credible?* Is it credible that God did this thing, if He
did not go further with it? Is it credible that, after ages
upon ages of waiting, during which the weary earth groaned
to heaven with the weight of sin upon it, and after an
infinity of labour in preparing the nations for His Advent,
He should come and depart in such sort as to leave us a
cruel inheritance of perplexity about Himself, His commands, His work, His wishes? It means that, coming to
visit and redeem His people, He tabernacles among them
for a brief space "as a wayfaring man that turneth aside
to lodge for the night," and then goes His way! Thus
the very memory of His presence, His strange beauty,
His piercing words, become a trouble haunting men's
minds. He raises our hopes, only to cast them to the
ground. He adds yet another riddle to the tragical
enigmas of life. He comes to cast fire on the earth, and
His light shines in the darkness ; and then, like other lights

before and since, the darkness overwhelms it, and it is gone—leaving, let us say, a name in history, a topic for disputation, a worthy subject of study and research.

To some readers this will seem mere satire. It will seem that the refutation of such a conception of Christ's coming and work is to kill the slain, or to seek to kill what never lived. But this is not so. All Anglicans are compelled, as it seems to me, to adopt this conception of Christ's mission in greater or less degree. I found it the prevailing opinion of Anglicans at Oxford, though admitted only grudgingly and painfully by some religious minds as the least intolerable and least impossible explanation of the divisions among Christians. Others felt no such hesitation. They were eloquent on the *normal* duty and privilege of every man to discover the truth for himself from the Scriptures and the Fathers and Reason. And in that sense they boasted of their Christian liberty and dignity. The traditional Catholic doctrine of the Church's *magisterium*, and any conception of faith as an obedience, as a submission of the reason, found no favour with them. The religious anarchy of Anglicanism was best palliated by boldly elevating it into a virtue. The *magisterium* of the Church was a "Western growth," "legal and Roman," "unknown to St. Athanasius and St. Chrysostom and the East generally." (Surely, too, the commission *Qui vos audit, me audit* must be a Western interpolation, and the entire history and *Acta* of the early Councils Western forgeries!) More boldly still this was said: "It is a thing to be expected that Revelation should come to us crossed by the same difficulties and uncertainties as Natural Religion" —an assertion which ought to make Bishop Butler turn in his grave, so perversely does it misrepresent his mind. Thus my inquiry was a most practical one. Is the Incarnation of the Son of God historically credible when examined under the limitations imposed by this Anglican point of view? It was with extreme pain that I was driven to confess that to me the Incarnation, when thus regarded, ceased to be credible. The value of all historical evidence is relative to the intrinsic probability of the event. But there is an overwhelming antecedent improbability, as Newman politely expressed it, in Almighty God announcing a Revelation, and then equivalently revealing nothing. Deny the doctrine *de ecclesia* (as and so far as an Anglican denies it), and the Incarnation becomes incredible to me, not for want of extrinsic evidence, but for want of intrinsic possibility. It is dishonouring to God; for it implies that He left man with no adequate means of knowing the truths which He came to reveal, that He left us worse off than were the Jews before, that He frustrated the purpose of His own work and deceived us with highsounding promises destined to come to nothing.

My readers will see the dilemma which now confronted me. Let me remind them that I am not defending Catholicism. I am narrating facts from my past story. I am tracing, with the sincerest accuracy to which my memory, with the help of some old letters and memoranda, can reach, the stages in the growth of a mind. I found that the Christian *ecclesia*, living in some way by the breath of Christ Himself, teaching with authority His own infallible truth, ruling the souls of men by His power and in His name, is contained as it were by an inner necessity in the doctrine of the Incarnation; that the natural Body

involves the mystical. Both or neither!—such were the
conditions by which I saw that I was limited in my awful
decision.

For the sake of brevity I will not here enter upon the
arguments which compelled me to refuse—indeed, to regard
at length as an intellectual absurdity and a moral suicide
—the latter of these alternatives. Only the former was
admissible. The issue, then, became further narrowed to
this: "Where is this *ecclesia?* As an Anglican am I
within the limits of this visible Christian *ecclesia*, so that
therein and thereby I may be 'taught of God;' or am I
excluded from that august company, an alien to that
Divine teaching?" I made every possible effort at this
stage to justify to myself the religious isolation and the
doctrinal confusion of Anglicanism. It would be wearisome to enumerate the successive pleas which I adopted
and abandoned. They could not take root in me. I
always came back to my first principle. If the Christ has
come, He must have provided us, here and now, with
ready and certain means of access to His revealed truth.
Moreover, what my reason demanded, His own word had
promised and guaranteed for all time. No "appeal to
Antiquity" could survive that test. For you can make
no adequate use of the early Christian records for this
purpose without immense labour. Do what you will, you
must distinguish between essentials and accidentals, the
permanent and the temporary elements, the explicit and
the implicit; you have to estimate how much is due to
exaggeration, to reactionary influences within, to local and
secular influences without; you have to deal with schools
of thought, differences of practice, novelties and individual

mistakes. You cannot aim simply at a blind reproduction of all that was currently accepted and practised during a certain more or less arbitrarily selected century or age. You must largely exercise your critical faculties. And then, what principles are to guide you in this work of discrimination? And where are you going to stop? You will have embarked on an enterprise of a lifetime, with no prospect of attaining any certain result at the end of it.

A concrete example of these difficulties, and one which made a deep impression upon me at the time, and will serve to illustrate my meaning here, is concerned with what a non-Catholic would call the origin and growth of Sacerdotalism in the Church. What can be learnt from the early Christian documents as to the powers left by Christ to be exercised by His ministers in the economy of redemption? Certainly it is a sufficiently vital question. It was Dr. Lightfoot's little treatise on the Christian Ministry (in his Commentary on St. Paul's Epistle to the Philippians) which first revealed to me some of the difficulties of this subject. Here was a profound scriptural and patristic scholar "appealing to Antiquity;" and with what result? Startling to me as were then his conclusions as to the origin of the episcopal order, far more so was his judgment that no traces of distinctive "Sacerdotalism" (if the word may be allowed) occur before Tertullian, nor any clearly defined evidence before Cyprian, and that it was a foreign element imported into Christian belief and practice from paganism and Judaism. One need hardly remark that these conclusions are by no means peculiar to Dr. Lightfoot, nor is there any lack of opponents to

his view.   But the effect of the dispute was to impress
upon me forcibly the ambiguities of these early documents
and the difficulty of piecing together the fragmentary
evidence which they afford.   In other words, both the
process involved in a prodigious "appeal to Antiquity"
of this sort and the uncertainty of the ultimate result more
than sufficed to condemn such a method of learning God's
revealed truth on a matter of vital importance to all men
—not, let it be observed, a matter of merely speculative
interest or the like.   I was sincerely seeking for the truth.
Most assuredly I was not in the position of a man seeking
for premises which will establish a previously determined
conclusion.   I was perfectly ready to believe, if necessary,
that Lightfoot was right, and to deny the *Sacerdotium*.
My only fixed prepossession was the conviction that there
must be some less cumbrous and less uncertain method
of answering this question, one way or the other.

Among my High Church friends and guides I found
a marked difference in their methods of dealing with this
question of the *Sacerdotium*.   What may be called the
New Oxford party, which boldly reduces to the lowest
minimum the idea of ecclesiastical authority, would endeavour to overthrow one by one Dr. Lightfoot's arguments, and pursuing the same method of inquiry (though
with less erudition) would conclude that he had misinterpreted the evidence.   I have said enough already to show
why I could not rest satisfied with that method of arriving
at the truth.   But the mind of the Old Oxford party was
far less Protestant in its attitude.   Their answer to Lightfoot might be worded as follows: "The scantiness of the
early evidence, and the guarantee of Divine assistance

promised to the Church as the depository of the Apostolic teaching, justify us, in a case like this, in reversing the order of our inquiry. Every one admits the highly sacerdotal character of the doctrine and institutions of later ages, *e.g.* the fourth or fifth or sixth centuries. *Therefore* the earlier ages also were sacerdotal. And if they seem to be otherwise, it is either because insufficient evidence has come down to us, or because these elements were for various reasons more or less implicit at first, and thus have escaped your notice."

It is an excellent reply, and the only proper reply, I think, on the part of one who really believes in the Christian *ecclesia*. But it is a reply which no Anglican can consistently make. It is to expose himself instantly to this retort from the opponent of sacerdotal doctrine : "You tell me that subsequent agreement by the whole Church is alone adequate proof of earlier acceptance, at least of implicit acceptance. If that is so, why, then, have you yourself abandoned the later for what you conceive to be the earlier expressions of the Church's mind ? Why have you set yourself in opposition to all Christendom, on the plea of a return to primitive purity ? By the same right that you deny the papacy, I deny the episcopate and the priesthood. The clearness and universality of the later evidence for priesthood and episcopate and papacy may conceivably be destructive of your position and of mine—but certainly not of mine alone. I will go further : taking the New Testament and all subsequent evidence down to the end of the third century, I say that there is stronger evidence for the institution, *jure divino*, of the papal primacy than for that of episcopacy or of the priestly

from "the obedience of faith," from the homage and service to which Jesus Christ called me

> ". . . Beneath Mary's smile,
> And Peter's royal feet " ?

There were only imaginary difficulties left (which are now hard even to remember, so purely imaginary were they), and the inevitable pain of flesh and blood. . . . I made my perplexities known to one of St. Philip's devoted sons in London, Father Gordon of the Oratory, and he, after the example of Philip himself, sent me to St. Ignatius. "You have studied too much," he said. "Go and pray. Make a retreat at the Jesuit Novitiate at Roehampton." Father Gordon told me afterwards that he had little hope that I would follow his advice. But by God's grace I went, and in the course of that retreat I saw the folly of my cowardice. It was Father Richard Clarke who helped me through this last ordeal. I told him my story, and said that I believed, or was ready to believe, the whole Catholic faith. He produced a copy of the Penny Catechism, asking me to read it very carefully. At this I laughed, protesting that I was familiar with it already ; would he not question me on Perrone's "Prælectiones Theologicæ," which I had been recently studying ?

"No, no," he cried, "let us stick to the Catechism. I knew you would say something like that. But I treat you exactly as Father Coleridge treated me, when I too was a catechumen."

I made my renunciation of heresy, and was reconciled with the Catholic Church before the retreat ended. It was on the Feast of the Transfiguration, and fervently I prayed with St. Peter, "Lord, it is good for us to be here." With reluctance I left that holy place. Two years later I had the happiness of again entering Manresa, and of being admitted among the novices of St. Ignatius.

C. H. K., M.A.

THE first real doubt of my position as an Anglican arose while studying for Orders in the Theological College of Cuddesdon, near Oxford. We had been studying the early heresies, and were somewhat perplexed by the many and nice metaphysical distinctions which in so many cases separated Truth from Error. I could not but see, however, that the primary cause of the final destruction of these heresies was the direct action of Church Authority, which was both organized and effective. Furthermore, I noticed that the rulers of the Church knew that they possessed this authority, and were moreover certain in their own minds of what really was "the Faith once delivered to the Saints." I could not but contrast this "*certainty*" and this "*authority*" with the uncertain teaching prevalent in the Church of England, as, *e.g.*, on such important dogmata as the Eternity of Punishment, the Inspiration of Scripture, the Eucharistic Sacrifice, and the Communion of Saints, to say nothing of the equally tenable but vastly different views held by Churchmen on Justification and the Sacramental System.

I remember interviewing our much-esteemed Principal (the present Bishop of Lincoln) on the subject, and asking him where at the present time was that motive power which was so effective in the past, that Divine Authority which so successfully protected the original deposit of faith. He quieted me at the time by assuring me that, up to the time of the great Schism that rent in twain Eastern and Western Christendom, the Church had undoubtedly possessed the precious gift of Infallibility, on the strength of which all heresies had been condemned which attacked the fundamental doctrines of Christianity, and that now, if we wished to be assured of the Truth, all we had to do was to study the early Fathers who had written, and the Councils which had defined, before that lamentable separation had taken place. I say it quieted me for a time, while I gave myself up to study and prayer in the daily routine of college life, but ever and anon doubts and perplexities would arise and take possession of my mind, during which I could not help realizing that, as regards myself at least, I was not in firm possession of that certainty which was clearly the privilege of the Primitive Church.

At the same time, I thankfully acknowledge I derived much spiritual comfort and strength from the reception of the Anglican Sacraments, not distinguishing then the difference which exists between the grace coming directly from the Sacraments and that which rewards the pious effort of the recipient ; and so I deluded myself with the hope that, divided as Christendom might be, I had all that was necessary for my sanctification and salvation. Under that quieting delusion I was ordained deacon by Dr. Wilberforce, and devoted myself to the pastoral duties which fell to my lot as curate in a parish near Maidenhead.

L

It was a shock, however, to find that my good old vicar,
a pronounced High Churchman, who, by his writings, had
done good service in the Tractarian movement, and more
particularly in bringing out a little devotional book on the
benefits of the Sacrament of Penance, enjoined on me to
be most careful, in my visits to the parishioners, never to
allude to the subject in my conversations with them.
And again I could not fail to see a vast contrast between
his undoubted maintenance in the pulpit of the doctrine
of the Real Presence in the Holy Eucharist, and his
practical treatment of that Adorable Mystery. I compared
all this with the practice of the Roman Church, who so
carefully in her rubrics protected the Adorable Presence
from the least profanation, and who, by her zealous
missioners, was ever attracting penitents to the Sacrament
of Reconciliation. I left this curacy in consequence of
my distress, and returned once more to Cuddesdon, by the
kind permission of the Bishop of Oxford, who did his
best to convince me that work, and work alone, was the
remedy for all my ills. With his advice and leave I took
duty under a more advanced and consistent High Churchman, the Reverend James Skinner, of Newland, near
Great Malvern. Here we had a daily Celebration, very
good musical services, and a most lovely church to
worship in. During the year and a half spent in this
place a constant conflict was going on within me. All
my sentiments and affections, as well as my worldly
interest, seemed to wed me to the Church of England ;
but my conscience and reason were ever in rebellion,
urging me to look for a more perfect ideal of the Church
than that in which I was—an ideal where all Church

members believed alike, and where authority was exercised to repel all strange and erroneous teaching. Never shall I forget the shock it was to me when a neighbouring vicar refused my invitation to be present at our Evensong, on the occasion of a visit by Dr. Gray, late the Bishop of Capetown, on the ground that we at Newland preached a different gospel from that which he had received and taught. Where was the living authority of the Church to decide which of us was preaching error? What was the use of the High Churchman denouncing "private judgment" when it was the foundation of all our different beliefs? If the principle was wrong in itself, it did not become right when exercised on the writings of the Fathers any more than when confined to the private interpretation of Scripture. It seemed to me that, as long as one remained apart from that Church which had undoubtedly come down in its chief See in an unbroken line from the Apostles, and which had even claimed the allegiance of mankind on the basis of Divine Authority, it was impossible to escape from making "*self*" and "*private judgment*" the sole arbiter in matters of faith. It was leaning on a very fallible and insecure foundation. Christ had "*taught with authority, and not as the scribes,*" and He sent forth His first representatives armed with like authority to make His supernatural Religion known to all nations. "*He who heareth you heareth Me, and he who despiseth you despiseth Me;*" and "*Lo, I am with you all days, even to the consummation of the world;*" "*If a man will not hear the Church, let him be to you as a heathen man and a publican.*" These were the words which kept ringing in my ears as I vainly strove to do my duty as

a minister of the Church of England ; but struggle as I
would to fancy that the Church was my guide and teacher,
I was bound to confess that it was a Church of a bygone
age, a Church of my own imagining, and which now no
longer invited unless (and dreadful was the thought) the
living Church of Rome was it.   Then, too, I was forced to
acknowledge that if the voice of the Church was hushed in
consequence of its divisions, it was utterly impossible for
the nineteenth-century Christian to know for certain what
the Revelation of JESUS CHRIST really was, and faith was
no longer attainable.

It was an awful crisis to which I had come. I had
dug down to the foundations of my belief, and found them
based merely on the sands of my own private judgment.
I was completely unhinged. Where was Truth ? Was it
to be found in some modern sect which professed to have
found it ? Was the religion of Edward Irving a true
revelation ?   Were perchance the Quakers right ?   Or
worse still, was it all a dream, and Christianity but a fiction
of men anxious to know the unknowable ? If Christ had
really revealed a supernatural religion and intended it for
me, it could only be brought home to me (if I was to
have certitude, or, in other words, *faith*) by some living
organized teaching Body preserved from error, and so
infallible.   To find this I had to go back to the Church
which had sent Augustine to England, and which, up to
the time of the so-called Reformation, had taught with
Divine Authority throughout the length and breadth of
the land ; and so, by the mercy and goodness of God, I
was led to look for the Rock out of which all dissentient
Churches at one time or another had been hewn—to the

Rock of Peter, which alone now and at all times was able to withstand the destructive forces of the ever-active mind of man. It was, of course, intensely painful to leave all that was most dear, and oppose the will of those one loved best and admired most in the world; but "*fiat Voluntas Tua*" was all one could say and pray; and so I made my way to Edgbaston to be further enlightened and consoled by the saintly Newman, to be by him in due time reconciled to "the Church of the Living God, the pillar and ground of the Truth."

It is now thirty-two years since that event took place, and I can truly say that each day, as it comes and goes, adds to the debt of gratitude I feel for the unspeakable mercy of God in thus calling me into the Unity of His Mystical Body. *Deo optimo et maximo gratias in æternum.*

Mrs. HELEN LANGRISHE,

Of Knocktopher Abbey, Co. Kilkenny.

BELIEVING as I did in the necessity of valid Orders for valid Sacraments, I could not, once I had begun to ponder on these matters, remain in the Church of England, whose Orders are repudiated not only by the *whole* of Christendom, but also by half her members and many of her clergy.

The risk to my mind was too great. Rome might err, but she could give me true Sacraments ; no one could dispute that. And what doubts or difficulties I might have to encounter could come up to those I faced in the Anglican Church, as to whether her Sacraments were genuine or not ? What greater evil could befall me than the risk I might run if they were not ? And so unhesitatingly I went over to the old faith ; and I can safely say, once in the true fold, all doubts and difficulties vanished. Everything seemed to become clear, and I saw things in such a light, that if I did not remember how they once appeared to me, I should fail to understand how it could be possible to question the Catholic Faith.

Mrs. CUTHBERT LESLIE,

OF HASSOP HALL, DERBYSHIRE.

WHEN, before my conversion, I had to define for myself, and for others, the reasons which forced me to enter the Catholic Church, I wrote down several statements, the substance of which I now give; as they bring out very clearly the motives which urged me to leave the Church of England and to join the Church of Rome.

First of all, I could not understand any Church being the true one in which the professing members are allowed to hold such contradictory opinions on the most important subjects.

Secondly, I had a very strong feeling that a Church cannot be called *Catholic* in which there is no pretence even of one central authority which all the world is bound to obey, and in which every one is allowed what is called liberty to accept one fundamental doctrine and reject another, and in which such different and contradictory practices are tolerated in dealing with the most sacred subjects—as, for example, Holy Communion and Devotion to Our Lady.

Thirdly, I never could understand the possibility of a

Church teaching a consistent body of doctrine without the presence in that Church of a teaching authority which should not only be *Universal* but *Infallible.* The Church of England was to me the best example of the chaos and confusion of thought which result, and must of necessity result, from the absence in a Church of an Infallible teaching authority which all are bound to obey.

Fourthly, I hoped and expected to get greater comfort from the Catholic Church than I had ever got from the cold formalism of the Establishment; but I did not argue that because the Catholic Church would be more consoling, it must therefore be the right Church; but I argued thus: "If it be the Church of God, it will as a matter of fact satisfy all the longings of the human heart better than the Church established by law in this land."

The Rev. T. LIVIUS, M.A.,

Oriel College, Oxford; Priest of the Congregation of the
Most Holy Redeemer.

I PASSED the years of boyhood amongst the associations of
Church-of-England Evangelicalism, with which, through
circumstances, I was surrounded, but which had no effect
upon me intellectually or morally. Before going to Oxford,
I drifted into sentiments of attraction to the Puseyite
movement, and the Branch theory of the Christian Church.
To prepare for Anglican Ordination, I read theology for
some time with Mr. Woodford (afterwards Bishop of Ely),
who held very orthodox views, especially on the Incarnation and its relation to the Church of Christ. From that
time these views stood by me.

During the nearly five years of my Anglican ministry
at SS. Kenwyn and Kea in Cornwall, I held on to the
" Branch theory," with moderate High Church teaching
and practice ; trying my best to conform them with what
I knew of Catholic doctrine.

Ere long I began to be troubled and dissatisfied on
many points, and especially that there was no recognized
mode or system in Anglicanism for reconciling the sinner's
soul with God ; and on many other matters.

I went to Oxford to see Dr. Pusey, and made my confession to him. But I saw that this was a most exceptional step, whether for the clergy or laity; and I became more and more convinced that, save the Sacrament of Baptism, Anglicanism was not a religion of Sacraments at all; and that when it is attempted to make it so, it is only a hollow outward imitation and sham.

Since I became a Catholic, received the gift of faith, and read something for myself on the whole question, I have seen that the notion of the Church of England having anything to do with the Holy Catholic Church in its origin or principles, is the most absurd that can be conceived. A very superficial glance over its history from its first start in the sixteenth century abundantly shows this; and that its founders were actuated by the very same Protestant anti-Catholic spirit as the continental reformers, whom they even exceeded by their persecutions, and in their destroying and plundering everything that Catholics most cherished.

After a very brief glance over the history of the Church of England, it has never appeared to me worth while to take any notice of the various points of Anglican controversy for their own sake. It has seemed to me a frivolous and useless waste of time to go into them; and all the more so, because the hypocritical first reformers, with a view to give a show of venerability to their new system, tacked on to it certain external customs and practices which they had borrowed from antiquity.

When one began to learn something of what true Christian faith was, it became very clear that Anglicans had it not, and, indeed, could not have it in any proper sense; for it is quite evident that a Divine supernatural revelation absolutely demands, for man to believe it, that there be a Divine, external, infallible authority to set forth to him the Divine supernatural truths and obligations which it contains.

This infallible authority, once given, must ever exist in the world, to preserve this Divine revelation, one and the selfsame in its integrity and purity, free from error, and to teach and explain it to men of all generations in every land and age.

I saw that there is such an infallible authority, and that there can be but one only—and that this is the Roman Catholic Church, which has ever made itself known to be such throughout the world from the beginning of Christianity; whereas it is held as a first principle in every other so-called Christian Church, and in the Anglican amongst the rest, that there is no such Divine infallible authority existing on earth at all, and consequently no means for man to know for certain what was divinely revealed, and what he is properly to believe. For it appeared to me utterly unreasonable and absurd to think of believing with Divine infallible faith supernatural mysteries, that are above the reach of reason, on merely human and fallible teaching.

Another argument connected with the above, that forced itself on my mind, is the marvellous harmony which the authoritative teaching of the Church shows to exist between the various Divine mysteries and supernatural truths of revelation, one with another; and at the same time that there is no contradiction discoverable between any of these and human reason, though they are impenetrable to man's finite reason: for if there was, he could not believe them, since God is the Author of reason as well as of faith, and faith must be reasonable.

How different is all this outside the Church! There, there is no religious certainty; but all is opinion, doubt, and contradiction.

These were some of the motives which, through God's assisting grace, led me to become a Catholic.

MARIA G. LODER.

HAVING been asked to contribute a short statement of the condition of mind that led me to join the Church, the following is a brief outline.

It was by degrees, and through long years, that the fact forced itself upon me, that it was not possible to find in the Anglican Establishment to which I belonged, the marks of the true Church founded by our Divine Lord. The anxieties, searchings, heart-rendings, and despondencies that led me to this conclusion are common to so many that I need not describe them, although they weighed upon me and occupied my troubled mind for the best part of a life. I *tried* to see what in truth I did *not* see ; to rely on the statements of others, though unconvinced by their arguments, and so to hug the belief that I might go on safely, and put my doubts aside. Happily, after a while, I was awakened from this slumbering condition, and resolved, by prayer for light, and by examination of doubts and misgivings—consulting works of standing and ability on both sides—to judge for myself on such vital points.

It was a time of anxious care, and I took no one into my confidence for solid reasons. Not until I had passed year after year so occupied, and had come to the conviction that salvation was not to be found where I was, did I for the first time approach a Catholic priest. By that time I was convinced beyond a doubt that submission to the Holy See would bring me into union with the One Holy Catholic and Apostolic Church, and a partaker of those blessed Sacraments which she alone can dispense. It remained, therefore, but to crave for admission to that Communion after which I had been groping so long. *Deo gratias !*

HERBERT H. MAY, Esq., M.A.,

AND LATE SCHOLAR OF WADHAM COLLEGE, OXFORD; PRIVATE
TUTOR FOR PASS EXAMINATIONS AT THE UNIVERSITY.

I WAS brought up for seventeen years in the Evangelical section of the Church of England, and found an insuperable difficulty in deciding what exactly justified one in making the assumption that one had obtained salvation.

Subsequently I went to confession to an Anglican in Oxford, and was satisfied that I had an assurance of pardon on the part of the Catholic Church which God could not repudiate.

I then took Orders, and became a curate in a High Church, but I was much exercised about the sentence: "Do you feel that you are moved by the Holy Ghost to take upon you this ministry?" (After I had become a Catholic it was pointed out to me that the Holy Ghost could not move a man to preach a false religion.)

I was given by my vicar Salmon's "Infallible Church," and I borrowed from a Catholic acquaintance Milner's "End of Controversy," and I bought the "Catholic Belief." This last book with great difficulty I persuaded my wife to read; then we went together to the Catholic priest's house and asked to see a priest, and when he came I said: "I wish to be taught the Catholic Faith." He gave us a lecture on "Go and teach all nations," to prove that there was one body of men established by Christ as a Divine Teacher; and another on "Thou art Peter," to prove that where Peter's successor was, there this Divine Teacher was. My wife was at once convinced and received. I took a holiday from my clerical work, went abroad for a few days to see the Church in a Catholic country, read ceaselessly works of controversy, but finally was received at Weston-super-Mare by a priest whom I had known from a boy. I need hardly say that to me my faith is the pearl of great price. Though, after my conversion, I experienced many temptations against faith, yet they were never logical; nothing could ever break the syllogism—

All things taught by the Church are true.

This is taught by the Church.

This is true.

As links in the chain of my conversion, I remember when a boy being much struck by my brother's explaining to me the verse "Thou art Peter;" that Catholics think their Church the voice of God, or something to that effect. I always called the Catholic priest at home "the holy father," and loved him, though he never said a word to me about religion. And I always thought the Holy Communion the sole service instituted by our Lord. I remember a sermon preached by a Protestant clergyman, in which he said that the words "Do this in remembrance of Me" meant "Offer this sacrifice." When I was convinced of the necessity of confession and the truth of the Real Presence, it seemed to me that the Church which taught these doctrines always and everywhere was the true Church, rather than a Church which, like the Church of England, taught them recently and partially. Lastly, I attended several death-beds, and felt my powerlessness to do anything except pray ; and when it was suggested to me that a confession should be exacted from the dying (not to me, for I was a deacon), it followed to my mind that it would much more usefully be exacted from *every one* and *in time of health.* It is with unwillingness that I speak of myself, but I shall be glad if these few notes make it easier for any one to submit himself to that Divine Teacher, Who says of His Church, " He that heareth you heareth Me."

M

R. S. MOODY, Esq., M.A.,

CHRIST CHURCH, OXFORD; FORMERLY A CLERGYMAN OF THE
CHURCH OF ENGLAND; LITTLE MALVERN.

PERHAPS the only thing worth mentioning would be that I worked out the problem entirely by myself. I did not know any Catholics, and I never spoke to a priest till within a few days of my submission.

What, then, led me to take the step? It was a belief in the Visible Church, in the absolute necessity for that Church having a Visible Head, and in the irresistible evidence in favour of the supremacy of the Pope. This is all. All other questions seemed to me to depend entirely upon this one.

As to the steps that led up to this train of thought:— I was at Oxford from 1840 to 1843, and I felt some attraction to the movement then at its height, mainly owing to my hearing it so persistently abused. But I did not belong to a religious set; very few Eton men did so in my day.

Towards the end of my Oxford days circumstances occurred which induced me to think of taking Orders in the English Church, and I went to the Wells Theological

College for a year or more. Of course, there was constant discussion on the leading Church questions of the day, mainly on doctrine. There was no interest felt then in Ritualism and Church millinery. We were strong in Baptismal Regeneration and Apostolical Succession.

My first curacy was under Lord Charles Thynne, at Longbridge Deverill, Wilts. He afterwards became a Catholic. After this I was in sole charge of the parish of Radnage, Bucks., where I managed to rouse the suspicions and opposition of some of the neighbouring clergy. Lastly, I was for a short time at Aston, Salop.

I was not long in detecting the weakness of the Established Church. I thought a married clergy a great mistake, but what particularly disgusted me was the want of pluck in the High Church party as shown in the Gorham case, when the Bishop of Exeter, having brought us all up to the fight, basely turned tail and instituted the very man whom I had denounced as a heretic. All this made it plain that the Royal Supremacy was a very real Power.

I made up my mind never to sign the Thirty-nine Articles again, and when an illness took me abroad, I finally severed my connection with the Established Church in 1854, in Rome.

Of course, there followed the usual family estrangements, more common then than now, together with alteration of wills and the great difficulty of getting anything to do. Still more painful was the strange feeling of finding oneself in an entirely different state of society, and having, so to speak, to begin life over again.

As to my reading :—I think that Robert Isaac Wilberforce's "Doctrine of the Incarnation" was of more help to me than any other book ; but, of course, I read a great deal of the controversial literature of the day. There are too many books published now. I always advise people in doubt to read the Bible, use their reason, and say their prayers. If an exhaustive statement of the case is needed, Allies' " Per Crucem at Lucem " gives it. I can say no more.

A. T. M.,

M.A. OF CAMBRIDGE.

PROBABLY my experience is, in many respects, that of others, who, after " seeking rest and finding none " in false and imperfect religious systems, have at length found peace in *the One True Fold*. The leading motives which prompted me to abandon my former religious position, and that, too, when in my sixtieth year, and when I had been more than thirty-five years a clergyman in the Anglican communion, were, briefly stated, as follows:—

Using my reason and judgment in weighing evidence as I felt bound to do, I came to the conclusion that the Church of England is the creation of the State, and so is a department of the State ; that she had no existence prior to the Reformation, at which time she separated herself from the rest of Catholic Christendom. Believing this, I could not possibly remain longer in a communion which, I was convinced, was not the Church founded by Christ and His Apostles,—not the venerable and historic Church of this country, but a mere creation of yesterday. I had been from childhood brought up in the belief that the Church of

R. S. P. M.

WHEN as a child in an Irish Dissenting Sunday school I sang, " God moves in a Mysterious Way," I little thought that in later years those words would have a very special personal significance, and that my own spiritual career would be a wonderful exemplification of the truth of the old and familiar hymn.

Having been regularly sent to church and Sunday school by my parents, who were deeply religious people, I soon became thoroughly acquainted with the Bible, and, by the time I was fourteen years old, I had passed many searching examinations in its history, and secured a very large number of prizes. I was thoroughly conversant with the lives and actions of the Biblical heroes, and, in fact, knew the sacred volume from cover to cover.

I had always been taught and believed that the Protestant version of the Bible was the very Word of God ; that it contained all things necessary for salvation ; that it was the only revelation of God's will to man ; and that it was the veritable sheet-anchor of religion. Coincident with these articles of faith, I was instructed that although it was the Word of God, it was necessary to construe its meaning by the light of reason ; so that when a passage came up for criticism, there was no appeal to anything higher than my own intelligence, or that of some commentator, or that of an uninformed but self-sufficient Sunday school teacher.

It is little wonder, therefore, that when doubts suggested themselves to my mind, and my minister or teachers were unable to solve or answer them, I gradually fell away into disbelief. There was much which I could not reconcile with reason pure and simple ; and, as I had always been taught to look on my own judgment as the final arbiter, I naturally arrived at the conclusion that the Bible had no other claim to credence than that possessed by any other ancient volume.

Brought up as a Protestant in Ireland, I was also taught that Roman Catholics—Papists !—were ignorant and deluded idolaters, kept in mental and spiritual darkness by cunning priests who flourished at the expense of their flocks, and who were allied in one huge scheme of imposture in order that they might wring money from the peasantry for themselves, their bishops, and the Pope, who, we were told, was the living representative of the Scarlet Woman. In addition, I was taught to look down on Catholics as inferiors—socially and mentally. *They* were not allowed the inestimable privilege of private interpretation ; it was an open question if they were even permitted to possess a Bible ; and it was perpetually dinned into my ears that the prosperity of the Protestant community was intimately associated with what was termed an "open Bible," the poverty of the Catholics being attributed to their real or supposed lack of Bibles. Further, were not the " Papists " thirsting to elevate all the Protestant heads on pikes, in obedience to the orders of the Inquisition and the Jesuits!

Is it matter for wonder, therefore, that, breathing such an atmosphere, it never entered into my mind to place my doubts before a Catholic priest, and that, later in life, after a long course of Paine and Voltaire, I joined the ranks of active opponents of Christianity? Doubts grow by what they feed on, and, having convinced myself that revealed religion was the enemy to be crushed, I became associated with the late Mr. Bradlaugh and his party. For a number of years I was a very active member of the National Secular Society, and willingly gave money and time to Freethought propaganda. Like St. Paul, I honestly believed that I was doing my duty in "exposing" the hollowness of a great sham, and that the more minds I unsettled the greater and nobler became my work.

This went on for some years—years in which I utterly disbelieved in spirit or in a hereafter, when I became interested in spiritualism. Now, whatever be the source of the phenomena termed spiritualistic—whether it be angelic or devilish, I am unable to say—it performed this important service for me : it opened my eyes to the fact that there are intelligences outside ourselves, who in many respects resemble us, and yet who are invisible. After a fair examination of the subject in its various phases, I became convinced of the existence of a future life, and also came to the conclusion that some spirits, under certain conditions, which are not and may never be properly understood, are permitted to communicate with living people.

From inability to extract definite information from the

spirits—many of whom lied in a most unblushing manner when under interrogation—I gradually ceased to interest myself in the subject ; but my materialism had vanished, and I had taken a step—but how great a step !—nearer a true conception of spiritual life.

One memorable Easter Monday I was passing the Oratory in the Brompton Road, when something induced me to enter, accompanied by my wife and son. I had not been in a Catholic church for over twenty-five years, and thought I would like to have a look around ; but my feelings of curiosity quickly gave place to sensations of quite a different nature. I had barely opened the door when I seemed to have entered the spiritual world. I felt myself encompassed by the Unseen, and an awful feeling took possession of me. I could hardly speak, and felt humiliated and crushed. Then did I realize what was meant by the power of the Spirit, and I remained under its influence about an hour, unconsciously communing with that One Whom I had all my life rejected and de-spised. Profound sorrow took possession of my soul, and I felt that here at last was Peace.

When leaving the Oratory, I bought a copy of " Catholic Belief," which corrected many of the absurd notions which I had entertained with regard to the faith and practices of the Church. Here, also, I was made aware of the fact that the Catholic Church is, above all, a teaching Church, and that her doctrines to-day are the same as those which she taught before the sacred books which form the Bible were collated and issued under her authority.

I had always thought that Protestants were in an utterly false position, there being no logical middle ground between absolute authority and rationalism. When I was thus happily brought to see that the Church possessed the authority which she claimed, I felt it my duty—in the highest exercise of my reason—to submit myself to her discipline, with the best results to myself individually.

Leading as I do a very busy life, I have not the necessary time at my disposal to study Catholicism as closely as I would wish ; but the more I see of the Church, the greater is my satisfaction. A larger-hearted charity is taught than in the protesting communities, and her system is meant as an everyday religion. The sermons which I hear are not eloquent discourses to which art and literature contribute, but plain words of warning, eminently calculated to make a man do his duty to his God, to himself, and to those with whom he comes in daily contact.

Once accepted, it will be found that the Church gives everything to be desired, requiring in return merely the love and obedience of her children.

M.,

A PRIEST.

I DO not think I can lay anything like a sufficient claim to being a "famous convert;" however, I will give you my experiences such as they have been.

I was brought up in what would now be considered very Low Church, not to say Nonconformist, principles and ideas. On looking back, I do not think I was any better or worse than the average Protestant boy. I learnt, and generally. said, some simple morning and night prayers. I learnt to tell the truth, but also, I fear, to look upon religion generally as a somewhat depressing exercise, to be avoided on any possible pretext.

At an early age I knew portions of the Bible by heart, and, I suppose, could have drawn a map of Palestine blind-fold. From reading a certain class of Protestant literature, the idea became fixed in my mind that somehow Catholics were mistaken, and oftentimes wicked people, yet with a certain amount of historical romance attached to them.

Losing my parents at the age of eighteen, I resided for a time with some relations—Irish Catholics—whose faith was of a very simple practical character. Under God, I attribute the beginning of my conversion to their example, and to the quiet influence of the priest of the place (whom I had known from my boyhood). He was an old man, an Oxford convert of the Tractarian times, of ripe learning and saintly life.

About this time I was very much engaged with matters pertaining to my secular profession. What made me *think*, however, was, that I was asked by the authorities of the Low Church I sometimes attended, to fill a temporary gap in the teaching staff of the Sunday school. I reluctantly consented. Bible-reading was all very well, but when it came to teaching my class something definite, I found out the truth of the saying that " no man can give what he hasn't got." I had no definite belief—no dogmas of my own, and I could impart none.

I fear my efforts as a Sunday-school teacher were not a success, but they made me *think*, and shortly afterwards I placed myself under instructions with the priest to whom I have referred. He kept me three months under careful and constant instruction, during which I had to learn the " Penny Catechism " by heart, page by page. This was a salutary discipline, and it would be well, I think, if we had more of it.

I soon found that I had really nothing to unlearn, and was simply ready to receive what I was taught. What impressed me most during my instructions was the "Teaching Authority of the Church," its obvious existence in the world, and its necessity. In matters of devotion, I think that the "Real Presence of our Lord in the Blessed Sacrament" and "Prayers for the Dead" drew me most powerfully. I remained a layman for a couple of years before I contemplated studying for the priesthood. I then

did a year's private study with the venerable priest who
had received me into the Church, and whose memory I
shall always hold in respect, gratitude, and affection. He
most kindly resuscitated my Latin, and put me through a
course of Church history and through an elementary one
of dogmatic and moral theology ; so that I started my
college course less handicapped than might otherwise have
been the case. And now, looking back on some sixteen
years of life as a priest, I can only say in the words of
the Mass, "Quid retribuam Domino pro omnibus quæ
retribuit mihi ? "

truth before me, and I thank God that I did not reject it at this the turning-point of my life.

I was extremely elated with the discovery which I had made, and which had caused the scales to fall from my eyes; in fact, the truth and its beauty were quite intoxicating to me.

I saw clearly how the Catholic Creeds fitted the teaching of the Catholic Church and no other, and why so many of the doctrines they contained were left untaught by the Protestant sects.

I was also struck by the contrast between the clear fulfilment in the Catholic Church of the Saviour's promise: "the gates of Hell shall not prevail against it," and the statement in the Homily of the Church of England, that "all Christendom, old and young, ecclesiastics and lay people, had been drowned in damnable idolatry for the space of eight hundred years or more." Where, I asked myself, was our Saviour's promise?

Soon after reading the "Catholic Belief" I paid a visit to my friend, Father Meagher, the Catholic priest at Simonstown, and expected that when he heard the news I had to tell him, he would forthwith receive me into the Church. To this expectation I received a rude shock, for, to my astonishment, he sent me away, telling me kindly to look well into the matter, and to come again in a fortnight's time, if of the same mind. But when I called again in the hope of being received without further formalities, I received another shock. He told me that I must now, if I would indeed be a Catholic, put myself under instruction, and commence by learning the Catechism. He quoted the text of Scripture, "Except ye be converted,

and become as little children, ye cannot enter into the
Kingdom of Heaven." I found that I had to become
again as a little child, and to sit down and be taught. I
learnt the Catechism by heart, and went to him daily
to repeat my lesson.

The good priest also lent me several Catholic books—
the first I had ever read in my life—and I began to study
history from the Catholic point of view. The first thing
that struck me was the fairness of Catholic historians, their
books being full of references, and mostly from the works
of their opponents. The Reformation period caused me
no little surprise and indignation. Indeed, I found so
much to learn and to unlearn, that it took me six or
seven years of hard reading to get myself up to date. But
I had the happiness, after three months' instruction, of
being received into the Catholic Church—on St. Joseph's
Day, 1887, the year of the Pope's and the Queen's
Jubilee.

It is often said that we Catholics are such "priest-
ridden" people. I answer: If this is because we honour
and obey our priests, and because we ask their advice
in things spiritual and temporal, we certainly are priest-
ridden, and we are proud of it. We obey our priests in
things spiritual, because Jesus Christ said, " He that heareth
you heareth Me, and he that despiseth you despiseth Me"
(St. Luke x. 16) ; and, "If he will not hear the Church,
let him be to thee as the heathen and publican" (St.
Matt. xviii. 15–17). We honour our priests, because they
are the anointed of the Lord, who daily offer the Body
of our Lord in the Holy Sacrifice of the Mass. I know
that it is difficult for the non-Catholic to grasp the exalted

position which a priest must ever occupy in the eyes of a good Catholic. He is honoured, not because of any good qualities which he may personally possess, but because of his holy office and of the position which he holds in the one Church of the Redeemer.

GEORGE HARE PATTERSON, Esq.,

FORMERLY A UNITARIAN MINISTER.

WHEN a convert, looking back, sees the path by which he has travelled homeward, notes its devious course, its pitfalls, and its snares, and realizes that by the mercy of God he is safe in the fold of Mother Church after all, he feels impelled to chant his Te Deum in joy and thankfulness. But when such an one is asked to tell how it all came about, what tended to produce so great a change in his life, he is at first almost at a loss for a reply. The Holy Spirit's leadings and promptings are in most cases so subtle, that it is extremely difficult to say definitely: This or that made me a Catholic.

But, having been asked to make some attempt to answer this question, I will endeavour to give briefly some of the reasons which weighed most strongly with me in making this great change. I shall not pretend to present arguments, writing, as I am, for inquirers rather than for controversialists, but simply bear my testimony so far as it is based upon personal experience.

As a Unitarian I invariably made a point of seeking to understand both sides of any question of importance

that presented itself to me, and so, upon casually forming
acquaintance with a Catholic priest, it struck me as being
a good opportunity of getting to know "the other side of
the question" in the matter of Catholicism. I therefore
asked him to suggest some book that would briefly and
concisely give a statement of the actual claims and teaching of the Church, and he recommended to me Father
Bruno's "Catholic Belief." I secured a copy, and read it
very carefully, with as fair and open a mind as was then
possible for me, and it taught me at least to understand
and to respect the Church's claims, however strongly I
might be inclined to dispute them. But this certainly
was a point gained, the full value of which I was to
experience later on. Not long after this I came to realize
the force of a view held by so many Unitarian thinkers,
that "between Rome and Reason there could practically
be no alternative." But at that time Reason seemed to me
to be an all-sufficient guide. I was then serving as a lay
preacher for the Unitarian cause, and when, after several
years of study and experience, I entered upon regular
work, it was to take charge of the Domestic Unitarian
Mission Church at Belfast. I was now called upon to
study human life in its various phases—not as it is
presented in books, but as it really is, and to an extent
that had never been possible to me before. I was not
long in discovering that the views which I held, and which
I was earnestly seeking to inculcate amongst my people,
were to a great extent in flat contradiction to those held
by my predecessor, and this was by no means an encouraging discovery. But, strange to say, the awkwardness
of such a state of things had never before occurred to

me ; on the contrary, I had rather gloried in what appeared
to me to be but the legitimate exercise of my individual
liberty of judgment. But how great seemed the difficulty
which now presented itself to me! While teaching from
the pulpit what I believed to be truth, it was my duty
to tell my people that they must after all think for
themselves as to what was truth and what was error.
And this to a working-class congregation, most of whom
were beset with difficulties and temptations on every hand,
and many of whom were enduring the terrible hardships
and privations of life!

To me, the existence of God and of the human soul
were certainties, and, as a spiritualist, I believed in the
reality of a spirit-world, in which we would have to reap
the fruits of our conduct and of our aspirations in this
earthly life. I would as soon have doubted my own
existence as to have doubted this. Hence my keen sense
of personal responsibility in the matter.

As time went on, there was brought home to me, with
increasing force, the full significance of the great divergence
of opinion which prevailed among our ministers regarding
the most fundamental and central truths of Religion. The
miserable inadequacy of Unitarianism, when brought to
bear upon the evils of life, became increasingly apparent
to me as my work as a missionary led me among the
very poorest and distressed and vicious of mankind, and,
in spite of many prepossessions and of deeply rooted convictions, I was made, after a while, to feel the absolute
necessity of dogma. How to help poor struggling
humanity in face of all the terrible problems of pain, sin,
and death, without setting forth some objective truth,

seemed to me to be a question pressing for solution. Some dogmatic basis of operation, some kind of infallible truth, seemed to me to be the one thing needful; but where was such a basis to be found?

At this time, Orange influences were well in evidence in Ireland, and the Ulster Unitarians, in spite of their profession of liberality in religion, were to a great extent impregnated with the Orange taint. It was this spirit amongst my own people which more than anything tended to drive me into Catholic society. Almost innumerable were the libels and charges trumped up against Catholics and their Church, and, but for my previous familiarity with Catholic teachings, I might have been imposed upon and imbibed the same poison. As it was, I often felt bound, in the interests of common fairness, to contradict many a vile assertion, and also to strongly condemn such gross violations of the law of charity as were involved in the utterances of what I knew to be malicious slander. Need it be said that I soon became an object of suspicion to many who should have known better? In spite, however, of the tongue of scandal which was at work, I persevered in my ministry; but those with and for whom I was working little knew with how heavy a heart. The daily familiar sights of poverty, disease, and vice, visitations of the dying, and the witnessing of death-agonies, together with the sorrows of the bereaved, left, I think, indelible impressions upon me. Indeed the strain and distress of mind became at times almost unbearable. "Is it possible," I asked myself, "that in God's wide universe there is neither help nor remedy? Is there no hope or inspiration beyond what is to be gained from scientific speculation and from guesses at truth?" I had, indeed, the undeniable facts of Spiritualism to fall back upon; but, real as they were to me, they were far too meager, and the truths they demonstrated altogether too indefinite, to meet the wants of the case. I knew, moreover, that they were put aside as mere superstition by the majority of both ministers and laymen in the Unitarian body. There was left, then, no basis whatever to work upon, and there could be no united effort of any kind in the least likely to meet our burning necessities. Generous material help there was, indeed, forthcoming from kindly hearted men and women; but, taken by itself, how sadly inadequate it was! Philanthropy, if confined to the merely material plane of life, is clearly not the whole of Religion, however necessary an adjunct to it it may be. True charity is the love of man for God's sake, and when it is prompted by supernatural motives, it has a Divine uplifting power. Without it, how shall the broken-hearted find comfort, the tempted receive strength, the dying find peace and forgiveness—how shall the bow of promise be made visible above the yawning grave?

I found many valuable and sympathetic friends among Catholics, specially amongst the Passionist Fathers of Ardoyne, at whose monastery I was a frequent visitor. But they never spoke to me on the subject of doctrine. The initiative was in every case taken by myself. Vague misgivings and forebodings were beginning to make life almost intolerable to me. The very enthusiasm with which I had hitherto advocated Unitarian principles was making the present experience all the more painful to me. I looked with inquiring eyes at all the Churches, and

although I found good and earnest men in all, helpful
agencies here and there, I found only one Church whose
news had a clear and certain sound, an unequivocal claim.
With a distinctness, as though it was whispered by spirit-
voices, came to me the question, " Is it not possible that
this despised, calumniated old Church may be the true
Church after all ; that in her is to be found Divine
helpfulness and—truth ? "

> " I at least believed in soul,
> Was very sure of God."

And, granting the existence and reality of these, it was
clear to me that the soul must have been created for an
end ; and if for an end, how was man to know and attain
it, save by a revelation which in its own nature was infallible ? Such were the questions and suggestions which
prompted a reconsideration of my whole position.

The re-reading of theology, of Christian history, very
soon led me to see that if the Catholic religion were not
true, the greater was the pity of it. Still the obstacles in
my way were considerable, it being no easy matter for a
rationalist to break away from the old moorings and to let
go his old ideals ; it was both a painful and a humiliating
process ! The task was made easier for me in that I did
not trouble over mere side issues, but went straight for the
main point : Authority and Divineness of commission. My
investigations were primarily directed to the credentials
of the Church, seeing that if they proved sound, all else
must follow in logical sequence. Granting the reality of
the Church's claim, no matter how great the difficulties involved, there could be no longer room for doubt regarding

anything contained in the'deposit of Faith. I came to view the Church as a living organism, following the natural laws of development and of assimilation, yet ever preserving its identity unchanged, by virtue, as I afterwards discovered, of the perpetual indwelling of the Holy Ghost. In no other way could its marvellous vitality be explained or accounted for.

I cannot, of course, attempt to set down the entire *rationale* of the process by which I arrived at these conclusions. This has been most ably done by other pens. For the information, however, of any of those who are travelling along a similar road, and who may be disposed to reconsider their position, I would mention some works which have helped me materially in bringing my inquiry to a successful issue. They are Hettinger's " Revealed Religion," and " The Existence of God " by the great German Jesuit Father Hammerstein. These two I found simply invaluable. I would also particularly mention Cardinal Manning's " Temporal Mission of the Holy Ghost," and his smaller but very pithy volume, " The Grounds of Faith." The book, however, that above all others helped to clear away my intellectual difficulties, and that showed me the soundness of the Church's position, together with the Divine nature of its mission, was Newman's " Grammar of Assent." The grace of God did the rest.

But besides the influences thus indicated, there were all this time other and, if I mistake not, still more potent factors at work, deep down in the recesses of my inner life. They are, however, of so sacred a nature that I almost hesitate to set them down. There are some experiences in life so tender and so holy, that right feeling would seem to forbid their being placed in detail before the public gaze. Suffice it to say that I had a little daughter who, strange to relate, had received the grace of Catholic baptism. After four brief but very happy years, she was taken from me. After that—I could not have given a reason why—I often wandered into Catholic churches, for it seemed to me as though I was nearer to her there than in any other place on earth, and that He too was nearer to me there as the Father of consolation and of comfort. A deep sense of peace, the significance of which I could not then comprehend, at such times stole into my inmost soul. The initiated will readily understand.

> "God has His mysteries of grace,
>   Ways that we cannot tell ;
> He hides them deep like the hidden sleep
>   Of him He loved so well." [1]

It seems but fitting that a word should be added as to my experiences as a Catholic. To me it has been indeed a taking up of the cross in the truest sense. But what of that? I have found a deeper peace and a greater all-pervading happiness, have found stronger incentives and more powerful aids to pure living and high thinking. I have received greater consolation in sorrow and, certainly, an intenser realization of the Divine Presence than I have ever known before in the history of my life. A fuller light has for me been thrown upon the intricate problems of humanity, and a key has been

[1] From " The Burial of Moses," by Mrs. Alexander.

given me which, like the magic *sesame*, will open the doors of the King's treasury, whence there are brought forth for me jewels rich and rare. I have exchanged sophistry for philosophy, chaos for order, uncertainty for certainty. The Church has satisfied the deepest wants and longings of my nature.

THE RIGHT REV.

JAMES LAIRD PATTERSON, D.D., M.A.,

TRINITY COLLEGE, OXFORD; LORD BISHOP OF EMMAUS;
ST. MARY'S, CADOGAN STREET, S.W.

I WAS born in 1822, and brought up in the ordinary
Protestantism of the period on the "Bible only." When
I went to Oxford in 1840, and was asked, before signing
the Thirty-nine Articles, what they were, I answered that
they were "a protest against Catholic errors," which was
considered a satisfactory statement. In the set to which
I belonged (the scholars of Trinity) I heard for the first
time of the principle of authority as the basis of religious
belief, and I immediately, as by a sort of instinct, adhered
to it as a philosophy of belief and a rule of life, never for
an instant doubting that the exponent of this principle
was "the Church"—that is, the Church of England as by
law established. In the course of my first three years'
residence at Oxford, the conversation, and, above all, the
excellent example of my contemporaries, gradually developed more and more fully belief in the primary truths
of religion—the Trinity, the Incarnation, the Redemption,
the Sacramental System, Prayer, Almsgiving, Fasting,
reverence for holy things and persons, the Communion

of Saints, and Forgiveness of Sins. At the end of that
time a course of lectures on ecclesiastical history, given
by the Regius Professor, Hussey of Christ Church, and
a good deal of reading on cognate subjects, mediæval
architecture, archæology, and especially the study of our
ancient Churches in frequent excursions, brought home to
me the perception of the great difference which there is
between the mediæval religion and that of the existing
Church of England ; it especially struck me as extraordinary that the outcome of the changes of the sixteenth
century, which we were told to esteem as excellent and
admirable, should evidently have been an immense de-
crease of religious belief and religious practice throughout
the land. I had attached myself to one of the Oxford
parishes, and in 1845 I offered myself as a candidate for
Orders. This necessitated a reconsideration of the claims
of the Church of England to my allegiance, and, when I
presented myself to the Bishop of Oxford, I felt it
necessary to acquaint him with the fact that I had some
doubt as to the validity of those claims. The Bishop
(Wilberforce), however, overruled them, more by a show of
authority than by any process of reasoning, and I was
ordained deacon in December of that year. The ministry
and its obligations did not, as I was told it would, tend to
settle me, but, on the contrary, increased my doubts. Under
Dr. Pusey's direction I obeyed his counsels to leave aside
controversy and apply myself to active work in the parish of
St. Thomas' where I was curate ; but, from time to time, the
old difficulties returned, and the more I read and reflected,
and also (in visits to the Continent) saw and heard of the
working of the Catholic Church, of its absolute unity in faith

O

and discipline, the more I perceived the absence of those characteristics in the Anglican Communion. The strain on mind and conscience broke down my health, and in 1849 I was advised to go abroad for a year to rest. At that time a number of us " Anglo-Catholics," as we called ourselves, were full of a speculative idea that we should find in the East communities who, while they, like ourselves, were not in union with the Papal Church, yet boasted of a great antiquity and of Catholic doctrine and discipline. I therefore, in company with a friend, like-minded, and very earnest, went to Egypt and thence to Palestine. We found a great variety of ancient local churches and representing some of the earliest heresies, often mutually contradictory, but all agreeing in rejecting the supremacy of the Pope. On the other hand, the Catholic Churches, whether following the Latin or the Greek, the Armenian, the Syrian, the Coptic, the Abyssinian, Maronite, or any other rite, were absolutely one in doctrine and in obedience to the Pope as Vicar of Christ and Supreme Head of the Catholic Church. If we were sometimes welcomed as brethren by the Copts, etc., it was as Protestants and Anti-papalists. The way towards the Church was thus no doubt made plain, but as yet the hour of grace had not arrived. It was in Holy Week, 1850, that we found ourselves at Jerusalem, and there, in the midst of the scenes hallowed by the Passion, Entombment, and Resurrection of our Saviour, that we received and obeyed the Divine call, and submitted to the One, Catholic, Holy, and Apostolic Church.

On looking back to that time, I see no reason to accuse myself of bad faith before the crisis came ; but neither can

I hope to give reasons which would satisfy others for the long delay in the process of conversion to the faith. Doubtless God uses second causes to bring about His merciful ends in the souls of men, but the whole is a supernatural operation, and those who have undergone it can only sum up all in the words of the man born blind : " One thing I know, that whereas I was blind, now I see."

C. KEGAN PAUL, Esq., M.A.,

Exeter College, Oxford.

"THE END OF WANDERING" (1890):

Being the Concluding Chapter of his Work, "Memories," published by Messrs. C. Kegan Paul, Trench, Trübner, & Co.

WHEN I came to London I was able for the first time, during many years, to consider my position calmly and fairly. While doing my duties as best I could, it had not been easy to realize how completely I had fallen away from the faith. Now, as a layman, with no external obligation to use words in which it was necessary to find some meaning consistent with my opinions, the whole services of the Church of England seemed distasteful and untrue. The outward scaffolding on which I had striven to climb to God, every sacramental sign under which I had sought to find Him, had crumbled into nothingness. I was in no conscious relation to Him, God had practically no part in my life; though I did not deny Him, nor cease to believe that a First Cause existed : simple atheism is a rare, and perhaps an impossible position. I was content not to know, and to wait.

But in the mean time certain things were abundantly clear. Human relationships exist—the family, society, the country, the race ; towards all these we have duties which must be organized ; some conception of history, philosophy, and science must be framed, if not depending on God, at least in relation to man. The system formulated by Auguste Comte had long attracted me on its historical and social sides ; a friend who, in and since my Oxford days, had swayed my life more than he knew, had found it sufficient for himself, and he placed before me the religious side of this grave and austere philosophy.

It is not a paradox, but sober truth, to say that Positivism is Catholicism without God. And it does, after a fashion, give order and regularity to life, inculcates simplicity of manners, aims at a certain amount of discipline, and caricatures, unconsciously, and with some effect, the Sacraments, the *cultus* of Saints, the place of our Lady in worship, making of humanity the ideal woman, the great mother and mistress of us all.

It should, in fairness, be said that in this faith, if so it may be called, men and women live high, restrained, ascetic lives, and find in humanity an object, not self, for their devotion. Like the men of Athens they would seem ignorantly, and under false names, to worship God. And for myself I may say that I doubt if I should have known the Faith but for Positivism, which gave me a rule and discipline of which I had been unaware. The historical side of Comte's teaching still remains in large measure true to my mind, based as it is on the teaching of the Church. Comte had the inestimable advantage of having been Catholic in his youth, and could not, even when he tried, put aside the lessons he had learnt.

So long as my Positivism lasted I brought in to it a

fervour and enthusiasm to which I had been a stranger, and I was therefore long in discovering that these were unreal and forced. On many Sundays, when the service was over, I was wont to walk home with a younger friend, whose experiences had been largely my own, save that his loss of faith had arisen from revolt against the extreme Calvinism which had been presented to him in his youth. He also had wandered out into Agnosticism, and discovered that he needed an external rule against the temptations of life which for a while he thought to find in the religion of Humanity. In long walks across the park homewards in summer and winter noons we both found that the fervour of the services evaporated, and left nothing behind them ; there was none of that sense of a power abiding within us which the Catholic worshipper brings away from the tabernacle, even if he cannot always maintain the intensity of devotion which has been granted him during the action of Holy Mass or in the Benediction Service.

Once more I saw that my soul was stripped and bare, when it had seemed fully clothed. Such also was my friend's experience, and God had given him grace to find, as I have found, the truth after which we were both seeking. Positivism is a fair-weather creed, when men are strong, happy, untempted, or ignorant that they are tempted, and so long as a future life and its dread possibilities do not enter their thoughts ; but it has no message for the sorry and the sinful, no restoration for the erring, no succour in the hour of death.

In the training of my intellect and literary faculty, such as it is, one man had always held predominant sway. Those young men who entered on their Oxford careers

towards the end of the decade, 1840–1850, found that one
prophet at least had gained honour in his own country,
even if he had experienced also scorn and rejection. John
Henry Newman was a moving intellectual force along
with Tennyson, Browning, Ruskin, and Carlyle. I came to
know the two poets as I know my Bible, if it be not
irreverent to say so, in such a way that, after a time, I
needed no longer to read them, because the exact words
surged up in memory when thought was directed to them,
and there was no need of the printed page. Ruskin and
Carlyle delivered their message and passed on, but
Newman abode, and his intellectual influence developed
into one that was moral and spiritual, preparing my soul
for the great grace and revelation God had yet in store.
Like Thomas à Kempis, so Newman, studied day by day,
sank into my soul and· changed it. Since Pascal none has
put so plainly as he the dread alternative—all or nothing,
faith or unfaith, God or the denial of God. I had not
denied Him, but had left Him on one side, and now as it
were God took His revenge. This is no place to explain
in detail how in sorrow and desolation of spirit God left
His servant alone for a while to clutch in vain for some
help in temptation, for some solution of doubt, and find
none, if it were not God and the old creeds. It were to
lay the secrets of the soul too bare to declare minutely
how each hesitation to submit to what was becoming
intellectually clear was followed by some moral or spiritual
fall, as though the Father would allow His child to slip
in miry ways, if nothing else would teach him the need of
guidance.

But, apart from the direct leadings of God's grace and

the general effect of the " Imitation " and Newman's writings, it may be well to specify more closely some of the arguments which weighed with me to accept the faith I had so long set at nought.

First, and above all, was the overwhelming evidence for modern miracles, and the conclusions from their occurrence. A study of Pascal's life, when I was engaged in translating the " Pensées," directed my special attention to the cure of Pascal's niece, of a lachrymal fistula, by the touch of the Holy Thorn, preserved at Port Royal. It is impossible to find anything of the kind better attested, and readers may judge for themselves in the narrative written by Racine, and the searching investigations by unprejudiced, and certainly not too credulous, critics, Saint-Beuve and the late Charles Bread.

Next in importance were the miracles of Lourdes, one of which, as wrought on a friend of my own, came under my notice. I do not mean, especially in the former case, that these facts proved any doctrines : that the miracle of the Thorn made for Jansenist teaching, or those at Lourdes for the Immaculate Conception ; but rather, that the Thorn must, from its effects, have been one that had touched the Sacred Head, that the spring at Lourdes could only have had its healing powers by the gift of God, through our Lady. It was not that miracles having been declared in the Bible made these latter occurrences possible, but that these, and in times so near our own, made the Bible miracles more credible than they were before, adding their testimony to that which the Church bears to Holy Scripture. And it was on the testimony of a living Church that I would accept the Scripture, if I accepted it at all ;

for surely, of all absurd figments, that of a closed revelation to be its own interpreter is the most absurd.

The books which mainly aided me at this period, when I had accepted in a more definite way than ever before the being of a God Who actively, daily, and visibly interposes in His own creation, were the "Grammar of Assent" by Cardinal Newman, and "Religio Viatoris" by Cardinal Manning. Both works postulate God and the human soul, and on that foundation build up the Catholic Faith. They are very different in their method, and perhaps, as a rule, helpful to different classes of mind, but both aided me. The re-reading the "Grammar of Assent" as a theological treatise, and with the wish to believe, was quite a different matter to my earlier study of it on its publication, when I regarded it only as an intellectual effort, interesting as the revelation of a great mind, but not as yet recognizing that it had any special message for me. But in these later days it proved to be the crowning gift of the many I received from that great teacher, who had been my guide through the years of my pilgrimage, little though I knew it.

It is not possible to state precisely the moment at which definite light came upon my soul in preparation for the fuller day. As Clough says truly of earthly dawn—

" And not by eastern windows only,
　　When daylight comes, comes in the light ;
　In front, the sun climbs slow, how slowly !
　　But westward look, the land is bright."

About 1888 I had light enough to attend Mass pretty frequently, but even then was not definitely Catholic in my belief and sympathies. There was one of my own

family, having a right to speak, who distrusted my evident
leanings, not so much from want of sympathy with religion,
as from a fear that, as my opinions had been so long in a
state of change, this also might be a passing phase. I said
to myself, whether rightly or wrongly I cannot judge, that
a year should elapse before I made up my mind on the
question, though I began to see which way it must be
answered. This was in the spring of 1889 ; but so weak
is memory that towards the end of the year I was misled
by a date, and supposed it had been in the late summer.

In May, 1890, I went for a short tour in France, as
I had done for some years past, and a profound sense
of dissatisfaction with myself filled my whole soul. In
other days the cathedrals and their services, the shrines and
their relics, places of pilgrimage, venerated images, had all
been connected with a faith in which no one who studied
the workings of the human mind could fail to take interest,
but they had no relation to my own. Now it seemed to
me that I was an alien from the family of God, unable to
take a part in that which was my heritage, shut out by
my own coldness of heart, my own want of will. And, as
had long been the case, what attracted me most were just
those things in the cult of Rome which most offended my
companions.

A distinguished ecclesiastic was talking in Rome with a
lady who, while in England, had shown some disposition
towards the Church, but lamented that in the Holy City
she had seen much that was to her quite disedifying, and
quite unlike the pious practices she had known at home.
He replied, " *Ah, madame, il ne faut pas regarder de si
près la cuisine du Bon Dieu.*"   It was this which interested ·

me and drew me to it. At Tours the heap of crutches in the house devoted to the *cultus* of the Holy Face, the pathetic agony of the engraving of the same, seen in so many churches of that diocese, appealed more to me than the celebration of High Mass in the cathedral ; the rude image of our Lady at Chartres more than many a fairer statue.

At Beaulieu, near Loches, the end came. We had walked there from Loches, and while my companions were resting under the trees in the little *Place*, and taking a photograph of a neighbouring mill, I remained in conversation with the *curé*, who was superintending some change in the arrangements of the altar. We spoke of Tours and St. Martin, of the revived cult of the Holy Face, of M. Dupont, "the holy man of Tours," whom the *curé* had known, and at last he said, after a word about English Protestantism, "*Mais Monsieur est sans doute Catholique ?*" I was tempted to answer, "*À peu près ?*" but the thought came with overwhelming force that this was a matter in which there was "no lore of nicely calculated less or more ;" we were Catholics or not. My interlocutor was within the fold and I without ; and if without, then against knowledge, against warning, for I recognized that my full conviction had at last gone where my heart had gone before. The call of God sounded in my ears, and I must perforce obey. But when ?

The promise which I had made to myself that I would wait a year was binding on me as though made to one for whose sake I had made it, and the date at which the promise would expire seemed far off. But early in August I discovered that I had been in error as to the time, and that I was already free. On the 12th of August, at

Fulham, in the Church of the Servites, an Order to which I had long felt an attraction, I made my submission with deep thankfulness to God.

It was the day after Cardinal Newman's death, and the one bitter drop in a brimming cup of joy was that he could not know all he had done for me—that his was the hand which had drawn me in when I sought the ark floating on the stormy seas of the world. But a few days afterwards, as I knelt by his coffin at Edgbaston and heard the requiem Mass said for him, I felt that indeed he knew, that he was in a land where there was no need to tell him anything, for he sees all things in the heart of God.

Those who are not converts are apt to think and say that converts join the Church in a certain exaltation of spirit, but that when it cools they regret what has been done, and would return but for very shame. It has been said of marriage that every one finds, when the ceremony is over, that he or she has married another, and not the bride or groom who seemed to have been won; and Clough takes the story of Jacob as a parable representing this fact. We wed Rachel, as we think, and in the morning, behold it is Leah. So the Church bears one aspect when seen from a distance, *ab extra;* another when we have given ourselves into her keeping.

But the Church is no Leah, rather a fairer Rachel than we dared to dream, her blessings are greater than we had hoped. I may say for myself that the happy tears shed at the tribunal of Penance, on that 12th of August, the fervour of my first communion, were as nothing to what I feel now. Day by day the mystery of the Altar seems greater, the unseen world nearer, God more a Father, our Lady more tender, the great company of saints more friendly—if I dare use the word—my guardian angel closer to my side. All human relationships become holier, all human friends dearer, because they are explained and sanctified by the relationships and the friendships of another life. Sorrows have come to me in abundance since God gave me grace to enter His Church, but I can bear them better than of old, and the blessing He has given me outweighs them all. May He forgive me that I so long resisted Him, and lead those I love unto the fair land wherein He has brought me to dwell! It will be said, and with truth, that I am very confident. My experience is like that of the blind man in the Gospel who also was sure. He was still ignorant of much, nor could he fully explain *how* Jesus opened his eyes, but this he could say with unfaltering certainty : "One thing I know, that whereas I was blind, now I see."

The Rev. CHARLES POYER,

PRIVATE SECRETARY TO HIS EMINENCE CARDINAL VAUGHAN,
ARCHBISHOP'S HOUSE, WESTMINSTER, S.W.

I JOINED the Church from two motives only: the first the *authority* of the Catholic Church, and the second her *unity of doctrine*.

These two facts seemed to me to require explanation, and after trying to discover authoritative teaching and unity of faith amongst Low Churchmen, Broad Churchmen, and lastly with the High Church party, I finally turned my attention to the Catechism of the Council of Trent. This gave me, what for many years I had been seeking for—a clear and logical reason for submitting my private judgment, in matters of faith and morals, to that Divine Institution which was founded by Jesus Christ to "teach all nations."

Where that Institution was to be found, the unity of its doctrine, its infallibility, its power, its sanctity, and other prerogatives, were truths which, by the grace of God, became to my mind logical conclusions from following step by step those marvellous explanations of the teaching of the Holy Roman Catholic and Apostolic

Church which are contained in the Catechism of the
Council of Trent.

The mind was convinced, but that was not sufficient.
The heart had to be converted. How this miracle was
effected only those will understand who have, in prayer,
sought for that peace which the world cannot give.

The Rev. C. E. RIVERS, M.A.,

ORIEL COLLEGE, OXFORD; CATHOLIC CHURCH, ACTON, LONDON, W.

I was born in South Africa, in the year 1863, my father being on the Governor's staff, and my childhood was passed there until I was sent home to prepare for an English public school at the age of ten. All the Anglican influences of those early days were High Church. The Bishop of Capetown had a convent of Sisters, and the services in the cathedral were certainly not of a Protestant description, though at the present day they would probably be termed very moderate. Choral services, Processions, the cross carried before the officiating ministers : this was the utmost that was attempted in the way of ritual development. I was taught to look upon the Dutch Calvinists, who abounded there, as worthy but misguided people ; and what I remember of the inside of their places of worship was a very dreary expanse of pews, a huge pulpit, and a general absence of artistic or musical accessories. I pitied them, and thanked God that I was born an Englishman, and that I was not of the Dutch Reformed persuasion. The

Superior of the Anglican Convent was good saintly Mary Buller, Sir Redvers Buller's cousin, and my elder sister was her pupil for several years in the first-rate school which she had started in the neighbourhood. One of her other nuns, Miss Andrews, is now Sister Mary Monica, of the Assumption Convent, Kensington Square, who was received into the Church quite late in life, and who at once joined a religious order in spite of her advanced age.

On coming home to England I had a strange religious experience—even for a child. My aunt, Lady C——, with whom I was to stay until the return of my parents, attended service at a certain West End church, where the present Bishop of Manchester then ministered. Here everything was different: an entirely new religion was presented to me. There were long and very learned sermons ; no ceremonial of any kind, and the doctrine, little though I understood it then, was of the broadest and most latitudinarian type. I heard it whispered that I had been brought up with very High Church ideas, and that I was almost like a Roman Catholic boy, all of which made me yearn for whatever that might mean, so much did I dislike the cold, unattractive parish church, and its unintelligible pulpit discourses. To comfort me I was told that "the vicar was a very clever man, and that people came from the other end of London to hear him." Since then, my aunt, through the influence of her daughter, has in her old age adopted the extreme of Ritualism, and now worships in a church in which the Anglican archbishop's "opinion" as to incense, portable lights, and reservation are contemptuously defied.

P

On going to school, I very soon discovered that there
were two distinct religions taught and practised there.
Each Sunday morning the boys were told off to go to
two different churches. One of the masters, I discovered,
was High Church, the other Low Church, and it was
in this way that the respective parents holding to these
different schools of thought were satisfied. By express
agreement with my relations in London, it had been
arranged that I was to attend the Low Church services,
which seemed worse to me even than the Broad Church
régime which I had experienced during the holidays. On
Sunday mornings, at 10.30 a.m., we were drawn up in
double line in the garden of the school, one party to
follow one master, the other the other—to St. Peter's, or to
Holy Trinity, Bournemouth. Fortunately, I had made
friends with Tommy B——, the eldest son of the present
peer, and he knew what a torture I endured at the
Evangelical place of worship. So in his unselfish little
heart it was devised that we should stand side by side in
the two lines, and that we should exchange places the
moment word was given to depart. I do not think that
we were ever discovered in this shocking act of deception
by either of the masters, and I rejoice to say that Tommy
was not killed in the Boer war with the many thousands
of his namesakes who have fallen on the field of battle,
but that he has returned home safe—unhappily, only to
receive a disastrous defeat, when standing for a Radical
constituency in the South of England. I am inclined to
think that he really did prefer Holy Trinity church, seeing
that he could sleep and even snore there in comfort during
service.

My next experience was Marlborough, where the spirit of Farrar yet abode. Religiously that spirit was sensuous and æsthetic, and devoid of doctrine of any sort. Dry moral truths only were inculcated ; no real Christianity was either taught or practised. The natural virtues and Natural Religion were the highest things that were ever aimed at. The music in the chapel was admirable, and it was generally well rendered ; but I remember well the amusing incident of my once being the innocent cause of my neighbours in chapel coming to blows, when service was over. The boy on my left had, like myself, High Church leanings, although he was really a worthless fellow. As a protest against our compulsory attendance at church twice a day, he used to spend his time in reading a sensational novel which he had carefully done up in the cover of an old Bible. On this occasion he was aroused from these profitable studies by the boy on my right hand, who was Low Church, stamping on my toes on account of my having bowed low at the "Gloria Patri"—a custom which I had adopted years before in the cathedral, Capetown, and which I had never relinquished. He was a precocious little villain, this champion of mine, and I wonder where he is now!

As I grew older I used to go to various London churches, the more advanced in Ritual the better ; but it was only when I made my first Communion that I began to think seriously about the doctrinal basis of religion. First of all there came to me the all-important question : What was it that I received in Holy Communion? Was it God or was it Bread? and if the first, why should I not go into His Presence as often as others did, instead of following Him from afar off, when He was "made known to the faithful in the breaking of bread"? So I adopted without hesitation the practice of non-communicating attendance at the Anglican Communion Service, and thus came unexpectedly upon a book compiled by Carter of Clewer, "The Treasury of Devotion." Here was Catholicism in full bloom—everything but the Pope, Our Lady, and the Saints; and even *they* were spoken of with respect, although kept at a respectful distance.

Before going up to Oxford, where I matriculated at Oriel College, I went to a tutor's in Germany to learn that language thoroughly. The "Culturkampf" was at its height, but never before had I seen such faith and devotion, the churches being crowded, and devout multitudes hearing Mass from outside the sacred buildings. (Numbers of Catholic Churches had been handed over to the schismatics of 1870, who held with Döllinger, Reinkens, and Co.) My tutor was a freethinker—although he posed before my uncle, who was making terms with him for my sojourn under his roof, as an Evangelical Protestant, whatever that may mean. His text-books in Theology were Strauss and Renan, and there were two copies of the "Vie de Jésus" on the shelves of my bedroom. He looked rather contemptuously at the crucifix which I had with me; but he was a kind and genial man, a musical genius and good scholar (an authority on Aristophanes), and he had a supreme contempt for the new "old Catholic" sect, which he described as being composed of tepid and lukewarm Romans, who, finding the restraints of their own Church discipline irksome and troublesome, were inconsistent and unreasonable in not going as far as he did towards modern unbelief. His wife turned out to be a fervent French Catholic, whose life was a living sermon, and who, although refusing to enter into controversy with me or her husband, had nevertheless a quiet way of answering questions which was most impressive and dignified. The good woman has since died, and the professor has married a German of his own way of thinking.

While at Heidelberg, which was my headquarters, I made several pleasant holiday excursions, in company with a young Englishman, a nephew of one of Mr. Gladstone's peers, who has since become a London doctor, with a fashionable practice. He professed no religion at all, and scoffed at revelation, but was clever and highly cultured, and devoted 'to music and art. What little I know of either I attribute to him. A visit to the cathedral at Worms, during the octave of Corpus Christi, showed that ancient Catholic building to be well used, as though Luther had never existed ; while no one seemed to trouble to look at the Reformer's monument, which had been subscribed for by his admirers in other countries, and which occupies a commanding position in the town.

On my return home I took up residence at Oriel, where my religious difficulties at once began. I had imagined this, as the home of Newman, Pusey, and Keble, to be an ideal place as regards religious teaching, but I found to my amazement that no such instruction was even attempted. The chapel was a hideous bare building ; the Holy Communion was celebrated only three times a term, and the sacred vessels, whether empty or not, were removed immediately after the service by one of the college servants, whose duty it was to cleanse them at his own convenience in the college kitchen. This was a shock to the feelings of the several young men, who, like myself, believed in some sacramental presence; we soon, however, discovered the existence of Mr. Noel's church, St. Barnabas', and, confining our attendance at the college chapel to what the strict letter of the law required, we were happy for a time in what we saw and found in that stronghold of advanced Ritualism.

But now the question came to us practically, What was the teaching of the Church of England? Was the Anglican priest, who said Mass and heard confessions, right, or were the ordained ministers, who held sway in the Oriel College chapel, right? Who was to decide between them? Kind Dr. King, of Christ Church, now Bishop of Lincoln, cheered us by "comfortable words" as to our duty of improving the Church of England, and of making it truly Catholic, seeing that it was for the most part given over to the Protestants. Amongst our number were Aymer Vallance, who became a clergyman later on, and was then reconciled to the Church; H. L. Leverton, now a vicar in Cornwall; young Cunninghame Grahame, brother of the Socialist M.P., and a few others similarly minded. I remember Frank Russell, son of the late Chief Justice, expressing surprise at our eating fish on Friday in Hall. I suppose he meant that, not being Catholics, there was no obligation upon us to observe the Church's laws.

A matter which greatly perplexed me about this time

was the following practice which Dr. King had adopted.
I could not imagine how he could justify it to himself.
At 8 a.m. he would celebrate communion in Christ Church
Cathedral after the Low Church type, without any external
marks of reverence or adoration.   At 11 a.m., he would
be present at a solemn High Mass at St. Barnabas',
behaving just as any priest would to-day at the Brompton
Oratory.   It seemed to my juvenile conception of things
that either gross irreverence was committed at the early
hour, or else shocking idolatry at the later service.   I
mentioned this to one of the extreme party, who was
supposed to be a "ductor dubitantium," and he thought
that these things were, after all, merely external and
non-essential ; but I reflected afterwards that, if that
were so, how came it that the clergy of the same
school were ready to go to prison for their opinions,
and why was the English Church Union spending
thousands of pounds yearly for what was not really
worth fighting for ?

But before long Dr. King went to Lincoln, and I went
over to Rome, where things are managed differently.   It
was very soon brought home to me that there must be
absolute truth somewhere ; that there must be an unvarying
moral standard ; that we must know what we are to
believe, and how we are to act.   I began to wonder if,
after all, the Roman Church might offer some security as
regards these matters, though I was told that most of her
clergy in this country were very ignorant, and a good
many grossly immoral.   At any rate, I determined to
find out something about her in the proper place—the
Jesuit Church, St. Giles', Oxford.   Father Humphrey, S.J.,

happened to be preaching that very evening on the subject exercising my mind, from the text, " Many are called, but few are chosen," and I began to see things in a new light. I read much of Newman's books, the "Apologia," the "Essay on Development," many simple manuals and catechisms. I studied the devotional aspect of the Church's life; I spent a holiday or two abroad in an entirely Catholic atmosphere. I also examined a good deal of the anti-Catholic literature, from various points of view—the school of Charles Kingsley and of Robertson of Brighton, the pious Evangelical view of the matter. I saw Dr. King several times; I had an interesting correspondence with the great Dr. Liddon. All disagreed with one another, but all agreed against Rome. *She* must be wrong. She was the stone of stumbling, and the rock of offence. I was certain that the Christian Revelation was Divine, but it was clear that the Church of England was only a human institution. There was no definiteness and certainty in her message. God was clearly calling me to come out of her. I made my submission to the late Father Garnett, of the Oratory, on the 17th of December, 1883, and joined the Catholic Apostolic and Roman Church, of whom I am now, though all unworthy, a priest and servant.

What we should seek to point out to inquirers in the present day is that the Catholic Church has all the good that is contained in the various sects outside her pale.. We are High Church in the sense that our ceremonial observances are sublime and elevating, that the teaching of our spiritual writers and mystics is lofty beyond words —"so high, who can attain unto it?" Yet we care not for ritual for its own sake, but as the necessary attendant upon the Heavenly Mysteries, and their expression and accompaniment.

We are Low Church in the sense that we can descend to the level of the humblest intelligences. We give missions to the poor and the unlettered; we have plain low Mass and devotions in the vernacular. The great founder of the Friars Preachers is himself styled "Evangelicus Pater Dominicus"—a true teacher of the simple words of God.

We are Broad Church in the sense that there is nothing provincial or insular in our gospel—"latum mandatum tuum nimis," within the bounds of the Church's dogmatic definitions all is free and wide; "controvertitur" is the summing up of many a discussion of the schools —the theologians differ; but not concerning the Real Presence or Real Absence in the Blessed Eucharist, or as to whether there are two Sacraments or seven, or if the Christian ministry implies a sacrificial priesthood or just the reverse. These are matters which are vital and essential; they mean life or death, not only to the Oxford student and undergraduate, but to the servant and the tradesman; not only to the refined and educated, but also to the coarse and rough; either there is one Church, infallible, eternal, or Christ has been a false prophet—the gates of hell have already prevailed against her.

The Church has her conservative side, in that she cannot change; she is radical, in that she goes to the root of all questions, social, political, scientific, and moral. She appeals to all classes of society, and chooses her clergy from every rank and station of life.

However long the Anglican compromise may still continue to exist, it is surely clear that it has the seeds of decay and death within it. Its testimony does not agree ; it is of the earth, earthy: a mere State creation, doomed to failure and catastrophe. Unbelief, official and authoritative, is taught unrebuked by many of its clergy.[1] The Incarnation, Eternal Punishment, the Blessed Trinity, the very existence of sin and virtue as such are denied. May its best children leave it, and may they soon learn to know with Catholics throughout the world, of every nation and people and tongue, what is the length, and breadth, and depth, and height of the all-embracing love of Christ ; may they receive that unction from the Holy One which shall enable them to know all things, being made wise unto salvation !

[1] See the case of Mr. Beeby, of Yardley Wood, and the Bishop of Worcester, exposed by Lord Beauchamp, but with no result ; the former, though a Unitarian in his views, still retaining his opinions, and writing and preaching these deadly heresies, with the Bishop's tacit approval and sanction.

THE RIGHT REV.
Monsignor W. CROKE ROBINSON, M.A.,

AND FELLOW OF NEW COLLEGE, OXFORD; HAMMERSMITH, W.

IT is difficult to know where to start in a subject so large
and profound as the change of one's faith and the process
by which that change came about. I will endeavour to
trace the beginnings from which were evolved eventually
five conclusions which led me to the Catholic Church.

I must premise that I was brought up as a Low Church
Anglican, but that a very little serious thought brought
me to what is known as Tractarianism, as distinguished
from Evangelicanism on the one side and Ritualism on
the other, with neither of which I had any sympathy. I
thought the one narrow-minded and illogical, and the
other illogical and dishonest; and I think so now. I very
soon began to be disturbed and unsettled by the confusion
worse confounded of Anglicanism. I asked myself, Can
Almighty God be the Author of this confusion? Can our
Divine Saviour's promise be fulfilled, "that the gates of
hell shall not prevail against His Church"? or His prayer
be answered, "that they may be all one, as Thou, Father, in
Me, and I in Thee; that they also may be one in Us:

that the world may believe that Thou hast sent Me"?[1]
I could neither explain this difficulty nor get it explained. As yet the Catholic and Roman Church, for
whatever reason, never entered into my thoughts. These
early troubles were the beginning of what I may truly call
my ten years' agony. For it took me all that time—that
is, from 1862 to 1872—to find my way from darkness to
light.

It was not very long before it dawned upon me that
every Anglican, of whatever school, was in reality a law
to himself, and that he acted on his own authority; and
then it was that the question of *authority* became to me the
"*articulus stantis vel cadentis ecclesiæ*," and ever afterwards.
I asked every one I met, "By what authority dost thou
believe, and doest thou these things?" Sometimes, on
my inquiry of this or that divine, I was referred to the
Prayer-book as my authority, sometimes to the Fathers
of the Church, sometimes to the Primitive Church. It
took me some years to discover the fallacy of such appeals
to authority; why, I cannot think. But that is always the
way when one becomes a Catholic. One is sure to feel
and say, How could it have taken so long to discover
what a moment's serious thought and the exercise of a
little common sense ought to have revealed? How is it
that every Anglican cannot see it? The answer, of course,
is that they have not the gift of faith. They even might
see it—that is to say, might be intellectually convinced of
the fallacy of such appeals, and moreover of the logical
standpoint of the Catholic Church; and yet, for all that,
they will not and cannot become Catholics. For—and

[1] St.1John xvii. 21.

here I must be pardoned for making a considerable digression—intellectual conviction is not faith. It cannot be too strongly insisted upon at this present moment (January, 1901). There are thousands and tens of thousands to-day who are intellectually convinced, that of all bodies of men calling themselves Christians,"the Catholic Church alone is logical and unassailable in its credentials. But they do not, and will not, ever become Catholics because they have not faith. Let us give a homely illustration of the difference between intellectual conviction and faith. A clever botanist, born blind, will discourse learnedly about, say, an oak tree, and will be able with marvellous accuracy to describe its appearance by the aid of his imagination. Meanwhile those of his audience, who have eyes, see. This similitude explains itself. God alone can give the faculty of seeing as well in the order of grace as in that of nature ; and until He gives it, no man can attain to it by any process of scientific inference. And here, let me observe, many of the so-called apostasies of our days are to be explained. They are not really apostasies. It is simply this, that certain men have reasoned themselves into the Church and then have reasoned themselves out again. They were merely intellectually convinced, and were received on the strength of this conviction by priests who possibly took too much for granted, and who neglected to satisfy themselves about the faith of their neophytes, accounting such precautions as superfluous in the case of educated men or members of the Universities. But these people are not apostates, for they never had the faith. When a man has once the real gift of faith—that is to say, the gift of God's grace, which elevates his reason above its natural powers and attainments so that it rises and passes from intellectual conviction into faith, which is an act of the reason but different in *kind* as well as degree from intellectual consent,—when, I say, a man once has this great gift of God, it is impossible for him, so I think, to lose it, and to relapse into any form of Protestantism. He may lose it by wilfully and persistently sinning against the faith, and being punished by judicial blindness, become an infidel. This, of course, is true in the abstract. But, in the concrete, it may well be doubted whether this or that person among the exceedingly few apostates of to-day has really lost the faith. For myself I do not believe they have.

But to return to my subject. At length I saw through the fallacy of any appeal to the Prayer-book, or the Fathers, or the Primitive Church, or the Church of the Ritualists. To begin with the last. A Ritualist has always seemed to me to be one who forms for himself his own theory of the Church, and then religiously obeys, not the Church, but his own theory of it. He is as much a law to himself as the extremest Evangelical. His is merely a case of obedience to self once removed. All Anglicans likewise form their own theory of the Prayer-book, their own commentary on the Fathers of the Church, their own account of the Primitive Church. They are simply a law to themselves, and the slaves of a self-imposed obedience. This conviction of my mind was, I know not why, very slow in its growth, but it came at last, and was indeed a disillusionment! But, besides this, it occurred to me to inquire of what practical use is the dead letter of any book, whether Prayer-book, or Patristic writings, or even the Bible itself?

For any practical purpose, what is wanted is the living voice of authority to determine infallibly what the book means or does not mean in the case of Holy Writ ; and what is true or false doctrine in the pages of all other writers, even those of the Fathers of the Church, all of whom—with the solitary exception of Saint Gregory Nazianzen—we as Catholics know have more or less committed themselves, here and there, to false doctrine. Where is the living voice among Anglicans ? Echo answers " Where ? " It is quite past my comprehension how such men as Lord Halifax fail to see what is so obvious, and keep on appealing with wearisome monotony to what the Prayer-book teaches, or the Church of England teaches, when the fact must be patent to him, as it is to all the world, that there is no living authorized interpreter of either, and never can be, unless it be the Crown, which of course they repudiate. Here I find I must relinquish the continuous narrative of the process of my conversion for want of space. I will proceed to notice one or two of the chief difficulties which occurred to me on the march to the Catholic Church, and the solution of them which satisfied me, but may not, I am perfectly aware, satisfy everybody.

The first difficulty occurred to me in the condemnation of Private Judgment by the Catholic Church. Catholic teaching on this point seemed to me inconsistent with itself ; because at one moment it insists on the use of Private Judgment, and in the next it absolutely forbids it. The answer, however, is very simple ; though it was some time in coming home to me. Of course, a man must use his reason to examine the credentials of the Catholic Church. When he is satisfied with them, and has found the true Church, he gives up his Private Judgment, and submits to the judgment of the Church. As Cardinal Newman writes in his own inimitable style : " Those who are external to the Church must begin with Private Judgment : they use it in order to ultimately supersede it ; as a man out-of-doors uses a lamp on a dark night, and puts it out when he gets home. What would be thought of his bringing it into the drawing-room ? " [1]

I was puzzled for a time with another plausible contention. It occurred to me that it might be said, " You admit that by Private Judgment a man finds out the Catholic Church. Well, then, although he subsequently lays it aside, yet what was Private Judgment in the first instance must always be Private Judgment. By Private Judgment he began ; Private Judgment, therefore, is the real foundation of his subsequent belief." But I saw before long that this objection proves a great deal too much. It seems to imply, at least to me, that, in the last resort, truth is nothing more to a man than what seems to him to be truth. A most dangerous doctrine, truly, as well as utterly false ! It spells Idealism in Philosophy ; Licentiousness in Morals ; and Anarchy in Politics. Surely truth is not dependent for its being on Private Judgment. By Private Judgment we attain to it, but the truth was there before we discovered it, and no matter what we think about it ; and, the moment we arrive at it, we rest upon the truth, not upon the Private Judgment which brought us to it. By Private Judgment, at some time in my life, I apprehended the authority of the English Crown ; the moment I did so, I gave my

[1] " Loss and Gain," p. 203.

intelligent allegiance to it. Henceforth, I rested upon the
authority of the Crown, not upon my mental apprehension
of it. I am now a British subject, not because mentally I
have come to that conclusion, but because of the *fact*. Or,
to adopt another illustration : by means of a ladder I
mount a platform ; I am then standing on the platform,
and not on the ladder which is left down below. By
Private Judgment, then, a man must find out the Catholic
Church. When he finds it, it is a huge *objective fact*.
All men must be agreed about it as a gigantic organization, which has existed these nineteen hundred years.
For all that time—the name and date of every Pope being
historical facts—it has been a chief factor in the history
of Europe. All that time it has taught with the living
voice, and ruled with an incomparable discipline. There
it is to-day as of old, independent altogether of what men
may think about it ; a stubborn, undeniable, unmistakable
fact. Whether it be true or false in its doctrine is beside
the mark : there it is, and there it will be ; that is all we
are maintaining. Well, then, a man discovers this Church ;
he makes his allegiance to it, and is formally accepted by
it. Henceforth he rests upon the authority of the Catholic
Church, not upon his mental apprehension of it. He is a
Catholic, not because he thinks he is, but because of the
fact of his formal reception into the Catholic Church.
Whereas an Anglican rests, not in facts, but in his theory
of facts. Not one of the objects of his religious allegiance
really exists except in his imagination. He will say,
Surely the Prayer-book is a fact. To which I reply, Well,
of course it is ; but not the Catholic interpretation of it ;
for all men are not agreed about that—indeed, the great

Q

majority are violently opposed to it. As long as there is a Broad Church interpretation of it, or an Evangelical, so long the High Church interpretation of it must be a theory and not a fact. The same with the Fathers of the Church or the Primitive Church. These things are, of course, facts in themselves, but not to the Anglican, only the Anglican interpretation of them, which is a very different thing. From beginning to end, therefore, the Anglican is a creature of Private Judgment, not a child of faith ; and from the extremest Ritualist down to the most rabid Evangelical, he is a Protestant pure and simple.

But all this is reasoning in the mere natural order of things. Let us go to the supernatural. By Private Judgment, then, aided by grace—for without that he can do nothing—a man finds out the Catholic Church ; then Private Judgment is superseded by Faith, which, as has been already said, elevates and sustains the reason above the level of its own natural powers. It is on that platform that he stands ever afterwards, and Private Judgment is the ladder by which he reached it and is of no further use.

Upon this, another objection occurred to me, which may be worded thus : "That is a convenient way of getting out of a difficulty by appealing to faith which is not cognizable by any human sense. It may be or it may not be as you say, but that is not argument after all." To this I reply : "Quite so ; to every one but a Catholic it is, I grant, inconclusive. But, then, must it not of its very nature be so ? I cannot show anybody my faith, as I can show him a bunch of keys taken from my pocket. All I know is that I have it and that the non-Catholic has it not, and that that great gift of God is my foundation, and no longer Private Judgment, which is, *ipso facto*, driven out by faith just as darkness is by light."

I do not remember any other serious intellectual difficulty, or one that detained me for long. Bad popes and bad priests never troubled me for a moment. The office and the man are so obviously distinct, that the mind must be addled that does not see it at a glance. A policeman may be an immoral man, but the 'bus-drivers and cabmen will obey him, and rein in their horses at his bidding, because he is a policeman. The sentence of an immoral judge will avail to hang a guilty murderer, because it is the official act of a judge ; it is not invalid because the judge is a bad man.

But, before I formulate my five conclusions, I must here declare my greatest obstacle to my conversion, which was not intellectual but moral. I loved the English Church intensely. It was associated with everybody and everything dear to me from the first dawn of consciousness. From a worldly point of view, to change my faith was to lose everything dear to me, and to gain nothing. It meant the wreck of one's life, shattered nerves, and, for all I knew, absolute destitution. Can it be wondered that I felt reluctant to take the step? Whilst I cannot accuse myself positively of bad faith, yet I must own that the terrible prospect before me made me dilatory in the work of finding out the truth. I have always accounted it as nothing short of a signal miracle of God's grace by which a conversion such as mine was brought about. For ever and for ever blessed be His Holy Name! and the intercession of His Blessed Mother!

I come, then, finally to the five conclusions already

alluded to which pointed unmistakably—in the reputed language of Lord Macaulay after one of Cardinal Wiseman's famous lectures—to "*either the Catholic Church or Babel.*"

POINT I.—*If my soul is to be saved, God must show me the way. It is not for me to choose my own way, and offer that to God.* These words may seem a truism, but they are not really so; on the contrary, they are most useful as hitting off the Catholic and Protestant position exactly. The Ritualist, the High Churchman, the Broad Churchman, the Evangelical, the Nonconformist, all alike formulate their own views of religion, and offer them for God's acceptance as their account of salvation. The Catholic calls that putting the cart before the horse. The Catholic standpoint is this: that it is for God to reveal His own way of salvation, and all that man has to do, is to find out where that is, and to obey it. Further, that God *has* revealed it, and has committed this revelation to a competent authority upon earth, to guard it from error, and to enforce its observance. It is the duty of man to find out where this oracle of truth is, and submit mind and heart to it.

POINT II.—*When God does reveal the way of salvation, it will and must be* ONE—

> (1) One in *number*.
> (2) One in *unity*.

(1) One in *number;* i.e. "ONE LORD, ONE FAITH, ONE BAPTISM" (Eph. iv. 5). Nowhere does Scripture give a hint as to more than one Church. When St. John writes to the Seven Churches of Asia, he is, of course, writing to seven hierarchies of the One only Church. And so historians sometimes speak of the English Church

or French Church, meaning the Catholic Church in England or France. But mere common sense postulates oneness in number. It is impossible to imagine more than one way of salvation. Of course, it is conceivable that Almighty God could make many ways of salvation, because He can do all things ; but it is not conceivable how confusion worse confounded would be avoided if He did. Supposing there was one way for Europe, another for Asia, another for Africa, another for America, a man would have to change his religion four times in a voyage round the world ; and where could he tell where his good ship passed from one way of salvation into that of another ? Some spiritual Trinity House would have to mark the supremely important boundaries by buoys. I know this is fooling ; but, then, the theory I am trying to gibbet is fooling too.

(2) Next, if the revelation is one in number, it will be one in *unity* too ; that is to say, the earthly teachers of it will be one, and the taught will be one. Why ? Because it is the truth. Truth is one : one in the teachers, and one in the taught of its very nature. For instance, London is a city on the Thames. That is truth ; and so all schoolmasters are one in teaching it, and all scholars one in learning it. Why ? Because it is true. About God's way of salvation, then, wherever located on the earth—and located it must be somewhere—there will be unity in the teacher and unity in the taught. If I do not find unity in the teacher and unity in the taught, then I shall know that the truth is not there, from the very fact that there is not unity about it. Let us be quite sure about this. The following proposition is undeniable. Wherever the truth is, there must be unity of the teacher and unity of

the taught about it, because it is true. But the proposition, "wherever there is unity in the teacher and unity in the taught, there is truth," cannot, of course, be maintained as it stands ; because teachers and scholars may conceivably be agreed upon what is false. Yet, observe, in religious argument, even this last proposition is undeniable. For, as a matter of fact, no religious system of human opinion has ever succeeded in maintaining unity, and for this reason : because the moment you depart from the Divine rule of faith, wherever it may be, you are landed, *ipso facto*, in human opinion. There is no intermediate position possible. Now, human opinion must of its very nature be variable, because the human mind has been created by God as variable as the human face. When Dr. Benson, the late Archbishop of Canterbury, ordered prayers for unity in belief among his flock, I remember saying that he might just as usefully pray for *unity of countenance* among them. Therefore, in point of fact, though not perhaps in logic, the religious inquirer may be quite sure, that where there is not unity in the teacher and unity in the taught, there cannot be truth ; and that, conversely, wherever there is unity in the teacher and unity in the taught, there, *ipso facto*, is Divine truth.

POINT III.—*If God does make a revelation of the way by which the soul is to be saved, that revelation will be infallible.*

A. Infallible in its SUBJECT-MATTER—

(1) Because Almighty God delivers it. How can it be otherwise ?

(2) Because my soul wants nothing less. I cannot trifle with eternity. I cannot afford to make a mistake about it, which it is impossible to put right after death.

B. Infallible in its EARTHLY MOUTHPIECE—

(1) For of what practical use would be infallible truth with a fallible mouthpiece?

(2) How can Almighty God punish me for ever, if I refuse to believe a teacher who may mislead me? It is my solemn duty to refuse belief in such an one. Remember, we have to give an account of our faith as well as of our morals, and of faith before morals. "He that believeth and is baptized shall be saved : he that believeth not shall be condemned" (St. Mark xvi. 16). How can God punish me eternally for want of faith, unless He gives me an infallible teacher, whereby I can secure infallible truth? An infallible teacher of salvation is the most pressing of all the needs of the soul, and yet the very mention of an infallible teacher makes the average Englishman shiver in his shoes. This is indeed astounding. Well, then, somewhere on earth, and in some authoritative body of men, or in the office of one man, must be placed by Almighty God the infallible oracle of truth. The way of salvation, then, is reduced to great simplicity by this time. All a man has to do, is to find out where the oracle is, and then believe what it teaches, and do what it commands.

POINT IV.—*This way of salvation will be exclusive.* That is to say, it will be the only one ; and every other way of salvation will be false. This means that the true Church, wherever it is, will not only be the best of all Churches, but the *only* one. This point seems to require no further remark ; and yet I remember a catechumen once saying to me when teaching it, "Oh, Father, that is a tall order and no mistake!"

POINT V.—*To accept when once seen or wilfully to reject this way of salvation is a matter of life or death eternal.* This seems obvious from the words of Scripture already quoted. To see it not, by a man's own fault, is likewise to be lost. Once the solid conviction has crossed a man's brain, that if he inquired honestly into the credentials of the Catholic Church he would be convinced of the truth of it, and bound to submit to it in mind and will,—that man must go on in his inquiry, otherwise he will be lost. To see it not, not by a man's fault—that is to say, in a case where it has never occurred to a man's mind that his own religion is false or that any other religion can be true,—then, not to believe in the Catholic Church will not, of course, entail eternal loss on that account. All this was self-evident to me, but it may not be so to others. With that I have nothing to do.

My task is nearly done. Only a few words are needed to show that the Catholic and Roman Church alone can satisfy these five points or conclusions. Let the religious inquirer examine any system of religion other than that of the Catholic Church, he will find that it breaks down on one or more of these five points. Ask the Ritualist first, who is in many ways nearest to the truth (and yet of him I say, "Thou art so near and yet so far"), is he one with his brother Anglicans in faith? And what must he answer if he speaks the truth? Is he infallible, or the Church of his invention? Is the *Church Times* infallible? No; he breaks down hopelessly, and all his fellow-Protestants when submitted to the test of my five points. But ask next the Catholic Church if it can satisfy those same points, and you will soon see how perfectly she can stand the test.

POINT I.—This point, as we have already seen, is the Catholic standpoint *par excellence.*

POINT II.—Is the Catholic and Roman Church one? Yes; absolutely one in number and in unity all over the world, in every climate, in every race of men : one in the teachers, and one in the taught. It is this marvellous fact that in point of fact converted me. I have always considered this unity of nineteen hundred years as God's greatest miracle.

POINT III.—Is the Catholic Church infallible? Yes; and it has always claimed to be, and has acted as the infallible Divine teacher of truth from the time of Christ. The Catholic Church alone of all religious bodies claims infallibility. The very claim sufficiently proved its truth to me.

POINT IV.—Is the Catholic Church exclusive? Yes; it says, "I, and I only, am the one, true religion. All others are false, and not to be accounted religions at all."

POINT V.—Is it a matter of life or death eternal to accept when seen or wilfully reject the Catholic Church? The Catholic Church replies "yes." She alone. teaches this ; no other system of Christianity has dared to teach it.

Here I conclude the history of my conversion. I do not pretend to do anything more than show what led me to the Catholic Church. I do not lay down any law for others. All I know is that I have the faith, and in the profession and peace of it I have lived twenty-nine years. Not a shadow of a doubt in it has ever crossed my mind during that long time. In this faith I still live, and in this faith I hope to die. Amen.

ROBERT ROSS, Esq., B.A.,

King's College, Cambridge; Reform Club, S.W.

At a very early age I had an unusual predilection for hearing sermons; but I was always bored with the Anglican Morning Service, and I have never been able to understand the enthusiasm with which Anglicans refer to "our beautiful Liturgy." When I reached the age at which I was allowed to remain for the Communion Service, and the meaning of it was explained to me, although far from having an irreligious bias, I was more bored than formerly. I always preferred being taken to Presbyterian churches, where I was sometimes allowed to go with an aged servant who was Scotch. This was chiefly due to the absence of what I must characterize as the tedious offices of the English Church.

It was not, however, until I was about fifteen or sixteen that I thought at all seriously about religious matters, though I had always been fond of churches and interested in everything ecclesiastical. About this time I was fortunate enough to be taken by some Catholic friends to the services at the old Spanish Place Chapel, and here I remember hearing sermons which deeply impressed me, though I have no recollection, I am ashamed to say, of

what they were about, except that they inclined me to
study the Authorized Version of the Bible with greater
care and attention than I had hitherto done.

From this time I always had a distinct Catholic bias ;
but this was rather crushed for the moment by my being
sent to a High Church school, where the practice of
auricular confession was encouraged, and *grossly abused*.

I should say that I had always been given a religious
education, but on rather liberal lines.   At the age of
seventeen I held strong enough views to refuse Confirmation in the English Church ; but this was due to a
momentary wave of scepticism rather than to anything else,
and I became attracted by the ecclesiastical side of things
rather than the theological or purely *religious* aspect of
religion.   Conversations with excellent clergymen, High
and Low, convinced me that neither school was able to
answer for the *entire* Anglican Church on the important
subject of Transubstantiation, or the interpretation of
various passages in the Authorized Version of the New
Testament.   In a small book (the name of which I cannot
recall) I found perfectly definite answers, at all events, to
the questions I had asked my Anglican advisers.   But I
can honestly say that I read no books of controversy, and
the one I refer to was simply an exposition of Catholic
doctrine, with the various offices in English and Latin.
Careful reading of the New Testament (A.V.) and listening to Catholic sermons, and an intense dislike of the
Book of Common Prayer, produced the state of mind
which I had thus reached.   Being rather a precocious
reader as a child, I noticed that the saints, historical and
legendary, whose lives I only knew through Protestant

sources, were always spoken of with benevolent contempt or apology, and reading somewhere that "the English Church has never produced saints but good practical citizens," any lingering belief in Anglicanism, either as an interpretation of Scripture, a rule of life, or as a form of faith entirely disappeared from my mind.

Though interested in the controversy about ritual, I was never ritualistic; and I dislike music now, both in and out of church, and I would prefer all instruments banished from it.

I have recorded *tendencies* which led to my being received into the Church rather than reasons ; but, unless one is endowed with an intellectual and analytical mind, it is impossible almost to give reasons for arriving at the truth. A receptive power and temperament have, I think, more to do with the question than argument. Speaking for myself, I was never convinced by any argument in the world. I believe this (with brilliant exceptions) to be the case with most converts. They arrive at a certain condition of mind, spiritual or intellectual or emotional, as the case may be. If, however, reason enters into the conversion of ordinary converts such as myself, it is rather the absence of reason on the other side which renders the Anglican and Protestant position so unsatisfactory. The Anglican position seems to me to break down on its defence. The Protestant position breaks down in its attack on Catholicism ; at least, such has been my impression when I have followed discussion since I became a Catholic. Previous to being received I never argued ; I only inquired ; revolt against Sabbatarian tyranny being the only exception.

H. P. RUSSELL, Esq.,

FORMERLY VICAR OF ST. STEPHEN'S, DEVONPORT ; EDGVILLE HOUSE,
LEAMINGTON.

IF I must give a reason in few words I will say that,
starting with the belief that our Lord has established an
ecclesiastical kingdom here on earth, Visible and Catholic,
I came to see that it cannot be as a house divided against
itself, with antagonistic forms of government ; but that it
is indivisible, and that its unity consists, not in identity of
institutions such as an episcopal hierarchy and sacraments
(else would Donatists and others have been parts of the
Church, which Anglicans themselves do not allow), but
that it consists in an unity of polity and government—in
a word, in the unity of a *kingdom*.

Now, it should surely be obvious to every one that there
is but one ecclesiastical body politic, which interpenetrates
every part of the world, and unites men of every nation and
race in a religion which is everywhere one and the same in
faith and obedience; that there is but one ecclesiastical
kingdom which can with any truth be described as the
Visible Church Catholic.

So true is this, that Anglicans admit (and, I presume,
Easterns also) that they depend upon Rome for the Catholic

note ; that they would not, even though united with the Eastern Churches, form, without Rome, a Catholic Church in any true sense of the word, since such combination would still be confined as to locality and race. Rome, however, does not depend upon them for the Catholic note. She, without them, is a (the) Catholic Church.

And herein do we see the necessity to Anglicans of their contention that the Roman, Greek, and Anglican Communions form one and the same visible Church. But if the unity of the Church is the unity of a *kingdom*, we see also the absurdity of the contention.

Miss ADELINE SERGEANT,

THE NOVELIST.

I WAS brought up as a Nonconformist; then led by circumstances to become a member of the Anglican Church, from which I lapsed for some time into religious indifference and unbelief. But in 1893 my religious impulses reasserted themselves, and I associated myself with the Ritualist section of the Church of England—a section which had always attracted me. I became a member of various Societies and Guilds, and an "outer Sister" of a well-known English community. For two or three years at least I was completely satisfied with my form of belief, and I remember the friends amongst whom I worked with deepest affection and gratitude.

But I see now that, unknown to myself at first, a change was gradually taking place in my mind. My teachers "builded better than they knew." I learned a good deal concerning Catholic faith and practice from the devotional books which are largely used by Anglicans. In the book I used I found not only the English Communion Service, but the whole of the Canon of the Mass, Preparation for Holy Communion, Prayers (such as the *Memorare*), and

without a head, cut off from the main body of Christendom? Would not the quickest way to reunion be that of individual submission, if the whole body could not be moved to submit? Why not go over at once to the Holy Catholic and Roman Church, as I had heard it called in that stronghold of Ritualism?

"The Supremacy of the Pope" was the stumbling-block, my clergyman informed me; and so far he helped me very much, because he made me see the real point at issue. Henceforth it was on this subject that I thought most; and I must confess that it was the last obstacle to be removed out of the way.

In March, 1899, I visited the Holy Land, and, while kneeling at the Holy Sepulchre, I received so vivid an impression of the reality of the Church, and the futile isolation of Anglicanism, that I only wonder I was not converted there and then. Its only apparent result was to make me add to my prayers a petition that I might be directed into the true light; and later on, I formulated the somewhat presumptuous request that if the Roman Catholic Church were the true Church, I might be guided into the company of a priest who would instruct me, without my putting forth a hand to find one. I had no right to expect such a prayer to be answered, but I was very much afraid of doing what would be disloyal or unfair to my clergyman, for whom I have always had the strongest esteem and affection, or to the English Church. And as it happened, shortly after my return to England that summer, I was led, by circumstances which I could not control, into the society of a Catholic priest, whom I was obliged to see on business, and whom I could question on religious subjects without feeling that I had gone out of my way to do so. He gave me much help, and lent me several books of instruction. My distress of mind soon became acute, and I was almost glad that a severe attack of neuralgia kept me to the house for three weeks or more, and thus prevented me from either going to an Anglican church or seeking my Anglican confessor. The thought of the Anglican rite became intolerable to me, and yet I could not make up my mind to take the final step. Foolish as it may appear, it seemed to me then as though I were casting not only my Church, but my family, my friends, my country, behind me ; I beheld myself as giving up all I loved, and going into some far country which was desolate and strange. No home-sickness ever troubled me as did my desire, at the last moment, for the hymns and prayers of the Church of England. But—and it was my last argument—if the Catholic Church were of God, as I had been mercifully brought to believe, it was a Church for all nations and peoples ; and I had neither friends, family, tastes, nor opinions that I was not prepared to give up for the love of God. I did indeed feel as if I were casting myself into a gulf ; but I was quite sure that I should be held up by the Everlasting Arms.

It ended in my being received into the Church at Farm Street on October 23, 1899. To my friends the decision seemed a sudden one ; but it was preceded, as I have shown, by a long period of reflection. Indeed, it is now a matter of surprise to me that my hesitation lasted so long. I dared not move without complete conviction, and I am profoundly thankful that I did not wait too long, but was enabled to take the step which brought me into the haven of my desires, the Holy Catholic and Apostolic Church of God, in which I hope to live and die.

I have often heard curiosity expressed by Protestants regarding the mental and spiritual condition of converts after their reception into the Church. "Are you really satisfied?" they ask. "Is it all you expected? Are you disappointed?" "Will you never come back?" With these questions, I fancy, most converts are acquainted.

Answers in detail are apt to seem superfluous. But, for the sake of readers who may not yet know the blessing of the Catholic Faith, I will say a word or two in reply, although "my soul hath her content so absolute" that it is difficult to find words adequate for the "satisfaction" that I feel. Mind, heart, conscience, are at rest; no longer tossed on the sea of opinion, but safely anchored in the harbour of God's truth. But I cannot say that I realized my great gain all at once. Little by little the order and beauty and grace of the Church began to dawn upon me. I had accepted its Divine origin and authority before I loved it; therefore my life after I was received into the Church became a series of discoveries. I can almost remember the moment when I first said to myself, "This is more than I ever dreamed of! This is indeed the Church, the Mother of us all, the Heavenly City, the New Jerusalem, the Bride of God!" And more and more, as time goes on, I am permeated with reverence for the Catholic Church, and filled with joy that I am no longer a wanderer from that blessed Fold. For, when I consider the infinite scope of the Church's manifestation, the inspired wisdom of her counsels, the multitude of her

devotions, the care and tenderness lavished on the smallest
and weakest of her children—equally dear to her with the
mightiest upon earth; when I look at the roll of her
saints, evangelists, and martyrs, extending in unbroken
line from the days of the Apostles to our own, and thence
to the end of time; when I think upon the prayers which
ascend continually from the lips of her saints, living and
dead, crowned by the intercession of the great Mother of
God; last of all, when I adore upon the Church's Altars
the Sacred Body and Blood in which God's Presence
remains with us until the end of the world;—then indeed
I humbly say with St. Augustine, "Too late have I known
Thee, O Ancient Beauty!" while, at the same moment, my
soul re-echoes the Psalmist's exultant cry—

"*Beati qui habitant in domo tua, Domine: in sæcula
sæculorum laudabunt Te.*"

The Rev. A. B. SHARPE, M.A.,

Christ Church, Oxford; late Vicar of St. Peter's, Vauxhall, London; St. Mary's Church, Horseferry Road, S.W.

I FIND it difficult to give any clear or connected account of the process which led to my conversion. Some, perhaps most, converts have found themselves confronted, early or late in their career, with some definite fact or argument which stood clear-cut before them, and, like a sign-post, pointed out the only road they could conscientiously follow. Such was not my case. I cannot trace my conviction of the truth of the Catholic Faith to any single cause, or precise set of causes. It is the result, so far as it is due to any natural agency at all, of the innumerable influences which are perpetually acting on a man's character and modes of thought, and by which, concurrently with his own free will, he is moulded for eternity. My submission to the Catholic Church may very well have been immediately caused by one or other of those influences which in itself was among the least important of the whole series; as the face of a cliff is detached by the unnoticed and prolonged operation of the forces of nature, but is at last precipitated into the valley by a mere trifle—the fall of a stone, the touch of a finger, or the echo of a human voice.

As one grows old, many things become clear and certain which in earlier days seemed obscure, or doubtful, or impossible; and many others, which youth and inexperience took for substantial realities, are found in later years to be no more than the creatures of a dream. My dream was the catholicity of the Anglican Church; and the "soliditas Cathedræ Petri" was the reality that I found when I awoke.

I am thus unable to formulate any single argument as having preponderantly influenced me; and to give all the considerations which have helped to produce the final result would be to write an autobiography.

I can trace, however, with more or less distinctness, as I look back over the past thirty years, a progressive succession of states of mind, each of which seemed for the time to be final, but was really only a resting-place on a long journey. The processes by which I passed from one to another are too obscure and complex to be recorded here.

I. My first difficulty was with the Christian revelation as a whole. Though I had no deep tincture of philosophy, I had caught the infection of philosophic doubt which prevailed in certain places thirty years ago, and I could not accept without question the claim of the Christian religion to the possession of a Divine Founder. The argument which helped me most to a conviction on this point was that furnished by the continuous witness and unique persistence of the Christian Church—which phrase I then took to mean the aggregate of Christian societies, which, though they differed on what I supposed to be minor points, agreed as to the cardinal fact of the Incarnation.

II. I came, in no long time after this, to perceive that the Church could not be a mere congeries of independent units, or a polycephalous body; it must be an organism, not a mechanism; its local variations must be not organic, but merely functional. Thus I came to accept the High Church notion of a Church, divided indeed, but retaining a common form in the separate parts and a common life, of which that form is the external indication, and includes valid orders and sacraments, with a somewhat indefinite set of beliefs which is held to represent the faith of the undivided Church.

III. Then the question naturally arose, Which of the contending systems—Roman, Orthodox, and Anglican—was the true one? They undoubtedly were all true, so far as they were agreed; but in regard to the points on which they differed, which was right and which was wrong? This question I tried to answer by means of a prolonged study of historical controversy. I found that the facts which were the subjects of discussion were not themselves in dispute, but that controversialists fought one another about the deductions to be drawn from them. Thus the question I had to decide, if I could, was this: Were the historical instances of apparent opposition to the See of Rome, or of denial of modern Roman doctrine, on which Protestant controversialists relied, to be interpreted in their sense, or in that of their Catholic opponents? For a time I was content to accept the interpretations given by Anglican High Church authorities. How far my position during that time may have been the result of prejudice, of personal influence, or of disinclination to a revolutionary change in my life and circumstances, I do not know.

Possibly all three may have been at work in my mind ;
I can only say that I was not conscious of any of them.

IV. I came later to distrust all interpretations of
Church history, and all controversy. I thought that
probably the history that was truly illuminating had never
been and never could be written. Historical records tell
of the crises of the Church and of society, and of actions
which illustrate only imperfectly, at best, the principles
on which they are based. To construct the true features
of the Church of the present day from the salient events
of its past history is like estimating a man's character from
the diseases and accidents which have befallen him. There
had been, apparently from the first, a Papal and an anti-
Papal school of thought in the Church, which had between
them produced a state of manifold schism. But which was
the healthy and which the diseased system—which was the
body and which the excrescence? I doubted if any one
could solve the problem, and I was certain that I could
not do so for myself. I therefore decided to regard the
question as an open one ; possibly the truth might lie
midway between the extremes. For my own part, my lot
was cast in the Church of England ; and though much
might be said against the Anglican position, I could not
leave the body in which God had placed me, and the
work I had undertaken in it, without a certainty which I
did not possess, and which seemed to me unattainable.
For many years I remained in this state of mind. I
studied little, being fully occupied with active work, and
I avoided controversy in every form. In my practice
and teaching, such as it was, I almost insensibly adopted
more and more of the methods and principles of the

Catholic Church ; though I refused in this matter to go beyond the line which I had drawn, perhaps somewhat arbitrarily, as marking the limit of loyalty to Anglican formularies.

V. Finally, I came—I could scarcely say how—to see the Church in a new light. I perceived that there was no need to go to history, or to disputed points of theology. The Church, if it existed at all, was a living body, and must be sought for and tested as such. It could not, on its own principles, be subject to decay ; it claimed perpetual youth in virtue of our Lord's promises ; it must stand or fall by what it is to-day. Our Lord had intended the Church to be recognizable by all, learned and ignorant alike ; it was to be a city placed upon a mountain, a light shining in the darkness. It might, indeed, need practical reform on its human side from time to time, but it could never forget, or deny, or obscure the truth into which it was guided by the Holy Ghost, and of which it claimed to be the divinely appointed witness and teacher. Thus a Church which depended for evidence of its genuineness solely or mainly on historical research and learned argument was proved by that very fact to be no Church ; and a Church which was uncertain as to the extent of the revelation committed to it, or which failed to teach what it held to be Divine truth, by positive declaration on the one hand and by condemnation of error on the other, must equally forfeit all claim to be considered.

It is obvious that these considerations must be fatal to any form of Anglicanism ; and equally obvious that they point unequivocally to the Catholic Church as the only divinely accredited authority in religion. If theory is set aside, and regard is had only to contemporary facts, it is obvious again that the Catholic Church alone among all Christian societies bears the four notes of the Church visibly impressed upon her. She alone is everywhere, and goes into the whole world, preaching the gospel to every creature, as exercising her certain right and duty ; she alone can claim continuous solidarity with the Church of the Apostles ; she alone has an ideal of sanctity, and holds it up before the world in the multitude of her canonized members. And as to doctrine, the question as to the true Church must be decided before doctrine can be brought to any test. The Church is the pillar and ground of the truth, and the true doctrine must be that of the true Church, not *vice versâ*. To test the claims of the Church by the truth or falsehood of her teaching is to prejudge the whole matter, and would imply that revelation is either non-existent or superfluous.

Further, I saw that the Catholic Church was an institution that would work as no other would. It alone had authority which sufficed for the guidance of its members and for the due combination of its various forces. I perceived that though the possession of this authority was not of itself a sufficient evidence of the validity of the claims of the Catholic Church, yet its absence sufficed to rule all other claimants out of court. The one was a living organism, whose every part gave evidence of its common life ; the others were mechanical engines, more or less skilfully put together, which were unable, and scarcely even pretended, to show anything of that organic development and progressive adaptation to environment which is the surest evidence of life, and without which decay and impotence, such as has already overtaken all non-Catholic religious bodies, is inevitable.

In a word, I saw clearly that the Catholic and Roman Church was not merely *a* Church, or the best Church, but the only Church. If the arguments of Protestants against her were conclusive, the consequence would be, not that some other Church must be held to be the only true one, or a better one, but that there is no Church at all. But those arguments are not conclusive—they are answered as often as they are put forward ; and since the Roman Church was so evidently the true Church, that is to say, the only genuine form of Christianity, what should hinder me from accepting her explanations ? Surely nothing.

Many things taught by the Roman Church would, *à priori*, have appeared to me improbable. But since she teaches them as certain, being what she is, I felt that I could, and must, accept them as certain.

I had for long been conscious that my standing-ground in the Anglican Church was a very narrow one. But to be dissatisfied with Anglicanism is one thing ; to believe in the Catholic Church is quite another. So long as I could not make an act of faith in the latter, I necessarily clung to my foothold, slight as it had become in the former. No other refuge was open to me, strongly convinced as I was that individualism in religion is absolutely contrary to fundamental Christian principles. As soon, however, as I saw the true position and character of the Roman Communion, Anglicanism ceased to exert any influence over my mind. As a system, it seemed to shrink to nothing and vanish before the light of truth ; and I had no choice but to make my submission to the authority of the Church.

MRS. E. SCOTT STOKES,

NEW STANSTEAD, PURLEY, SURREY.

[THE following is by one who was brought up as a strict Anglican, but whose faith in holiness, and as a consequence, in God Himself, was much shaken between the ages of twenty and thirty. She has been a Catholic over three years.]

The need of a trustworthy and authoritative guide for oneself and for one's children, in facing the daily problems of life in all its relations, led me, at first by slow unconscious degrees, but later by rapid strides, to the following conclusions. Faultily expressed I know them to be, but they are the convictions by which I hope to stand and to be judged, not here alone, but hereafter also. They are these :—

I. The Catholic Church has the longest and the widest experience in philosophical and practical dealing with every problem of human life, public and private. To briefly substantiate this assertion, it needs only to point out that the theologians of the Church have for centuries been occupied with the philosophical aspects of faith and unbelief, of holiness and sin, as they affect the intellect and as they influence the heart. The Catholic clergy, regular and

secular, undergo a severe training, based on the teachings
of these centuries, for their duties in the confessional—a
training without parallel elsewhere. These duties bring
them in contact with all the so-called most modern problems
of the day :—the innumerable difficulties, for instance, that
beset the married life, the celibate life, and the much-
trodden yet unmapped country that lies between.

II. The uncompromising morality of the Catholic
Church, encompassed and pervaded at all costs by the
broadest and humblest charity, appears, in my judgment,
to be nearer to the spirit and teaching of Christ in the
Gospel than that of any other Christian communion.

The truceless war with sin, the lifelong endurance,
shown perhaps more often in sustaining a dreary siege
against temptation from without and within, than in
pitched and eager battle against the invigorating foe—this
on the one hand, and the meekness of charity to sinners,
well-nigh beyond and against all reason, on the other—these
are characteristics of the men who have the care of Catholic
morals which can hardly be known till the convert has spent
some time under their rule. But sufficient becomes discernible to make a mother recognize that the hearts and
minds of little children may here best find both grace and
discipline. And so it is. The joy of Christmas, the glory
of Easter, the wonders of the Incarnation, the unbounded
generosity of the Passion—imprinted by the use of the
rosary and by the habitual practice of other devotions
flowing straight from the fountain-head of faith—evidently
stir and expand many a child-heart with quiet and simple
enthusiasm which outlasts the changes and chances of life,
and is often only brightened by the fires of temptation.

Nor is this all. The foundations of the family life, and its very existence, depend upon our fidelity to the teaching of Christ Himself.

Many among us who are not Catholics cling, thank God! no less firmly than ourselves to Christ's doctrine. But they cannot make a lasting and effectual stand (neither can any save the infallible Church) against such infringements of God's law as man by custom or enactment chooses to sanction. For the children's sake and for our own, it is good to embrace and to hold fast by that religion which ennobles and sanctifies love in every relation, and which raises aloft the standard of modesty, simplicity, and charity. The Catholic Church holds the estate of virginity to be holier and higher than the estate of marriage ; but none the less she holds the estate of marriage higher and holier than do any outside her communion who profess and call themselves Christians, or who aim at ethical perfection.

III. The authority of the Pope and of the Councils of the Church, that authority to give dogmatic definition of the truth concerning God and His purposes, past, present, and to come, of which we speak when we call the Church infallible, seemed to me to be in no degree illogical or spiritually improbable. The definitions themselves may, being spiritually discerned, seem strange or even foolish, or again over-wise, to the natural man. But that the revelation of God, instead of ceasing should be expanded and developed, albeit in language no longer actually inspired, is no monstrous or incredible thing in a Church to which the gift of the abiding presence of the Holy Ghost Himself was emphatically assured. And once this presence, this revelation, be granted, there is no question of hesitancy to work in a dock parish, and, my degree taken in classica honours, had entered a theological college. I begge‹ the Principal to send me to that parish in all England where he thought I should be best grounded in parochia‡ work. He chose an immense parish, where severa‡ churches, and some ten curates, are under one vicar.

I set out on my career as the guide of souls. I soon found that my Church had not provided me with suitable armour or weapons. I could manage a savings bank. arrange a school treat, and other similar things. But that is not direction of souls. Helpless misery soon filled my own soul. Our pulpits rang each with a different doctrine. I asked myself, "What, then, did Jesus Christ teach?" My Church sounded an uncertain note, and I, the guide of others, could not guide myself.

Deep was my distress in visiting the sick and dying. The Protestant delusion which passes for " Faith only," but is not Faith at all, shut out from their souls the sense of sin. Our pulpits fostered this self-righteousness. My vicar, preaching on the "Mother of Jesus " in his vast church, taught us she was "no better than any respectable girl in our town." There is, then, no such thing as sanctity. How could I hope to raise my flock to higher things, whilst they were authoritatively taught that there are none?

I knew not that the missing weapon was the Sacrament of Penance—that two-edged sword which pierces to the depths of the soul. I knew not the health so often brought to the sick body by the Sacrament of Extreme Unction, as promised in Holy Scripture ; or, if that may not be, the strength and comfort given to the departing

soul. I knew not the treasures of Divine Love containec
in the True Sacrament of the Holy Eucharist.
    In my distress I sought my vicar. He, I think, saw
the real difficulty, and wished to turn it. His advice was
in visiting the sick poor, to place camphorated flannel in
my book ; I could then "recollect myself" in its pages
and combat the odours. Unsatisfied, I sought my
senior curate. He advised me to explain a Scripture
text. "On my second visit ? " I inquired. "Read
another." But we had "Bible-readers " for this. · I sought
a fellow-curate, a popular preacher. He said, "Pilate
asked, What is Truth ? " and appeared to think the
question was yet unanswered.
    During my distress, July 1878, the Anglican "Epis-
copate" met at the Lambeth Conference, and in their
"Pastoral Letter " implicitly approved what, in the Holy
Scriptures and the early Church, is called heresy and a
great evil, but, by Protestants, a virtue and the "*right* of
Private Judgment." They made no claim to the indwelling
of the Holy Spirit to guide them in the way of Truth.
    And now a friend sent me a little book.[1] Plainly, if its
statements were true, the "Church of England" had no
standing ground. I refer to the acts and claims of the
early Popes—*e.g.* of St. Leo the Great and St. Gregory
—and the manner in which those claims were admitted by
patriarchs and councils, Eastern and Western alike. The
"Church of England" professes to mirror the doctrines
and practices of the early Church. If, then, the early
Church admitted the Papal claims, the "Church of

---

[1] "Lectures on Ritualism," No. vii., by Father Gallwey, S.J. Burns
and Oates.

England" is plainly the veriest pretender ever set up by man to impose on his fellow-men.

I therefore resigned my charge, and devoted myself to the search for the Apostles, whom Jesus Christ sent to *teach* the whole world, and with whom He promised to dwell unto the end of time.

I consulted others, High and Low. I found few with any knowledge of the subject. A leading idea was, "The great Church of the great British nation cannot be wrong." Were, then, the Roman "masters of many legions" right; the martyrs, wrong? They defended an existing state of things; or, hoped "all would come right in the end." Again, one seemed to hear the Pharisees—"But we are so much better than others!" The catch-phrase, "You leave a pure for a corrupt Religion," satisfied many. But which *is* the pure Religion? And what means has Jesus Christ instituted to keep it pure? Some, plainly, had "married wives" or "bought farms," and therefore could not come. "And they began all to make excuse."

A leading Suffolk rector came to prove to me that "Rome has erred." He had two proofs. (1) He had once seen in the lanes a man, surely a Jesuit, who seemed tipsy. (2) The Church teaches that the Blood of our Lord is really present at Mass; yet she calls it "the Unbloody Sacrifice." I said quietly, "There is blood in my hand, but you would not call it a bloody hand." He said he had thought me a serious young man, but now saw I was an impertinent fellow, and closed the interview.

Dr. Littledale's book, "Plain Reasons against joining the Church of Rome," gave me a push. It was approved by all parties in the "Church of England." I found it a shameless mass of untruths, misrepresentations, and misquotations. I said so in the public press, and quoted from p. 48 : "It is impossible to find any serious warning against this danger and sin [*i.e.* of image-worship], much less any frank prohibition and condemnation of it, in any popular Roman Catechism or manual of doctrine." I then quoted seven answers from the authorized English Penny Catechism. The first five ordain the worship of the one, true, and living God, and forbid the worship of false gods or idols, and the giving to any creature whatsoever the honour which belongs to God alone. The last two, 188 and 189, regulate the use of Christian images : " We should give to relics, crucifixes, and holy pictures an inferior and relative honour, as they relate to Christ and His saints, and are memorials of them." " We may not pray to relics or images, for they can neither see, nor hear, nor help us."

Dr. Littledale replied : " I simply repeat over again my words, ' It is impossible,' etc. If my readers will look at the Penny Catechism, they will find my charge proved —that is, that the impression which is intended " [note the insinuation] " to be made on the mind of the child, is that there is practically no way of breaking the Second Commandment, except by being a Pagan outright ; and that no hint of any abuse of the kind being possible for a Christian is to be found." He added, " I have shown in my book that Catholics really do pray to pictures and images," and offered to correct any error in his book which might be brought to his knowledge.

I replied : " I can only say, that apparently no human

powers *could* 'bring an error to his knowledge ;' . . . otherwise he could not have failed to observe, that the very practice he adduces in his letter—that of praying to a picture or image—is categorically forbidden in those passages."

To conclude : I found the Catholic Church the Church of the New Testament.

1. She alone truly reverences it. She alone, sole heiress of the Jewish Church, chose out and arranged the books of the New Law. She alone preserved them down the ages. She alone to-day combats fearlessly for the preservation of their meaning and integrity ; alone, as her Divine Master, unmoved by the passing ideas of the world, and by fear of results.

The "Reformers" came not to Holy Writ as disciples, but as judges ; and would reject all that gainsaid their new religion: The judgment of Solomon must again decide between the two claimants—the one prepared to suffer all, if only the object of her love be safe ; the other prepared at once to sacrifice the object of pretended love, if only her enemy be spited.

2. Our Lord and His Apostles taught Catholic principles. The early Christians were Catholics heart and soul.

I found that the "Church of England" was not in earnest when it claimed to restore primitive Christianity. Its true aim was, if possible, to satisfy both sides.

I found that the presentment of the Protestant "Reformation," taken on trust by pious Protestants, is a myth ; that its agents and its methods were not marked by the seal of sanctity, the seal of Divine approval.

I remarked a general parallel between the refusal of

the Jews to consider the credentials offered by our Lord, and the refusal of Protestants to listen to those presented by the Catholic Church. The objections raised by the Jews against our Lord and His mission are those thrown at the Church by Protestants. I noted the same contemptuous certainty, and the same *à priori* prejudices.

I remarked that Protestantism has not applied its dissolving principles to the affairs of this world—*e.g.* commerce, politics, the army or the navy—and has, a few sectaries excepted, only pretended to do so in matters of religion.

To prefer to the Church certain chief aids of the " Reformation " and their work, is to cry again with the Jews—

" *Not this man, but Barabbas.*"

The Rev. W. O. SUTCLIFFE, M.A.,

St. John's College, Cambridge; Master of St. Edmund's House, Cambridge.

BROUGHT up as a child after the Evangelical way of thinking, I gradually became more "High Church," but it was not until I was within a year of taking my degree at Cambridge that the idea of the claims of Rome being even possibly valid entered my head. At that time I read a pamphlet by Father Gallwey, S.J., on "The Position of St. Peter in the New Testament." This was a revelation to me; I saw the meaning and importance of passages of the Gospels which had been familiar to me from childhood, but for that very reason, if for no other, had not impressed me before.

I was now struck by the great chain of passages bearing on the Petrine claims: Simon when first called by our Lord receiving from Him the promise that he should be called Cephas, "rock," Peter (John i. 42); Simon, at the calling of the Apostles, being specially mentioned as the first—"The names of the twelve Apostles are these: The first, Simon, who is called Peter" (Matt. x. 2); Simon receiving his name Peter and our Lord's promise that the

Church should be built upon him—" I say to thee, That thou art Peter; and upon this rock I will build My Church, and the gates of hell shall not prevail against it. And I will give to thee the keys of the kingdom of heaven " (Matt. xvi. 18, 19). A passage in St. Luke's description of the Last Supper seemed to me very striking, where our Lord said to St. Peter, " Simon, Simon, behold, Satan hath desired to have you, that he may sift you as wheat: but I have prayed for thee, that thy faith fail not: and thou, being once converted, confirm thy brethren " (Luke xxii. 31, 32). I was impressed by the fact that our Lord, while saying that all the Apostles would be tempted, promised to St. Peter alone the commission and the grace to strengthen the rest. Finally, St. Peter, after such preparation, received his commission ; the Good Shepherd being about to leave this world, commended His flock to the care of a man, and that man was Simon Peter: " Feed My lambs ; feed My lambs ; feed My sheep " (John xxi. 15-17).

It seems to me now striking, but I do not know that I noticed it then, that the Key-bearer of the House of David gave the keys to St. Peter ; He Who is the Foundation, than which no other can be laid, made St. Peter to share in the work of supporting the Church when He called him Rock ; and the Good Shepherd committed His whole flock, lambs and sheep, to the care of St. Peter.

From this time the claims of the Catholic Church were continually present to me. For about a year I did not pay close attention to them, as I was occupied with preparing for my tripos ; but during the twelve months succeeding, I was free, and gave much time to the study of the question. I considered the objections and the difficulties; the objections, for example, which are made to the Catholic interpretation of—"Thou art Peter, and upon this rock," and that which may be drawn from the fact that St. Paul withstood St. Peter to the face.

My early training and prejudices naturally provided me with difficulties, and Dr. Littledale's book, "Plain Reasons against joining the Church of Rome," which was recommended to me by clergymen on all hands, was a perfect storehouse of objections. However, this book finally helped me to become a Catholic; for knowing Latin and Greek, and having access to the best libraries, I was able to test his statements, with the result that I was horrified at what seemed to me his extraordinary misrepresentations or misunderstandings of the passages he quoted.

In course of time other reasons appeared to help to convince me of the claims of the Catholic Church; for instance, the great argument that the New Testament teaches that the Christian religion is to be preached to men *with authority*, and that they are bound to receive it under pain of eternal condemnation. Our Lord said to the Apostles, "Go ye into the whole world, and preach the gospel to every creature. He that believeth and is baptized shall be saved; but he that believeth not shall be condemned" (Mark xvi. 15, 16); and, "Going, teach ye all nations: . . . teaching them to observe all things whatsoever I have commanded you: and, behold, I am with you all days, even to the consummation of the world" (Matt. xxviii. 19, 20). But the Apostles to whom these words were said were soon to die, whereas the promise was to endure to the consummation or end of the world ; hence, I argued, the command and the promise were made, not only to the Apostles then living, but to their successors. Again it is written, "The gates of hell shall not prevail against it [the Church]" (Matt. xvi. 18) ; and, "The Church of the living God, the pillar and ground of the truth" (1 Tim. iii. 15).

From these passages and others, such as Luke x, 16 ; John xiv. 16, 17, 26 ; xvi. 13 ; xx. 21 ; Gal. i. 8 ; Eph. iv. 11–14 ; Heb. xiii. 17 ; 2 Cor. x. 4, 5 ; and all those, too, in which heresy and schism are spoken of as sins, it seemed clear that our Lord intended to found a Church with authority to teach and the promise of His perpetual assistance, and I could find this Church nowhere but in the Catholic Church. Those Churches of the East which are separated from Western Christianity could not appeal to me as representing the universal Church ; and other Christian bodies did not even profess to do so, Anglicans admitting that Roman Catholics and Eastern Orthodox are part of the Church, and other bodies, such as Wesleyans, Baptists, and Congregationalists, claiming the right of private judgment for the individual, as indeed do many Anglicans.

Again, it followed from the above passages that the Protestant principle that the Church had erred was untrue. But following the history of the Catholic Church back into the past, I found no break in its continuity from the beginning ; I found no point at which it could be said to commence except the Day of Pentecost ; it seemed clearly the continuation of the Church of the first centuries. Therefore as the Church cannot fail, but is the pillar and ground of the truth, the Catholic Church to-day had the same authority as the Church in the lifetime of St. Peter and St. Paul.

In the course of this year of consideration, I went to France to see Catholicism at home; for it seemed better not to visit Catholic churches in England, on the ground that the Branch theory might possibly be true and the Anglican Church a true branch of the Church, but there could be no objection to my visiting a sister Church. I spent six weeks in the guest-house of the Benedictine Abbey of Solesmes, and while there received a remarkable letter from an Anglican clergyman to whom I had spoken about my new ideas in England, and to whom I had written from the Abbey. He had no pastoral relation to me, but I had consulted him once or twice on matters of conscience besides the Roman claims. He explained to me afterwards that he had understood that I wished him to direct me, and thought that in France I had placed myself "under Roman instruction," but admitted that "we clearly misunderstood one another with reference to our mutual position." He wrote as follows: "God knows, I would a thousand times rather persuade than command you, but I must no longer delay lest I share in the guilt of any sin you may thus commit. In the name of God, therefore, and by the authority of our Lord Jesus Christ, entrusted to me through the English branch of the Catholic Church, I solemnly enjoin you to leave according to your first intention, and to take no further step whatever until after seeing me on your return. . . . Let me hear of your obedience soon." As I had never been taught that the Anglican clergy had any such authority, I naturally held that this command had no binding force whatever on me.

After my return to England, I consulted various other Anglican clergymen, including four well-known men, but none of them changed my growing convictions. Six or seven months after my return I asked to be received into the Church, and soon the doings of the Anglican Church became to me like the sound of waves falling on a distant shore.

J. E. T.,

BARRISTER-AT-LAW.

I WAS brought up amidst the narrowest of Evangelical surroundings, with few or none of the nobler elements of the older teachers of that school. But I was not influenced, save in the way of repulsion, by any clerical teaching in boyhood. At school I read a good deal of the Greek Testament, and especially the Epistles to the Romans, the Galatians, and the First to the Corinthians. At an early period I revolted from the Sabbatarianism which was made a chief article in the Christian Faith. I was attracted by the ideals of voluntary poverty and virginity, and I discovered in the First Epistle to the Corinthians a doctrine of the Real Presence. Certain newspaper controversies affected me, especially that between Dr. Pusey and Lord Sydney Godolphin Osborne ; but my interest was mainly academic. I was struck by the unfailing grace and courtesy of Dr. Pusey ; but I read little of his writings, and was never impressed by him. At Oxford, in the late sixties, I read the "Christian Year" diligently, and many of Newman's sermons. These and the "Lyra Apostolica" impressed me greatly. But I was not for any length of time a High Churchman, and have never been what may be termed a "clerical." In my later time at Oxford I was led philosophically by Mill, and thought his examination of Hamilton convincing. I imagined myself to be a Utilitarian, though the bent of my mind must have been far otherwise, as I remember an intimate friend's taking me to task for defending the theory. I used to go and hear Monsignor Capel sometimes, and was much taken by the argument that the Church was a σῶμα—a living organism ; not an εἶδος, or mere aggregation of particles or individuals. The real bent was perhaps indicated by the first book I ever took out of the Union Library, Butler's "Lives of the Saints," though I have read little of that book or any other lives of saints. For the last year or two at Oxford, and for some years after leaving the University, I was distinctly an agnostic. But throughout I took pleasure in Plato—the "Republic" and the "Theætetus" particularly. The preference, in the former, of justice and suffering over injustice and success, in combination with the statement in Newman's "Anglican Difficulties"—ridiculed, if I remember rightly, by Thirlwall—that the Catholic Church deemed the smallest venial sin as incomparably a greater evil than any physical catastrophe, immensely affected me. Certainly I owe more to Newman than to any one else, and among his books most to the "Grammar of Assent," the "University Lectures," "Loss and Gain," "Callista ; " but far above the others (of which a word presently) to the "Essay on Development." But I was repelled by his "Sermons to Mixed Congregations." Ward's "Nature and Grace" powerfully affected me. I was led to read it by Mill's reference to it in his "Hamilton."

From the practical and political point of view, Sir James
Stephen's " Essays in Ecclesiastical Biography " did much
to lead me to the Church ; and, even in boyhood, the often-
quoted remarks of Macaulay (in his essay on " Ranke's
Popes ") on the Church's power of utilizing every form of
enthusiasm whereby what in the Church of England
degenerates into a Joanna Southcote, is elevated in the
Catholic Church to a St. Theresa, had their effect. But
the last operative cause (speaking humanly) was my reading in succession, some years after I had left Oxford,
Butler's " Analogy " and Newman's " Essay on Development." The latter I still hold to be the greatest of Newman's writings. His " Letter to the Duke of Norfolk " also
greatly influenced me.

I have here dealt merely with what I read and thought
before I entered the Church. But for myself, then as
now, the alternative in the world of thought is the Church
versus Agnosticism or rather Nihilism, with its inevitable
Pessimism and Materialism ; and, in the moral and practical sphere, between the presence *versus* the absence of a
perpetual witness for righteousness against brute force, and
individual as well as national selfishness. If the Church
were not what she claims to be, she must have been
swept away long ago as a ridiculous anachronism. I
remember marking, in one of Goldwin Smith's lectures,
the prophecy that the end of the century would see the
disappearance of the Papacy. But the Papacy has not
yet vanished.

THE REV. O. R. VASSALL,

OF BALLIOL COLLEGE, OXFORD; A PRIEST OF THE CONGREGATION OF
THE MOST HOLY REDEEMER, ST. JOSEPH'S, BISHOP'S STORTFORD.

THIS paper was written in 1878, when the author was still an undergraduate, shortly after his own conversion, in the form of a letter to a friend, who subsequently became a Catholic and a priest. After the lapse of years he feels that he should say very much the same now to any one who, like himself and his friend, was already convinced of the Godhead of Our Lord Jesus Christ and of the truth of the religion which He revealed to men. The letter is therefore reprinted as originally written.

ON WHAT AUTHORITY DO I ACCEPT CHRISTIANITY?

I.

If I am not to accept Christianity *as a whole*, as taught by the One Catholic Church in union with St. Peter's See and on her evidence, *on whose testimony* am I to take it?

1. If on the testimony of the Bible and the Fathers, by whom are they to be interpreted?

2. If interpreted by myself, on what testimony is the person that cannot read to take it ? and (at least so far as regards the Bible) what becomes of St. Peter's warning that "no Scripture is of any private interpretation " ?

3. And are we not all bidden to receive the kingdom of God as little children ? but is it the part of a little child to interpret a vast number of difficult and ancient documents for himself ?

4. But if I am to accept Christianity on the testimony of the Bible and the Fathers, as interpreted by the nineteenth-century Church of England, why am I to accept this authority ?

5. Is it not a primary principle of the reformed Church of England that "as the Churches of Antioch and of Alexandria have erred, so hath the Church of Rome erred," and that, therefore, by a parity of reasoning, so may the Church of England err ?

6. Is it not another primary principle of the reformed Church of England, that as a matter of fact she *did* once err in various important matters (*e.g.* the authority of the Pope, and that "fond thing," as she now terms it, "the Romish doctrine of the Invocation of Saints ")? If, then, the Church of England thus grievously erred for (at the very least) a thousand years, what warrant have I that she cannot err now ; why should I trust her now ?

7. Again, to which of the authorities or sections in the Church of England am I to listen ? for is it not a fact that the Church of England, in its desire to be "comprehensive" and "national," admits all variety of contrarient beliefs and teachers to exist within its pale ?

8. Is it not also clear, that any body which claims to

tell me what Christianity is, must exist throughout the wide world to authoritatively deliver to other men the *same* message? but is not the Church of England merely a local or at best a Pan-Anglican body? Therefore if the Church of England be the Divine interpreter of revelation, it must follow that men, *e.g.* in France, cannot get the perfect message, but must needs, at best, put up with a "spurious Gospel."[1]

9. Will the history of the Establishment of the English Church as a body distinct from Rome in the reigns of Henry VIII. and Edward VI. bear investigation? Is there not some point in the contrast that the contemporary historian develops between the pure Spouse of Christ formed out of His Sacred Heart, and the Church re-formed from the vile lusts of a tyrant and his courtiers? Again, how can honest men who believe in "Sacerdotalism" bear to read the history of the reign of Elizabeth, with its butchery of more than two hundred priests for the crime of saying Mass, and yet accept Elizabeth and Parker's Church as the teacher of Divine truth?

10. But if I am to believe Christianity on the authority of the "Undivided Church," why am I to "hear the Church" before the Photian schism (or any other date you may name), and forget that obedience is better than sacrifice for ever after? Also, who is to tell me, in case I am unlearned, what the "Undivided Church" really taught?

11. But if I am to accept Christianity as taught by

[1] The absurdity of supposing that there are, as it were, several editions of Christianity (one to be used in England and a second in France, while yet a third is required for Russia, and another for the peculiar use of those uxorious people termed "Alt-Catholics") is surely transparent.

the "*Ecclesia diffusa*"—the term used by some High Churchmen to express the united authority of (1) the Eastern Churches, (1) the Catholic and Roman Church, (3) the Church of England and Ireland (?)—on what principle, I would ask, are these hostile bodies thus brought together by individual members of one of them ; and how, moreover, is it possible to learn what a thing is from three teachers who all contradict each other, who have not, and never have had, or so much as wished to have, a common voice, and who in no assignable respect illustrate the Apostolic assertion that "we being many are one Bread " ?

II.

But why should I not accept the testimony of the Catholic and Roman Church ?

1. The Fathers at the Council of Chalcedon cried out, "*Petrus per Leonem locutus est.*" Why am I to be forbidden to believe them ? Why am I to be forbidden to believe St. Ambrose when he says, "*Ubi Petrus, ibi Ecclesia*" ? Why am I to be forbidden to submit myself to the Shepherd to whom our Blessed Lord when about to leave this world committed all His sheep and all His lambs ; for whom He prayed specially that his faith should not fail, and to whom alone He gave a new name, and the keys of the kingdom of heaven ?

2. I profess in the Creed that I believe the Church of God to be One, and to be Catholic ; as a matter of plain fact, is there any Christian body which is one, and which is universal, save the Roman Church ? It was probably at the first Eucharist that Christ prayed that His Church on

earth should be by its visible unity a plain sign to men of the unity of the Godhead (St. John xvii.). Am I seriously to believe that the prayer of my dying Lord has been unanswered? If there is one thing on which the great Apostle St. Paul insists, it is the absolute necessity of unity. *"Corpus unum, sicut unus est Dominus, una fides, unum baptisma."* "Is Christ then divided?" he asks indignantly, when speaking of the deadly sin of schism, almost as if he could foresee the time when "the divisions of Christendom" should be a trite commonplace of discussion. But can any one, on the one hand, pretend that the *"unum ovile sub uno pastore"* is to be found apart from the unity of Rome? on the other, dare any one deny the supernatural unity of faith, of worship, of discipline, among the children of the mighty Mother? As in the Apostles' days, so it is now; Roman Catholics, so far as their creed goes, are undeniably of one heart and one mind.

Next, can any one deny the Catholicity of the Roman Communion? There is no other Church in the world which is not merely national. The Roman Catholic priest alone dares grapple with his Saviour's command to teach *all* nations.

3. I also profess my belief in the Creed that the Church of God is Holy, and that she is Apostolic. Now, with regard to sanctity as a simple matter of fact, *who* is the Mother of the Saints? To look merely at the purely *modern* Roman Church—where, out of her fold, can you find the like of St. Ignatius Loyola and St. Francis Xavier, St. Theresa and St. Catherine, St. Francis of Sales and St. Vincent de Paul, St. Alphonsus Liguori, St. Paul of the Cross, and St. Philip Neri? You will,

I think, search in vain outside the Roman Church for sanctity such as that of the three Jesuits—St. Aloysius, St. Stanislaus, and the Blessed John Berchmanns—as you will search in vain for examples of heroism that may be compared with the martyrs of Japan and of China. Many good and kindly men as the Church of England has in these latter days possessed, who would think of comparing even the best evidences of her highest type of character with, for instance, the saintly Curé d'Ars? With regard to Apostolicity, I am not going now to examine the claim of the Anglican Establishment to that note of the Church; but I presume, at least, that no one would think of denying it to the Church of Rome.

4. If I apply St. Augustine's test as to the true Church, and ask which Church is called "Catholic"[1] in popular parlance, what answer do I receive? If I ask "the British Church" what I am to do, shall I not be told, in the words of the Council of Sardica (A.D. 347), "to refer to the head, that is to say, to the See of Blessed Peter"?

5. If the Church is, as St. Paul teaches, the "*columen et firmamentum veritatis*," and *if* the doctrines of the Real Presence and the Sacrifice of the Altar be truths,

---

[1] The term "Catholic" is to-day as generally understood in Constantinople, St. Petersburg, or London, as in Vienna, Paris, or Rome. The schismatic Greek Church may call itself "Orthodox;" but the title "Catholic" it has never ventured to arrogate to itself (for *it*, at least, is no *sham*). A certain party of recent growth in the English Establishment, it is true, loudly proclaims itself "Catholic," or "Anglo-Catholic;" by the outer world, however, this school has been known successively and according to its various phases, as "Tractarian," "Puseyite," "Ritualist" (its designations as shifting as its principles), but "Catholic" never. That title still is, as it ever will be, reserved for another and very different Communion. In this matter of names we may fairly say, "*Securus judicat.*" The world knows at least who's who. For St. Augustine's words, see Appendix.

which, as a matter of historical fact, is the Church that has been "the pillar and ground" of these verities, and which is the Church that has by an almost consistent tradition rejected them?

6. Has any *adequate* explanation from the non-Catholic point of view ever been so much as offered, of the growth, perpetuity, and ever-vigorous life of the Roman Catholic Church—of that organic Society which Lord Macaulay admitted to be, in his judgment, the most remarkable phenomenon presented by the history of the world? Are not the very vicissitudes of her fortunes, and her constantly recurring and unparalleled triumphs over every difficulty which has temporarily threatened to bar her way, the very strongest proof that she alone it is to whom it was promised that the gates of hell should never prevail against her; as also the most magnificent witness to the Divinity of Him Who (at a time when she existed only potentially) promised her that Divine aid which should enable her to perfectly accomplish her supernatural mission, even unto the end of the world?

7. Finally, are not the reasons which are usually given for not submitting to the Roman See either sentimental or baseless? Sentimental, surely, is the unwillingness to disbelieve in the efficacy of "sacraments," that after all depend on the validity of Orders, which latter hardly any one has ever recognized save those who lay claim to them, and which must, therefore, at the best, be purely hypothetical.[1] And are not those reasons which are

---

[1] It can hardly be necessary to say that Catholics believe that God often gives to those in good faith grace *with* (and not *through*) the Anglican ordinances.

not sentimental baseless? That is to say, have not a host of candid inquirers, who were all originally strongly biassed against Rome, examined them carefully and found them one by one fade into thin air? Such inquirers as Schlegel, Newman, Manning, Wilberforce, Allies, Oakeley, Ward, Faber, Coleridge, and many others, can hardly *all* be dupes, nor can they be classed amongst wilful deceivers. As *the Evidences of Christianity are all when examined equally evidences of Catholicism*, so may we not leave to Voltaire or to Rousseau, and, alas! to many free-thinking Englishmen in our own day, the two-edged sword of scepticism, which (originally directed against the Catholic and Roman Church) is but too surely meant by the unseen and diabolic hand which guides the blow to pierce the personality of Christ our Lord, to sap the very foundations of Christianity, to lay low the belief in the Incarnate Son of God Himself.

"Too late have I known Thee, O Thou Ancient Truth; too late have I found Thee, O Thou First and only Fair!"

Appendix.

The following is the language of St. Augustine with respect to the name "Catholic," which is referred to at p. 278 :—

" For inquirers it is enough that there is one Catholic Church, to which various heresies apply different names, while they themselves, as they cannot deny, are called each by their own names. And hence it is given to impartial judgments to understand to whom the name of Catholic, to which all aspire, ought to be assigned." [1]

And, again, when speaking of the reasons which then kept him (reasons precisely similar to those which keep Catholics now) in the Communion of the Catholic Church, he says—

" The agreement of peoples and nations keeps me there; her

[1] St. Aug., De Util. Cred., c. 9.

authority, founded by miracles, nourished by hope, increased by love, strengthened by antiquity, keeps me there ; her succession of priests, from the very See of Peter the Apostle, to whom the Lord after His Resurrection committed His sheep to be fed, down to the present Episcopate, keeps me there ; lastly, this very name of *Catholic*, which, not without a cause among so many heresies, that Church alone possesses—so that all heretics wish themselves to be called Catholics, yet if any traveller were to ask where the congregation meets at *the Catholic Church*, none of the heretics would dare to show him either his own Church or house." [1]

As also St. Cyril—

" The faith has delivered to thee, by way of security, the Article, ' And in One Holy Catholic Church,' that thou mayest avoid their wretched meetings, and ever abide with the Holy Church Catholic in which thou wast regenerated.   And if ever thou art sojourning in any city, inquire not simply where the Lord's house is (for the sects of the profane also make an attempt to call their own dens houses of the Lord), nor merely which the Church is, but where the Catholic Church is.   *For this* is the peculiar name of this holy body, the Mother of us all, which is the Spouse of our Lord Jesus Christ," etc. [2]

How any man who professes reverence for " the Fathers " can acquiesce in his position in the " Church of England," after reading such passages as these, is indeed an intellectual puzzle ; but let *us* always remember that it is through no merit of ours that we have been brought out of our darkness, which was once as dark as theirs is now, and let us without any thought of bitterness say again and again from our heart of hearts, " Rabboni, that they may see ! "

I should now like to add to this letter that I was helped into the Church especially by reading, as a child, a story called " Father Clement " and the Waverley Novels. These books, together with the history of England and of the Crusades, gave me, when very young, an interest in Catholicism which I never lost.   Later on, as a boy of sixteen, I devoured Newman's " Apologia " and his work on " The Development of Christian Doctrine."   From that

[1] St. Aug., Contr. Epist. Man., lib. i. c. 5.
[2] St. Cyril, Jerus. Cat., Lect. xviii. 26, Oxf. trans.

time on I knew in my heart that Christianity and
Catholicism were, in truth, convertible terms. Other books,
such as Milner's "End of Controversy" and Cardinal
Wiseman's Lectures, helped me also; but to Cardinal
Newman I always feel that, under God, I owe my very
soul.

O. R. V.

April, 1901.

The Rev. EDWARD J. WATSON, M.A.,

SOMETIME SCHOLAR OF CHRIST'S COLLEGE, CAMBRIDGE ; CALLED TO THE
BAR IN 1871 ; NOW PARISH PRIEST AT ST. EDMUND'S COLLEGE, WARE.

IF the reasons for conversion to the Catholic religion are
plentiful, the circumstances under which souls are converted
must be almost as various as those of human life itself.
They range, at least, from the lofty and sudden illumination of a Paul down to the simple and lifelong development
of early impressions or of an innate tendency. In any
account of a conversion which, like my own, must be
classed in one of the humbler categories, it must be
difficult to separate the circumstances from the reasons.
Let this excuse me from the charge of egotism or imper-
tinence, if I put into a somewhat autobiographical form my
answer to any one " that asketh me a reason of that hope
which is in me."

The idea of an innate tendency to Catholicism is not
likely to meet with much favour in this country, except
from those Philistines who consider Catholicism synonymous
with evil. Nevertheless I make bold to say, that the
patristic maxim, *Anima humana naturaliter Christiana*,
might as truly run, *Anima humana naturaliter Catholica ;*

283

and, if the fact is not noticeable, it is because education and the second nature (habit) are so much stronger than any religious tendency. Certain it is that children may be brought up Catholics just as easily as Christians in any other sense. Indeed, they take much more naturally and joyously to an acquaintance with the ceremonial, sacerdotal, sacramental systems, and the idea of the authority of the Church, than to the profounder mysteries of the Trinity in Unity, the Incarnation, the Redemption.

Protestant parents seem to feel this when they jealously guard, as mine guarded me, from even the slightest Catholic influence. My convert kinsfolk had not a chance with me. I scarcely knew them; yet no one but had a good word for the saintly-minded priest amongst them, who died young —dear to God, no doubt—and to whose prayers I largely attribute the mercy I have received.

Nevertheless, even in the nursery, probably through some crypto-Catholic nurse, I imbibed some genuine Catholic ideas: *e.g.* the existence of the Pope, and that our Lord called Peter a rock, and that that was all on the side of the Pope,—a seed which grew quite imperceptibly, but which by the time I was sixteen proved to be an ineradicable plant. I was also taken to Farm Street, to a service since identified as Benediction, and was very favourably impressed (whatever the critics may say about some people's ceremonies).

And the atmosphere of a public school, even a day-school, seems on the whole favourable to the growth of Catholic impressions. Hard work, not mere bread-work, obedience, reverence, and an intense regard for truth, are, I believe, relics of the ancient Catholic discipline, and however much a boy may resist them in practice, they must necessarily affect his mind; he feels instinctively that they are the right sort of thing. I fancy that I gave in my adhesion to the theory, and I got some other notions in the right direction from an elder brother (justly held up to me as a reproachful pattern), who, during my earlier years at Merchant Taylors' School, used to come back from Oxford for the vacations full of High-Churchism. He it was who led me astray from St. George's, Blooms-bury, to St. Andrew's, Wells Street; nay, even to All Saints', Margaret Street, and St. Paul's, Brighton. From him I learnt the doctrine of priestly absolution (though it was a very long time before I asked for that grace), and some great notions of the Church of England: "It was for the clergy to speak and the people to obey"—even he laughed at this—and that there were no such beings as Puseyites; and I nearly caught that peculiar squint which looks at things Anglican as though they were Catholic. Also during the last few years of my school life I found that other boys, too, were bitten with the Catholicizing mania, notably Walter Mathews, who, however, died Anglican Archdeacon of Ceylon (R.I.P.). And somehow we got hold of that key to the Thirty-nine Articles known as the *non-natural* interpretation—a blessed euphemism not imparted to us, and not blurted out on the house-tops at any time.

We learnt this important method just in time, for the master of the sixth lectured every Monday morning on the *natural* interpretation. With perfect fairness he would state the Catholic doctrine in question, and it always and instantly commended itself to my mind; as I should say

now, it seemed true and beautiful and lovable.   Nor did
he suspect that we possessed a secret prism which refracted
all his light, and which could be adjusted to throw the
desired hue on any particular article.

So it came to pass that, before I left school, I had
acquired a considerable amount of Catholic doctrine : not
only the orthodox belief on non-contentious truths, such
as the Blessed Trinity, which was established for us at
considerable length as against all the leading heretics,
Arians, Semi-Arians, and others with all their formulas ;
and an orthodox belief in the Incarnation as against
Nestorius and Eutyches (how well I remember that
Low Church clergyman insisting that Mary was not simply
χριστοτόκος but θεοτόκος !) ; but also a belief, Catholic so far
as I knew, in the Real Presence, the Sacrifice, relics,
images, Purgatory, the necessity of good works, and of
grace (with a sneaking sympathy, however, rather becoming
in a scapegrace, for Pelagianism).   Of the Petrine claims
I did not learn much, but I shall not forget the surprise
and scorn with which I first heard that the " rock " is not
Peter, but Peter's confession.

Thus, though my equipment of Catholic doctrines was
meager in quantity and probably inaccurate below the
surface, still Catholicity, as I imagined it, had become my
standard, and even as an Anglican schoolboy I was not
far off having the Faith implicitly.

Among the influences leading me to Catholicism which
have to be classed as sentimental, but are not less powerful
on that account, I reckon first of all Westminster Abbey.
Taught from childhood to admire it, I was deeply impressed with the sacred beauty of the place ; during many

a holiday I fairly haunted it, and, to my schoolboy thoughts, it seemed possible, certainly right, that monks should people it again and quicken it with everlasting song. And then George Herbert, with all his silly Anglicanism, sounded a note, especially in his poems of the Passion, which was entirely unlike anything I heard in any Protestant church, and so affecting that I seem now to recognize it as an echo of ancient love, in his day perhaps not quite forgotten. Thus everything Protestant grew more and more detestable, and especially sermons whenever domestic politics made it necessary "to hear Mass" at St. George's, Bloomsbury! But let me never forget my debt of gratitude to St. Alban's, Holborn, "the most Catholic" church, as it seemed, then accessible. I am still grateful for the relief and delight of the services, for the illuminating joy of so much true Catholic doctrine (though I remember some strange things which would not be said there now), and, above all, for the noble example of the clergy, whose manner of life became my ideal then, and my ideal is not much lifted to this very day.

Such was my religion when I went to Cambridge, and such essentially it remained till I changed it ten years later. Paley's "Evidences" and St. Mark's Gospel helped to strengthen my foundations; but what could a university course do for one whose real object of ambition (never attained) was a light-blue oar, with a degree in the background? Religion was reduced to a crucifix in one room, a statue of our Lady in the other, and occasional visits to St. Clement's, and (my nearest approach to piety) to the pretty Catholic church now so gloriously superseded.

But even in that undergraduate soul there had lain

dormant a half-formed purpose of some day "taking Holy
Orders;" and it was not till the time came to develop it,
that I seriously examined the grounds of the Anglo-Catholic
position in which I had grown up.

At once the Thirty-nine Articles (my old enemies) loomed
large across my path, and I sought a serious method of
getting over them without loss of the Catholic arms, supplies,
and treasures, which were to me of the last importance.
The difficulty (thought little of nowadays) was not one
of my own imagining.   At one pole of Anglicanism, Mr.
Capel Cure (then Rector of Bloomsbury), and at the other
the Rev. A. H. Stanton, of St. Alban's, both kindly warned
me.   I was recommended to read "Forbes on the Thirty-
nine Articles," and I read it eagerly, and Cobb's "Kiss
of Peace," and other such special pleadings, as antidotes
to Harold Browne, and in order to learn how to interpret
the Thirty-nine Articles in a Catholic sense, and to sign
them with a good conscience.   In the same way I balanced
a similar series against those works on the Reformation,
the Prayer-book, and early history which it was advis-
able to read for the Cambridge Voluntary Theological and
the Bishop's Examinations.

With such helps, and the argument *ad verecundiam*, in
view of the many men of high character who had gone
the same way, and the consideration that the Catholic
interpretation was known and tolerated, I made the assault,
and eventually effected my purpose.   Indeed, there seemed
nothing else for it, if one was to be ordained at all.   Had
not Döllinger, I argued (whose "tail was thought to draw
a third part of the stars of heaven"), lately proved Rome
(of which I knew little at the time) to be impossible?

Yes, "we must cling to the See of Canterbury!" High Heaven! how grand it sounded! And all the grander that the occupant was a heretic!

However, I had not been ordained very long, when, being out for a walk one day alone, I met a sly old fox. He used to prowl along the hedgerows near Frome in search of curates. Father Kyan, S.J., a holy old man, set me thinking about Anglican Orders, and, in particular, about the intention of a bishop in ordaining; for I could not but remember that my own ordainer (the then Bishop of Bath and Wells, Lord Arthur Charles Hervey), in a sermon preparatory to ordination, had spoken of Masses for the dead as a kind of crime into which a man might fall if he did not take care, whereas one of my chief objects in getting ordained was to say Masses for the dead. I set to work and read much, if not all, there was then to be read on either side of Anglican Orders. Dr. Lee and Canon Estcourt were my chief counsel for and against, without bringing me to a decision; nor did a letter to the former elicit all the satisfaction I wanted. But the Orders had not been actually condemned, and a wider and deeper question was presenting itself, and was peremptorily demanding an answer. Leaving the Orders in abeyance, I passed to the consideration of the whole Anglican position.

I had long suspected that the Roman theory (as we called it) of unity was the only logical one, and I had arrived at that suspicion by the somewhat circuitous route of the British colonies. If the present Church of England could justify her opposition to Rome as heiress of the mediæval Church, still how in the world could she have

U

jurisdiction in South Africa, New Zealand, Australia, India, Canada? It was futile to talk of the missionary spirit. Missionary spirit for England was missionary spirit for France and missionary spirit for Russia. Priority of occupation or diocesan limitation had never been regarded, nor could they be; and even if they could be sufficient as laws, they would still need an administrator and arbiter. The evangelization of the world brought home to me very forcibly the necessity of, to say the least, a central executive—another road that seemed to lead to Rome.

But we young men (I was still in the twenties) were always being cautioned against trusting to too much logic! There were other forces to deal with. I turned to history, and began a mild course with Robertson as a text-book; but the controversial questions were what I wanted answered. The answers were life or death to me, and I plunged into a perplexing series on either side. Mr. Allies, in his "Church of England cleared from the charge of schism," would have been conclusive, had not his "See of St. Peter" been unanswerable. "Janus," Père Gratry, *id genus*, would have been irresistible, had not the evidence for the Papacy, such as that collected by Colin Lindsay and others, and always turning up, been immovable. Then came a course of Newman, and, entering into the theory of development, I seemed to see the whole Papacy, infallibility and all, as a corollary to Butler's "Analogy."

But the work that settled all my doubts, perplexities, and hesitations was one of a lighter sort. In " Loss and Gain " I found my fears drawn out and marshalled in dire array ;

they pressed me close and pierced me through and through. And then I saw my old bugbear, Catholic subscription to the Thirty-nine Articles, in a light new to me indeed, but true beyond dispute. And what an ugly monster it was !—ugly and monstrous, not because it disclosed itself as a baser piece of quibbling than was ever invented by pettifogging attorney (though that was my ultimate and free conclusion), but because I saw that there is something lower than a quibble, and that is a religious compromise.[1]

Let it be granted that Catholic subscription is no quibble ; let it be supposed that men who really hold Catholic doctrines can sign without a qualm. Yet surely all the world of sense and honesty allows that those same Articles do at least admit of the opposite interpretation. Such astounding propositions, however, are made nowadays that it may be as well to illustrate my meaning. If it is

[1] It is most astounding that the truth of this statement is only now beginning to be recognized outside the Catholic Church. I have a vivid remembrance of hearing, some thirty years ago, a sermon even in St. Alban's in which it was claimed, in perfect innocence, that *res anglicana* (whether church, religion, prayer-book, or what precisely, I forget) was "a compromise." As recently as the autumn of 1898, a thinker of so high an order as the late Duke of Argyll wrote a public letter (?to the *Times*) which drew of course great attention, and in which with all sincerity he congratulated the Church of England on being "a compromise," one of her chief glories. I was immensely surprised and pleased that the *Spectator* repudiated the compliment. I had read that journal for years with the deepest interest, yet had never observed that attitude before. Now there was virtually a seal put on words which I had been allowed to say in the *Pall Mall* twenty-one years before, (may I be allowed to repeat myself?) that "no one can enter into a compromise in religion without being himself compromised." Simple and obvious as the truth is, its recognition by the *Spectator* promised to clear the air, but the pleasing prospect was almost immediately clouded by the substitution of the word "comprehensiveness." If that is anything but compromise in action, on what principle can the comprehensiveness of the English Religion be limited to narrower boundaries than the four seas ?

too much to assume that Article XI., to the effect " that
we are justified by faith only," was intended to teach
Luther's doctrine of justification by "faith alone," still
surely Luther's own words must be patient—at least patient,
I say—of Luther's own meaning, so that a Lutheran *can*
honestly subscribe that Article. The same might be said
of words about the sacraments, which apparently admit
Calvin's doctrine, and which have, quite lately, been shown
to be in Calvin's own words. Similarly of Article XXXVII.
If it is really a mistake to suppose this teaches the Royal
Supremacy, yet surely the attribution to "the Queen's
Majesty" of "the chief government of all estates of this
realm, whether they be ecclesiastical or civil, in all causes,"
saving only "the ministering of God's Word or of the Sacraments," *would* satisfy Henry VIII., or Elizabeth, or Sir
William Harcourt. Again, they who hold that the Church
should everywhere be subject to the State, may surely say
that "General Councils may not be gathered together
without the commandment and will of princes," even
though Article XXI. really means that they *may* be
gathered together without the commandment and will of
princes ; and people who do not believe in the infallibility
of General Councils may surely be allowed to say that
"they may err and sometimes have erred even in things
pertaining to God," even though the plain meaning of the
Article is that General Councils cannot err and never have
erred in things pertaining to God. Once more, if people
believe that the Sacrifice of the Mass is a blasphemy, they
may say that "the Sacrifices of Masses were blasphemous
fables." They who do not believe that Transubstantiation
is a true doctrine *may* say that "it is repugnant to the

plain words of Scripture ; " and if they do not believe that
confirmation, penance, orders, matrimony, extreme unction,
are sacraments at all, they may declare that they " are
not to be counted for Sacraments of the Gospel," and
" have not the like nature of Sacraments with Baptism and
the Lord's Supper." I say such Protestant subscription
is surely admissible by the Articles, even though the
Articles were really and only intended to anticipate and to
promulgate the decrees of Trent on all these matters of
faith. Yes, even though they be traced backward to the
Council of London, which required Wiclif's subscription
to Transubstantiation, or to Archbishop Peckham's injunc-
tions for general instruction (and it is high time for such
research to be made), or if it be shown that they never
have been subscribed, except in a Catholic sense, until
our own time, still I maintain that Protestant subscription
is admissible.

For me it was no mere academic question. The Articles
were not obsolete, nor mere forms ; nor was there any
declaration of authority to overrule the Protestant interpretation. Quite the contrary !—that was the prevalent
interpretation, and they were in full working order, and,
what was worst of all, I had given them my own unfeigned
assent and consent.

Therefore I could not, with some friends, stupidly beg
the question, and say, " The Church of England is Catholic,
therefore her Articles of Religion must be Catholic." If
her Articles of Religion admit Protestantism, *she cannot
be Catholic*. Nor could I agree with another, *Quieta non
movere*. Still less could I say with a third, "I don't care
what they mean." No ! the case was far too serious. I had

agreed, and solemnly, to let the truths I held most sacred be wrested to their very opposites, to a betrayal of the kingdom which is not of this world, into the hands of the civil power—a piece of treachery of which Wesleyans and the humblest Dissenters might make us ashamed.

I had agreed to let the Councils of God's Church be called fallible ; to let the Mass and the Sacraments be shamefully blasphemed, and the most pernicious false-hoods about grace and works be taught with my unfeigned assent and consent. There was no doubt about it. I came in personal contact with clergymen who did such things ; their religion was entirely different from mine, and so for that matter was the religion of many persons in the congregation, and the Church of England gave me no authority to teach them otherwise. The ugly monster was very much alive, and whichever way I turned there was no escape. Did men, I asked myself, make such arrangements in other circumstances of life ? If a man's own character is called in question, does he acquiesce in an ambiguous apology, which leaves it an open question ? Or, if the physician's prescription is illegible, and it is doubtful whether it means sal-volatile or strychnine, rhubarb or Prussic acid, iron or arsenic—the quantities and frequency of doses, too, being obscure—would the patient let the chemist's boy. do his best and take his interpretation of it ? Nay, even in matters of money, would a man invest in a company whose articles of association are so dubious that the directors can carry on any business they like, and as they like, some of them one way and some another ? No, not money, not health, not honour ; only the interests of the Christian faith were to be treated in such manner, and that, so far, as I knew (or know), only by the extreme section of the Church of England.

The genial, kindly, much-beloved Rector of Christ Church, St. Leonard's (Mr. Vaughan), and my chum among curates (John Forbes)—God rest them both!—did their best to console me. But I was past that kind of consolation, and the former was constrained to own that "I had swallowed the Thirty-nine and could not digest them." Most true, and I only had to get rid of them by writing a polite letter to Dr. Durnford, of Chichester, emphatically withdrawing all my assent. And I did so with the sense of having got rid of a disgusting burden. There was no doubt now which way to turn. I soon made an application to Doctor Newman (not yet a Cardinal), and received from him the honour of an invitation to the Oratory. Five days later, in St. Philip's Chapel, the venerable Father, with the assistance of Father Bittlestone, received me into the Church of the crucified and risen Saviour. It was the Feast of St. Thomas the Apostle, and all my doubts were at an end. *Beati qui non viderunt et crediderunt.*

C. J. WATTS, Esq.,

FORMERLY A BAPTIST PREACHER.

On the twenty-first day of June, 1890, I was received into
communion with the Holy Roman Catholic Church, after
having for nearly forty years been associated with the
various Dissenting congregations of this country.   This
may be of no particular interest to others, but, to myself,
it was the great turning-point of my life.   When a man
has passed the age of fifty, he is not expected to make
so great a change without due thought and consideration.
The reasons that led up to such a step I desire now to
set forth, in the earnest hope that others who may be wandering, as I once was, in the wilderness of Dissent and in
the quagmire of private interpretation and of free thought,
may be induced to consider their position, and, after full
inquiry, to find, as I have found, perfect rest and peace
in the "one fold under the one Shepherd."   It is only as the
time of famine and of the hunger of the soul is realized,
and as that dissatisfaction which is engendered by religious
uncertainty is experienced, that any really earnest attempt
is made to arise and to seek for the Father's House, where
there is "bread enough and to spare" for the hungry and
weary soul.

Dissenters, it is well known, have ever regarded Catholic worship, with its elaborate symbolism, as something excessively formal and unspiritual, and they have judged it so from the fact that the free and spontaneous utterances of their own unliturgical services have made them accustomed to such simple modes of worship. To them worship consists of the uninspired utterances of the human mind, expressive of want or entreaty, and addressed to the Divine Redeemer, Who, because of His Divine manhood, feels our sorrows and knows our necessities. Any pretence of priestly interference or anything approaching sacerdotalism is resented by them, and is regarded as a dangerous interference with the mediatorship of our Lord and Saviour (1 Tim. ii. 5). And yet a moment's reflection must surely show that each time a minister in prayer to the Almighty becomes the spokesman or the mouthpiece of others, he is in reality a " mediator " in a far truer sense of the word than he who reads a prearranged and fixed form of prayer which is known and followed by his congregation. It seems to me that it is simply the non-recognition of the fulness and perfection of the present intercessory work carried on by our Redeemer, in pleading the Divine sacrifice of Calvary and its precious efficacy, which accounts in some measure for this strange misapprehension. Dissenters are apt to dwell exclusively on the one offering made on Calvary—an offering made once for all, and never in any sense to be repeated. Their worship consequently lacks the necessary elements of *present* sacrifice, except perhaps sacrifice in the subjective sense, *i.e.* that of a humble spirit and a contrite heart. But I am not using the term in this subjective sense here, but in its true and

generic sense—sacrifice in the sense of a victim offered as
a means of propitiation. I have always found it difficult to
understand how, in the Protestant sense, an act accomplished
nineteen centuries ago could in any way be applied to me
individually so as to be incorporated in my very life, and
how I could thus be said to be made a *partaker of Christ*,
and to *appropriate* Him as *my* Saviour and *my* Redeemer.
Although I tried hard to persuade myself that it was by
faith only that I could appropriate an absent Saviour, and
by faith only share in the merits of His death, I nevertheless yearned for a *present* Saviour, and strained my
ears for the sound of the living Voice saying to me,
" Thy sins are forgiven thee ; go in peace, sin no more."
But with what certainty is this provided for in the Catholic
Sacraments of the Holy Eucharist and of Penance ! I
can give unhesitating testimony on this point, having
known the two states—that of yearning desire, and that of
realized certainty.   The question, therefore, resolves itself
into this : Does the worship of God Incarnate on the
altars of the Catholic Church present a real and true
source of strength to the human soul ?   Is it in its very
nature a means of grace of the highest order, filling the
soul with true joy and with calm rest ?

A correspondent wrote me shortly after I was brought
into the Catholic Church : " What have you found in the
Catholic Church that you did not find among the Baptists ?"
To which I replied, " When associated with my good friends
the Baptists my great wish was expressed in a single line
of a verse often on my lips, ' Dear Jesus, make Thyself to
me a living bright reality.'   And although I cannot but
acknowledge that I often felt a sense of restful repose in

the thought that in some way I apprehended Christ, yet, as compared with my apprehension of Christ now as 'a living bright reality,' it is overwhelmingly in favour of Catholic worship and doctrine." My experience of the Blessed Eucharist is this, that while as a Baptist I had to work myself up into a certain frame of mind and "feelings," in order that I might, as it were, take the Saviour with me to the Supper, I now find the Blessed Redeemer there in His Church waiting to welcome me, and to become mine in a way no language can express. It is an experience to be realized. It has often occurred to me since I have become a Catholic, that if non-Catholics who are in earnest, and who are disposed to inquire concerning the claims of the Church, would but ask themselves the question (a sort of corollary to my correspondent's question): What has any one of the many religious sects outside the Catholic Church got to offer that the Catholic Church does not fully and perfectly supply, and in a far more lasting and definite manner? such a question pondered over and thoughtfully answered would lead, I think, to very excellent results.

I will now quote a passage from Dr. James Martineau's "Seats of Authority in Religion" (p. 169), seeing that it is the testimony of one who is not only a non-Catholic, but also a non-Protestant in the ordinary sense of the term. He says—

"If somewhere among the communities of Christendom there is a sovereign prescription for securing salvation, the Roman Catholic Church has obvious advantages over its competing claimants for possession of the secret. Regarded merely as an agent for the transmission of an historical treasure, she has, at least, a ready answer for all her Western rivals and a *prima facie* case of her own. They have to all appearance quite a recent genesis, their whole tradition and literature lying within the last three centuries and a half; and, in order to make good their title-deeds as servitors of Christ, they must carry it over a period of four times as long during which it was lost, and identify it at the other end with the original instrument of bequest. Her plea, on the other hand, is that she has been there all through; that there has been no suspension of her life, no break in her history, no term of silence in her teaching; and that, having been always in possession, she is the vehicle of every claim and must be presumed, until conclusive evidence of forfeiture is produced, to be the rightful holder of what has rested in her custody. If you would trace a divine legacy from the age of the Cæsars, would you set out to meet it on the Protestant tracks, which soon lose themselves in the forests of Germany or on the Alps of Switzerland, or on the great Roman road of history, which runs through all the centuries and sets you down in Greece or Asia Minor at the very doors of the Churches to which the Apostles wrote? But it is not only to its superiority as a human carrier of a divine tradition that Catholicism successfully appeals. It is not content to hide away its signs and wonders in the past, and merely tell them to the present, but it will take you to see them now and here. It speaks to you not as the repeater of an old message, but as the bearer of a living inspiration; not as the archæological rebuilder of a vanished sacred scene, but as an apostolic age prolonged with unabated powers. It tells you, indeed, whence it comes; but for the evidence even of this it chiefly asks you to look at what it is, and undertakes to show you as you pass through its interior all the divine gifts, be they miraculous gifts or heavenly graces, by which the primitive Church was distinguished from the unconsecrated world. This quiet confidence in its own divine commission and interior sanctity simplifies the problem which it presents to inquirers, and, dispensing with the precarious pleas of learning, carries it into the court of sentiment and conscience, addressing to each candidate for discipleship only such prelimi-naries as Peter or Philip might have addressed to their converts —as if there had been no history between. No Protestant can assume this position; yet he can hardly assail the Roman Catholic without resorting to weapons of argument which may wound himself. Does he slight and deny the supernatural pretensions of to-day—the visions, the healings, the saintly gifts of insight and guidance more than human? It is difficult to do so except on grounds more or less applicable to the reports of like pheno-mena in the first ages. Does he insist on the evident growth, age after age, of Catholic dogma as evidence of human corruption tainting the divine inheritance of truth? The rule tells with equal force against the scheme of belief retained by the Churches of the Reformation; there is a history no less explicit and pro-longed of the doctrine of the Trinity and of the Atonement, than the belief in Purgatory and Transubstantiation. Does he show that there are missing links in the chain of Church tradition, especially at its upper end, where verification ceases to be possible? He destroys his own credentials along with his opponent's, for his criticism touches the very sources of Christian history. The answer of the Catholic Church to the question, 'Where is the holy ground of the world, where is the real presence of the living God?' 'Here within my precincts, here alone,' has, at least, the merit of simplicity, and is easier to test than the Protestant reply, which points to a field of divine revelation discoverable only by the telescope halfway towards the horizon of history. . . . It carries its supernatural character within it; it has brought its authority down with it through time; it is the living organism of the Holy Spirit, the Pentecostal dispensation among us still; and if you ask about its evidence, it offers the spectacle of itself."

This testimony from such a source had a great effect in helping me to make up my mind when I was inquiring into the claims of the Catholic Church, and, together with the lucid teaching of Cardinal Wiseman in his splendid lectures on the Catholic faith, and Cardinal Newman's "Apologia" and the lectures on "The Present State of Catholics in England," and Cardinal Manning's little treatise on the "Grounds of Faith," secured for me not only a ready and implicit assurance that it was God's Church, built upon the impregnable foundation of apostolic truth, which I was about to enter, but also furnished me with very explicit groundwork on which my mind could feel and know that the step taken was both a reasonable and a right one. I had long felt that there was no *via media* between the negations of doubt and the certain assurance of authority. The difficulty had hitherto been to find out this one abiding authority for Divine teaching, and I was forced to the conclusion that, if the concurrent testimony of history, together with the inherent vitality of a Church of nineteen centuries, did not prove the Church of Rome to be that authority, then there was no Church at all in the world, and God had left us all orphans indeed, piteously feeling about in the darkness, "with no language but a cry." Thank God that to me, too, there came the Divine guidance, and that the kindly light of faith dawned on my soul.

I was spending the season of Whitsuntide, 1890, at Stone, in Staffordshire, and one Sunday afternoon I strolled into the Church of St. Dominic and heard an address to the candidates for Confirmation. The priest who gave the address insisted on the presence and power of the Holy Ghost in the Church, it being a Divine organization for teaching the world, and he referred to the sacrament of Confirmation to be administered on the following Thursday as the blessed means by which Divine strength is imparted to the soul for its battle in life. The address was followed by Benediction, a service at that time not only new but exceedingly strange to me. However, I stayed for it, and the force of the thought which it suggested—the presence and power of the Holy Ghost in the Church—so acted upon my mind, that, on the following Thursday, I attended the same church, and witnessed the ceremony of Confirmation, given by the Bishop of Birmingham (Dr. Ilsley). The bishop, in his address, practically repeated what the priest had already expressed on the preceding Sunday. In the course of a few days I returned to London, but the thought of this Divine Presence and Power having a living embodiment in a visible organization I could not shake off, nor indeed did I wish to, and so I put myself under the instruction of a Catholic priest near my residence, with, to me, the happy result that, after forty years' wandering in the wilderness of religious doubt and uncertainty, I at last found rest in the certainty of the Divine unity of the one Church.

In conclusion, I should like to point out that : 1. The right of private judgment, so much belauded and so highly treasured by Protestants, and especially by Dissenters, is practically given up by them when, submitting their individual judgments to some one amongst the many teachers of their various and differing denominations, they are admitted to membership with some distinctive religious body. 2. That with non-Catholics, too, the realization of the deepest religious life is more or less connected with the ordinance and celebration of the Lord's Supper. 3. That the tendency of all non-dogmatic forms of religious thought is towards rationalism. 4. That there is no true religious sense of

rest and peacefulness enjoyed and possessed by non-
Catholics which is not far more really and fully enjoyed by
every devout and earnest child of the Catholic Church. 5.
That the entire testimony of history gives the Catholic
Church the prescriptive right to say: I am the exclusive
teacher sent by God to instruct men in the way of salvation,
and the only custodian of those Divine gifts by which they
can alone find rest and peace for their souls. 6. That the
Catholic Church has not only invariably achieved the most
brilliant victories over human vice and sin, but that it has also
done the most beneficent work in the field of philanthropy
and charity. 7. That there is really nothing good in any
one of the many sects of the Protestant Churches that has
not its source and origin, either directly or indirectly, in
the Holy Catholic and Roman Church. 8. That although
the Bible, and the Bible only, is alleged to be the rule of
faith among Protestants, this rule is almost always supplemented by some more or less defined creed which is said
to be drawn from the Bible only, but for the explanation
and defence of which the particular minister is appointed
and is made responsible.

The Rev. NORMAN WAUGH,

OF ST. ANNE'S CATHEDRAL, LEEDS.

THOUGH heartily in sympathy with the object of this publication, I cannot but feel doubtful as to how far anything I may have to record of my own experience will be either of interest or of use to others.

To begin with, I was not, as so many converts, a member of the Established Church. On the contrary, I had always been taught, what I still believe to be sound sense and good logic, viz. that if the Pope is not the Head of the Church, neither is the King or the Queen of this realm. Under God, I believe that I owed my conversion to the Catholic Faith to the startling originality of certain sections of modern Nonconformity. The idea gradually grew within me that if the doctrines, or rather the views, adopted by a number of the more advanced thinkers among educated and more thoughtful Nonconformists were indeed the reflected rays of Divine Truth, that then not until the nineteenth century had the Word of God been made manifest—and that to the few, and not to the many.

It was this impossible thought which first led me to

examine the claims of the Catholic Church to be the
divinely appointed guardian of and witness to the truths
of revelation. It was then I began to see that Holy
Scripture cannot be made to witness for and against the
same doctrines ; and that, as its inspiration is known only
through the testimony and teaching of the Christian Church,
so the Book and its truths are for ever sealed, unless
rightly interpreted by some time-lasting and divinely
appointed authority.

In my first contact with the Catholic Church I was
startled by what some would perhaps call its modern reality.
I found it difficult to reconcile the received idea and the
simplicity of primitive Christianity with the traditional
magnificence and ritual of the Catholic Church. But
Cardinal Newman's " Development of Christian Doctrine "
reconciled the oak and the acorn. From Newman I learned,
as others have learned, what his Lord and Master Whom
he loved so well had taught in the beginning, in the cradle
and on the cross. I learned that the Kingdom of Heaven,
as in the individual heart, so in the Church as a visible
society, is like unto "the smallest of seeds." And hence
one came to realize that, by a law of its being, vitalized
and made intelligent as it is by the Holy Spirit, the Church
of Jesus Christ must, from age to age, unfold and develop
within itself the mysteries of revealed truth and justice—
adding nothing, taking nothing away ; but putting forth,
according to the needs of nations, the fruits and foliage of
the True Vine.

This idea of development, as inherent in Christian
revelation, took a strong hold of my mind ; but it failed to
remove many difficulties on such subjects, I am sorry to

say, as the necessity of baptism, and Eternal Punishment. Again, Providence placed in my hands Father Faber's "Creator and Creature." Such chapters of this work, as "What it is to be a creature" and "What it is to have a Creator," were a revelation to the reader. To have read them was to understand that all the mysteries of faith are easy of belief when compared with the greatest of all mysteries, the one great leading truth of Christian Revelation. And that mystery is the incomprehensible fact, of which the Incarnation is the proof, that God, though He knows us through and through, loves us; and, though He is all-holy and needeth nothing, desires our love! Thus I came to learn in my own case the absolute truthfulness of Faber's words, in this key to all his works, when he says that "by far the greater number of objections which are urged against Catholic doctrine have their root in oblivion of the respective positions of the creature and Creator."

Now, after the lapse of thirteen years, I have more reason than ever to be thankful for the grace of submission to the Holy Catholic and Roman Church—Catholic in its circumference, and Roman in its centre. From then till now, religion, whether it regard what we should believe or what we should do for eternal life, has been—as it always was and will be—a matter of *fact* and not a matter of *opinion*. For, herein, in these two words, "fact" and "opinion," we have the essential difference between what is taught by Divine authority, and what is offered for our belief as the outcome of private judgment. May the solid realities of the Catholic Faith be the inheritance of all who pray that theirs may be eternal life in the knowledge of the only true God, and of Jesus Christ His only Son! It may be there are some who will read this publication, of which my own contribution forms so small and unimportant a part, who, whilst they pray for this great grace, will do well to remember one of Cardinal Newman's greatest thoughts, contained in two brief lines in his "Dream of Gerontius"—

" It is thy very energy of thought
Which keeps thee from thy God."

A. St. LEGER WESTALL, Esq., M.A.,

AND SCHOLAR OF QUEEN'S COLLEGE, CAMBRIDGE ; LATIN ESSAY AND
COLLEGE PRIZEMAN ; 2ND CLASS CLASSICAL TRIPOS, 1884; FORMERLY
CURATE OF ST. MARY'S, PLAISTOW, ST. MICHAEL'S, BRIGHTON, AND
ST. SAVIOUR'S, CROYDON ; MANOR PARK, E.

MY father was an Anglican clergyman of High Church
opinions ; and home training, inclination, and study combined to make me, at the time of my ordination as an
Anglican, an adherent of the most advanced High Church
school. For several years I worked as a curate, without
the smallest misgiving as to the soundness and consistency
of our religious position. The first shock came to me in
the course of an inquiry, undertaken from interest, not
from doubt, into the early evidence for the Papacy. I had
always taken for granted that the Pope's claim to be the
successor of St. Peter and Visible Head of the Church
rested upon no securer foundation than a dim and precarious tradition. I was therefore deeply moved by the
discovery that the historical evidence was at least as strong
as the evidence for the authenticity of any single book of
the New Testament—stronger far than the evidence for
several of those books. Another severe shock to my faith
in the Anglican position resulted from reading Father

Richardson's little work on the "Catholic Claims," written in answer to Canon Gore. Learning and scholarship lay with Canon Gore, but the victory appeared to me to lie with Father Richardson. If I had read at that time Cardinal Newman's work on "Development," which contained the solution of the difficulties I still felt, my submission to the Church would probably have taken place then, eight years earlier than it actually did. As it was, I did not see how to reconcile the claims and position of the Papacy in the nineteenth century with its position in the fourth or fifth, although I held that the Pope's primacy was derived by succession from Peter, and was not merely due to the consent of the Church. The latter was not the origin of his position, but the witness to it. I was a "moderate Gallican." As time went on I was compelled to abandon the Tractarian appeal to the Primitive and Undivided Church. The latter had ceased to exist for a thousand years. How was her voice to be heard? It was an appeal to documents, to writings, with the individual inquirer as interpreter. How did that differ in principle from the Protestant appeal to the Bible? In so far as it differed it was for the worse. It substituted hundreds of books for a score and a half. The former were to interpret the latter, and the interpretation was harder to come by than the matter to be interpreted. Eight hundred years were to be studied instead of eighty, and private judgment was the real interpreter of each several doctrine after all. I fell back upon the theory that, as three branches of the Church were living and teaching bodies here and now, the Churchman's duty was to believe every doctrine in which they agreed as a matter of faith; and where two were agreed against the third, to regard the matter as still *sub judice*. The chaotic condition of religious teaching in the Anglican Church made her testimony in all matters of dispute difficult to come by, and practically one had to go by the teaching of the Roman and Greek Churches, when they agreed. What was my dismay when I realized that they cordially agreed in the rejection of the Branch theory! They were also agreed that to be in communion with avowed Protestants was to be guilty of Protestantism—that is, of heresy. At this time, too, I began to see that the Anglican Church, as a Church, taught no definite faith at all. By the *Church* I found that Church-people always meant the Prayer-book ; and the Prayer-book not as traditionally expounded and acted on during the three centuries of its existence, but the Prayer-Book as interpreted by the extreme party. To me a Church meant a living body of men, women, and children, and the voice of that body was to be sought in its authorized and official teachers, and in its traditional interpretation of its documents. As far as our official teachers were concerned, any heresy might be and was taught without let or hindrance ; as far as immemorial tradition went, it was, at best, "moderate High Church" —that is, a timid heresy instead of a bold and uncompromising one. Furthermore, the mere allowance of heresy appeared to me to be fatal to a Church.

Matters were in this condition with me, when I suddenly realized that another conviction had taken firm possession of my mind. This was a realization that from the beginnings of Christianity until the Reformation, it was universally believed that the Church was one, in the sense that she was made by God to be One Visible Body or Corporation, incapable of division into warring fragments, and that this was her first or chief mark. One Church, one Faith, one Voice; that was the undoubted and undoubting testimony of all the ages. To teach or to allow two faiths was as impossible as to believe in two Gods; to be divided into antagonistic "branches," each with its own belief, was as impossible as to divide Christ into various antagonistic personalities. That our Lord founded one Society, which was to remain one; that He deposited in her one Faith, and endowed her with the gift of infallibility in order that she might ever teach this and no other; that such a Society still existed, and made these claims, and carried them into effect, and that no other Society so much as claimed the allegiance of the whole world; that this Society was the Catholic and Roman Church, and that her claims were those of the Primitive and Mediæval Church, while the Anglican position was diametrically opposed to both;— all this gradually took possession of me as indubitable truth. How else could we know what the Faith was that He delivered to His Apostles? When I had begun to grasp this as the crucial fact, other difficulties began to disappear. A Church, a visible organization, was the vehicle of God's revelation to man. From her I must learn it. Whether or not bishops are essential to the Church, whether there is a priesthood or not, whether Saints may be invoked or not, whether the Mass is a Propitiatory Sacrifice or not, whether the Pope is supreme or not,—all these questions can be answered for certain by the Church and by nobody else, for none but the

Church has Christ's authority to declare them. A case may be made out for and against any one of these, or indeed any other Christian doctrines ; study might lead one to form an opinion, and on many points the more careful the study the more difficult it is to decide between conflicting opinions. To give a decisive answer is the *raison d'être* of the Church in all ages and for all nations, and the Church in communion with Rome alone claims to do so, and acts on the claim.

Another feature in her seemed to me to point the same way. The Roman Church never stirred from her position. The separated Easterns, or many of them, had three or four times surrendered to Rome, most notably at Florence ; never had Rome surrendered to them. If the Anglican Church were in continuity with the pre-Reformation Church, then, on her own confession, she had agreed with Rome for a thousand years of her existence. The efforts of Church Defence lecturers to prove that the early English Church was anti-papal or non-papal, I regarded with unmitigated contempt. The popular Anglican falsification of early Church history led me to question very seriously the theory that "continuity," in any but an Act-of-Parliament sense, was preserved at the Reformation. It was a waste of time to trouble about Henry VIII. or even Edward VI. ; all had been put right under Mary, and the question, for all practical purposes, was confined to the Elizabethan "settlement." To put in a few words what took me many months, if not years, to grasp, I came to the conclusion that the State destroyed the old Church, and erected a brand-new one on its ruins.

When I had long been trembling on the brink of these

conclusions, the Papal Bull on Anglican Orders was published. I was well aware that the question of Anglican Orders was a very secondary one, and did not affect the questions of schism, jurisdiction, heresy, or the necessity of unity. Still, so habituated was I to being in a state of separation from Rome, that an acknowledgment of the validity of those Orders by the Pope would very probably have delayed or prevented my conversion, illogical as that would have been; indeed, I was quite aware of the fact, and yet allowed the question of Orders to have an undue influence. Probably it was due to the fact that I was a married clergyman with a family, and that the future, in the event of my conversion, looked so dark, that one caught at straws. However, the Pope decided against us, and the controversy that ensued convinced me that the Pope's decision was right. The Holy Father was attacked by Anglican speakers for being unhistorical, prejudiced, talked round by enemies; his arguments were called "shallow," "hollow," "exploded," "founded on fiction," and so forth. To me the Bull seemed a singularly clear and logical piece of reasoning, and in addition to that I had grasped the fact that doubtful Orders could no more be used than if they were certainly invalid. Rome had rejected ours for three hundred years, and now had set the seal upon that rejection; now the case had been tried by a Pontiff of lofty character, great learning, and a singular desire to treat Anglicans with as much indulgence as his duty admitted; then surely the Orders must be doubtful, to say no more. Finally, the study of the Councils of Ephesus and Chalcedon set all doubts on the subject of the Papacy at rest. By that time, indeed, I had come

to the same conclusion by another road, namely, that
the Church alone could give certain information as to
the prerogatives of her visible Head ; and that the Church
in communion with Rome was alone the Catholic Church.
This had become with me a matter of absolute certainty.

For years, therefore, I had been growing nearer and
ever nearer to conviction ; and the Papal Bull, by making
me realize that my daily ministrations were null and void,
forced me to admit a conclusion which I had held, without
realizing it, for a long time.

THE RIGHT REV.
THOMAS W. WILKINSON, D.D., B.A.,
Of Durham University.
LORD BISHOP OF HEXHAM AND NEWCASTLE.

Ushaw College, Durham, Nov. 11, 1900.

MY DEAR SIR,

It is quite true that I once had the misfortune of being a Protestant of the Established sect. I was born in 1825, educated at Harrow, took my degree in 1844, and was received into the Church at twenty-one from St. Saviour's, Leeds, in 1846, where I was supposed to be preparing for the Protestant ministry. I was ordained priest in 1848 from Oscott, where I studied under Dr. Wiseman, the then President and coadjutor Vicar Apostolic of the Midland district of England. Since then I have laboured in the mission in my own native county of Durham until 1887, when I was chosen Vicar Capitular to rule the diocese *sede vacante*, and in July, 1888, was consecrated Bishop. I fear I should find it now, in my seventy-sixth year, very difficult to give you the history of my conversion. I simply owe everything to Newman, "The Tracts for the Times," and generally the Puseyite movement.

St. Saviour's was founded and built by Dr. Pusey. It was opened in 1845. I was present at the opening, and remained there with the clergy till my reception in 1840. Mr. Macmullen and Mr. Haigh, founder and builder of the glorious church at Erdington, were received with me. I have nothing to say of my conversion. God be thanked for it. After fifty-two years of priesthood I can only say that I hardly as yet realize the great mercy God has extended to me, in bringing me out of the darkness of Puseyite Protestantism into the glorious light of the One True Faith, and making me a loyal and loving subject of my Lord the Pope.

I remain, your faithful servant in Christ,

(Signed)   THOMAS WILLIAM,

Bishop of Hexham and Newcastle.

The Rev. D. WILLIAMS,

St. Peter and St. Paul's, Newport, Salop.

I BELONGED to the Anglican Church until I was eighteen years of age. At the age of seventeen I saw, in the house of a Catholic acquaintance, several copies of Duffy's "Penny Lives of the Saints." I read one and borrowed the others. I was very much astonished at the sufferings of the Saints and Martyrs (Catholic) for the Faith. This was all new to me, and made a deep impression on me, and I began to ask questions of our minister, who was a very amiable man. On Sunday he preached a tirade against Transubstantiation, in which he said that all Catholics were *idolaters*. I had never heard of Transubstantiation before. Some time afterwards I ventured to put a question to a gentleman, with whom I was acquainted, on this subject of Transubstantiation. I remember well his friendly smile at my simplicity. He was not offended, he was not astonished, he was not amused, but I thought he was a little pleased when I repeated the question, and when he saw that I was in earnest. He was silent for a few minutes, and then, turning to his bookshelf, he took down Power's "Catechism" in two volumes, and said to me, "I think you will find what you require to know here." He lent me the two volumes. After reading them slowly through, I turned back to the "Holy Eucharist." This I read through repeatedly, until I almost knew it by heart in every detail. My faith in and my admiration for the doctrine of the Real Presence increased daily, and, at the age of eighteen years, I had the great happiness of being received into the bosom of Holy Church.

I have been a Catholic so long a time that I feel a little shyness in answering the question, "Are you a convert?" In compliance with the wish expressed, however, I may say that the above statement is, as far as I can remember, the way by which grace drew me into the bosom of Holy Church, and, although I hope it is in no way detrimental to say so, I feel grateful to the Protestant minister who preached the tirade against Transubstantiation.

Beatæ aures quæ venas divini susurri suscipiunt, et de mundi hujus susurrationibus, nihil advertunt.[1]

[1] "Imita. Christi," lib. iii. cap. 1.

T. F. WILLIS, Esq., B.A.,

Exeter College, Oxford; formerly Curate at St. George's
Mission, London Docks; 53, Caithness Road, W.

Short Summary of Reasons for thinking that the Church of England cannot be the Body of Christ.

I. Does she herself corporately assert, as our Blessed Lord did before Caiaphas, " I am " ?

Is it not clear (when we remember that the Church is not a collection of documents but a society of living souls, and that her true organ of utterance is her episcopate), that so far from asserting herself to be the Christ, she follows John the Baptist's example, who "confessed and denied not, but confessed, I am not the Christ." If she, then, corporately asserts that she is not the Body of Christ, how can I honestly assert that she is ? In other words, if she corporately disclaims these prerogatives, how can I teach that she undoubtedly possesses them ?

II. Submission of judgment in matters of faith, which is a primary necessity in, nay, a very test of, a true messenger of God, seems impossible in the Anglican Communion, because the Anglican Church does not claim infallibility. For to submit absolutely to, *i.e.* to credit with infallibility, one who declares himself fallible is surely unreasonable.

That this submission of judgment is a primary condition of truthfulness in God's messenger, is evident from our Blessed Lord's mysterious sayings even about Himself and the Holy Spirit. "The words that I speak unto you I speak not *of Myself;*" "He that speaketh *of himself* seeketh his own glory;" "He shall guide you into all truth, for He shall not speak *of Himself.*" If even within the Godhead it is in some mysterious way the law of truthfulness that the Person sent does not speak *of Himself*, but acts merely as the organ of the Person sending, how much more must it be an indispensable law of truthfulness in the Church which is the visible Image of God?

Therefore to be compelled to act upon one's own private judgment in regard to the substance of the message to be delivered, is fatal to one's own belief in one's Divine commission. But if we really and truly submit our judgment to the Anglican Bishops and echo their views, we must deny the essence of the Catholic Faith.

III. The most Catholic party in the English Church are now declaring distinctly that they ask for nothing more than toleration alongside of those who teach the exact contrary. Now, that is nothing less than a definite surrender of the proposition that "the Church of England is the Body of Christ." Can they who are commissioned to carry Divine truth to a world which is eternally opposed to God, and are commanded to seal their witness, if need be, with their blood—can they dare to ask for Divine truth to be *tolerated* side by side with its contradictory? Surely to do so is to deny that it is Divine truth. And if it is not Divine truth, it is not truth at all ; it is blasphemy.

Of course, the toleration of which we speak is not physical or civil toleration. It has nothing to do with the enforcement of outward conformity by temporal penalties. But clearly, if we are obliged by the expressions of doctrine, to which we are pledged either directly or indirectly, to hold that he who denies the Real Presence or the efficacy of Absolution can be a worthy communicant or a faithful minister, we are certainly prevented from holding that these doctrines are part of the Faith ; we are pledged to a toleration which is destructive of faith.

IV. The principles on which the separated position of Anglicanism is defended by various adherents are all contrary to Christian doctrine as found in Scripture.

Nationalism, which has been, all through, the theory of the High Church Tories, is plainly anti-Christian, because our Blessed Lord came to destroy all barriers of race, as far as religion was concerned, and to set up one world-wide heavenly kingdom. " There is neither Greek nor Jew, Barbarian nor Scythian ; " " He hath redeemed us *out of* every kindred and tongue and nation." The very idea of a *National* religion as an excuse for schism, *i.e.* as superior and not subordinate to the oneness of the Church, is a return to the pre-Christian state of things.

Congregationalism, which is practically the Anglican system, is the same thing, only narrower. It makes every clergyman a pope to his people, and throws to the winds the One Faith and One Body, even if it retain the One Spirit and One Lord and One Baptism. Also it involves " heaping to ourselves teachers."

Private Judgment in the individual as to the doctrines of faith is narrower still, and makes every one the whole Church to himself. It makes all faith impossible, except faith in oneself. And every defence of the Anglican position that can be given seems to rest ultimately upon one of these three principles.

V. It seems impossible to reconcile the oath of the Royal Supremacy, which all Anglican clergy take at their ordination, with a true belief in the Divine nature of the Church, especially when we look at it in the light of history and of present events.

VI. The *animus* of the Established Church as exemplified in the bishops seems so like the *animus* of the religion of ancient heathen Rome, which was an established form of worship in the interest of morality and good order, but tolerating every form of religious *belief*, *except* the special doctrines of the Incarnation, which it regarded as " blasphemous fables and dangerous deceits."

VII. The wording of the Thirty-nine Articles bears a most suspicious resemblance to the wording of heretical formulæ in all ages by its adoption of equivocal expressions. Heretical formulæ have always been designedly *inclusive*, Catholic formulæ designedly *exclusive*—the object of Catholic formulæ being to secure inward peace from doubt at whatever cost of outward ; and the object of heretical formulæ being to secure outward peace at whatever loss of spiritual peace and inward clearness of faith.

VIII. All through the Anglican system there is such a resting upon civilization, and worldly position, and respectability and public opinion, that it looks much more like a religion designed to make this world comfortable, than the religion of Him Who was born in a stable, and Whose kingdom is not of this world, and Whose maxim was, " He that loveth his life shall lose it."

IX. Anglicans are separated from the main body of Christendom, and their connection with our own pre-Reformation Church is very slight and indirect. It does not appear from Scripture that Apostolical Succession *alone* constitutes a valid ministry. All the early schismatical bodies had that. The thing which is evident from Scripture is, that our Lord gave the Holy Ghost unalienably to a Society, not to individuals, and that he who separates from that Society loses the gift.

X. The oneness of the Church in which we, in the Nicene Creed, express our belief must be an outward oneness (though of course it is an inward oneness too), because it is by this oneness that she *bears witness* to the initial truth of revelation, that God is one. Her *visible* oneness is the outward witness in creation to the invisible oneness of God. She preaches by her existence much more than by her words. It is by being the Image of God, the Body of God, the outward visible form which God designs to wear when He comes among His creatures, that the Church reveals God to the intelligences of men and angels. And, therefore, so far as the Church gives up her outward oneness she is untrue to the first object of her existence, viz. revealing the oneness of God : she practically denies the first article of the Creed, " I believe in One God."

Again, the grammatical position of the word "one" in the third part of the Creed implies that it signifies an *outward* oneness. "Catholic" and "Apostolic" both express characteristics of *outward organisation* rather than of inward essence, therefore it is natural to infer that "one" at least inclusively denotes a characteristic belonging to the same category.

This outward oneness of the Church Anglicanism seems by its position to deny.

XI. It is quite clear that the Ritualists are the only persons in the Church of England whose teaching and practice can be reconciled with Scripture and the faith of the primitive Church; but their position seems to be indefensible by reason of their want of submission to their bishops, which submission is the one most essential thing in the organization of the Church.

It is true that their attitude towards the bishops is remarkably parallel to our Blessed Lord's attitude towards His ecclesiastical superiors when He was on earth; but in order to accept this as a justification of themselves, they must assume that the cases are parallel, *i.e.* that they are commissioned by God to found a new order of religion foretold in the prophets. This was the assumption of the Montanists, of Luther, of the Irvingites; but how is it consistent with Catholicity?

BERTRAM C. A. WINDLE, Esq.

M.A., M.D., D.Sc., F.R.S., F.S.A.

PROFESSOR OF ANATOMY AND DEAN OF THE FACULTY OF MEDICINE,
UNIVERSITY COLLEGE, BIRMINGHAM.

*(Reprinted from an article in the " Weekly Register " of
March 9, 1900, entitled " Books that have influenced me.")*

THE most important book to me was that which eventually brought me into the Catholic Church, now more
than seventeen years ago. I am not going to narrate the
incidents which led to that important step, interesting
though they are to me. I think, perhaps, the first book
which turned my mind in that direction was Cardinal
Newman's "Apologia," a work which has doubtless had
the same effect upon many other minds. I read this
merely because, after I had taken up my residence in
Birmingham, I used to hear the Cardinal much spoken of,
and wanted to know something about him and his views.
But it was not the "Apologia" which brought me into
the Church. Interested in the question, I read many
other books, but without arriving at a conclusion. And
here I will break off for a moment to express my wonder
that at this stage of my life I never came across that
remarkable book, "The End of Religious Controversy."

Why it was never placed in my hands has been an unceasing source of marvel to me from the day when I first read it, some years after I had entered the Church, down to the present moment. Well may Dr. Salmon admit that our case is there presented in the most "taking" way. "Convincing" I should rather phrase it, for the solid learning, the irresistible logic, the grave earnestness of that work seem, to me at least, to be unequalled by any other book on the same subject. The solemn adjuration on the closing pages must certainly give pause to any one who thinks upon such subjects, and many are the men and women who can, from the bottom of their hearts, re-echo its closing words, "You will no sooner have sacrificed your own wavering judgment, and have submitted to follow the guide, whom your Heavenly Father has provided for you, than you will feel a deep conviction that you are in the right and secure way; and very soon you will be enabled to join with the happy converts of ancient and modern times in this hymn of praise: 'I give thee thanks, O God, my enlightener and deliverer; for Thou hast opened the eyes of my soul to know Thee. Alas! too late have I known Thee, O ancient and eternal Truth! too late have I known Thee.'"

But the book which was largely instrumental in making a Catholic of me was Littledale's "Plain Reasons against joining the Church of Rome," which some friend sent to me when I was embarked upon this course of reading. And certainly, after I had finished it, the step which I had previously regarded as at least possible, seemed now to be one which could never be taken. Whilst in this frame of mind I was walking down a street, idly looking into the shop windows, when, in those of a Catholic Repository, I saw a book which purported to deal with that of which I was then thinking. I went in at once and bought it, and I suppose I need hardly say that it was "Catholic Controversy," by the dear friend of my later days, Dr. Ryder. I carefully studied both these books together, and, baffled by their discrepancies, determined to select some dozen or so of the most divergent passages, and consult the original authorities with a view of seeing for myself which of the two authors was speaking the truth. A few hours spent in a good library stocked with the Fathers, sufficed to answer the question, and to enable me to make up my mind. The die was cast, and I was received into the Church. And now I should like to know which of those two books made a Catholic of me? For I should probably never have read "Catholic Controversy" if I had not first read Littledale. It is an interesting question to me, and I cannot solve it.

H. G. WORTH, Esq., M.A.,

St. John's College, Oxford ; formerly Chaplain to St. Katharine's
Anglican Convent, Queen's Square, Bloomsbury.

COWARDICE OR CONVICTION: WHICH IS IT ?

(A Letter to an Anglican Friend.)

My dear Friend,

You say that it cannot be right to leave the Anglican Establishment in order to join the Roman Catholic Church. You say that by so doing one leaves the Church of one's baptism, and acts in a most cowardly way, inasmuch as duty is neglected.

I will endeavour, in a brief manner, to answer these and like objections which have been raised.

In the first place, we are baptized into the Catholic Church ; therefore, so long as we remain Catholics, we cannot be said to have left the Church of our baptism. If the Roman Catholics and Anglicans are all members of the Catholic Church, the latter do not desert the Church by joining the communion of the former. If the Anglicans are in heresy or schism, then any one of them who submits to the Catholic Church, *returns* to the

Church of his baptism. If the Anglican is the only
true Church, then, of course, any one leaving her is leaving
the Church of his baptism ; but I do not think that many
High Church people, at any rate, deny that the Roman
Catholic is at least a portion of the Catholic Church.
We cannot be baptized into a particular diocese or
province, but into the whole Church.

You say, in the second place, that it is cowardly to
run away from duty.

This is perfectly true, if we are sure that it is our
duty to remain. If we are *sure* that a cause is right,
then it is cowardly to desert it ; but what if we think,
on due consideration, that the said cause is wrong ?
Then it would be cowardice to stick to it, as we should
be either lacking in courage to own ourselves wrong, to
face the contempt and disapproval of others, or we should
be guilty of sheer obstinacy.

The plea that we are bound to remain where God
has placed us seems plausible, but it might be argued
against Church-people by Dissenters with equal force.

Suppose any Dissenting preacher felt a drawing
toward the Church of England, would any Anglican
consider that he would be justified in remaining where
he was because he happened to be placed there, and did
so much good, and he felt that if he deserted his followers,
they might fall away into utter irreligion and indifference ?
Would such an one be considered justified in remaining
because he might thus in time bring many with him into
the Church ?

To argue in this way is practically to say that God
cannot possibly dispense with a particular individual, and

any one who says this of himself is open to the charge of conceit, in thinking that *he* is necessary to accomplish God's work. If God calls us to leave any position, we should be wrong in refusing to do so, however much good we might feel we were doing.

All agree that evil must not be done for the sake of good. If we feel that we are in a false position, we must leave it, otherwise we are tempting God, and instead of benefiting others, are probably encouraging them to blind themselves. If we neglect what seems like a clear call from God, we may lose His grace. We may *think* we are converting the souls of others, but are in great danger of losing our own.

If any one leaves the Church of England, *believing in her claims*, and joins the Catholic Church merely because he *prefers* the latter, he is acting upon sentiment only, and is guilty of self-indulgence. Anglicans as a rule believe that converts have no higher motive than this, even in the case of those whom before they have esteemed and held in honour. However high-principled, logical, and honest they may have been considered previously, no sooner do they "go over to Rome," as it is called, than they are credited with being weak-minded, sentimental, dishonest, and self-interested.

But, surely, Anglicans who remain should in all fairness allow that those who leave them are actuated by motives as honest as their own.

Abuse is no argument, and is generally only resorted to by those who are doubtful of their own position.

But it will be urged that Dissenters are in a different position from Anglicans, inasmuch as the latter have valid

Orders, whereas the former have not. Even if this were the case, we must remember that the possession of Orders is not everything ; the Monophysites and Donatists had valid Orders, but they were not considered as part of the Catholic Church : the former on account of their heresy, the latter because of their schism.

Before we proceed, we must consider what schism is. It is the being cut off from the unity of the Church.

The popular Anglican idea of schism is that it consists in being out of communion with any particular Bishop. They say that Roman Catholics in England are in schism because they are not in communion with the Anglican Bishops, whereas Anglican chaplains in France are in schism because they are not in communion with the Catholic Bishops of that country.

We must not, however, forget that, according to the teaching of the ancient Fathers, those who communicate with schismatics are guilty of schism. If, therefore, the Roman Catholic Church is schismatic in England, she is guilty of schism everywhere. The Pope and all the foreign Bishops who are in communion with him, recognize the Roman Catholic Bishops of England, not the Anglican ; if, then, the former are in schism, the Pope and all the Bishops and people who submit to him are in schism also.

On the other hand, it is clear that, on Anglican principles, the English Bishops in Canada are schismatic, therefore the Anglican Bishops who are in communion with them are in schism.

Now, the result of this must be either that the whole of Western Christendom is in schism and the Greek Church is the sole representation of the Catholic Church, or that there is no Catholic Church remaining anywhere ; or else either the Roman Catholic Church or the Anglican Church is schismatic.

If we accept the first two alternatives, we are forced to own that the gates of hell have prevailed against the Church, and that our Lord, when He said that this should never come to pass, spoke falsely. As also when He said that the Holy Ghost would guide the Church into all truth.

It remains, then, for us to consider, that either the Roman Catholic Church or the Anglican is schismatic, and that *everywhere*. Which is it ?

St. Cyprian tells us that those who are not with the Bishop, are not in the church. (Ep. Florentio, lxvi.) These words are quoted by Anglicans, to prove that they are not in schism because they are in communion with their Bishops.

But when there are two rival Bishops, as in the case of the Bishop of London and the Archbishop of Westminster, how can we tell which is the lawful Bishop ? One must be in schism.

St. Cyprian would tell us that he is the lawful Bishop who has not separated himself from his fellow-Bishops.

"For a man could not hold the episcopate, even after his episcopal ordination, if he should fall away from the body of his fellow-Bishops and from the unity of the Church." (Cyp. Ep. Antoniano, lv.)

The Anglican Bishops are not in communion with the Catholic Bishops throughout the world, therefore they are in schism.

St. Augustine, writing against the Donatists, says:
"You are with us in baptism, in the creed, in the other
sacraments of the Lord, but in the spirit of unity, in the
bond of peace—in fine, in the Catholic Church itself, you
are not with us." (Ad Vincent Rogat, Ep. xciii.)

Some people seem to think that schism is an unimportant matter; such should study St. Augustine's writings
against the Donatists. He shows that they might have
sacraments and the true doctrine, but being cut off from
the Catholic Church by schism they could not have
salvation.

"Extra Ecclesiam Catholicam totum potest præter
salutem, potest habere honorem, potest habere sacramentum, potest cantare Alleluia, potest respondere Amen,
in nomine Patris, et Filii, et Spiritus sancti fidem et
habere et prædicare, sed nusquam nisi in Ecclesia Catholica
salutem poterit invenire." (St. Aug. Sermo ad Cœs. Eccl.
plebem, vi.)

"Outside the Catholic Church you can have everything
except salvation; you can have honour, the sacrament,
you may sing Alleluia, and answer Amen; you may hold
and preach the faith in the name of the Father, the Son,
and the Holy Ghost; but nowhere except in the Catholic
Church can you find salvation."

If we consider this we see at once how absurd is the
commonly received idea among Anglicans that it is
wrong to attend Roman Catholic services in England,
but right when we are abroad, because if the Roman
Catholic Church is in schism in England, she is guilty of it
everywhere, and it would therefore be a sin to communicate
with her *anywhere*.

Anglicans say that the Pope is not the centre of unity, but that each Bishop is in his own diocese. But we may well ask, How can the faith be preserved entire in each diocese? If Bishop differs from Bishop, who can remedy this? Metropolitans may do so in their province, but who can unite the Metropolitans? On Anglican principles each province could have a different religion.

We sometimes hear Anglicans quote the Gallicans, and especially Bossuet, as if they were in their favour; but if these insisted on anything, it was on the necessity of communion with the see of Rome as the see of Peter: how, then, can those who consider such communion as not necessary gain any countenance from them?

Others, again, say that they are willing to accord to the Pope such supremacy as was accorded to St. Gregory the Great, and they lay great stress on the fact that the latter did not approve of the title "Universal Bishop." They seem, however, to ignore the fact that St. Gregory rebuked the Patriarch of Constantinople for taking to himself this title, but that of his own prerogatives he speaks in these words: "I know not who is not subject to the Apostolic see" (St. Greg. Epist. lib. ix. Epist. lix.).

Again, we must remark that if the Roman Catholic Church is not right in making the claims she does, she is heretical, for, be it remembered, the supremacy of the Pope is not considered merely a pious opinion, but an article of faith. Any body of men which insists on the necessity of believing what is wrong is an heretical body. If the Pope is not what he claims to be, he is an arch heretic; if the claims of the Roman Catholic Church are not Divine, they are diabolical.

If these claims are Divine, why do not Anglicans submit to them ? If they are not, why attempt to make terms with such an imposture ?

The Holy Spirit is the soul of the Church ; He cannot teach different doctrines in different places.

The Roman Catholic Church teaches the supremacy of the Pope as a dogma. The Anglican says this is not true. Both cannot possibly be right.

Many people seem almost to disbelieve in the Visible Church, though strangely enough they see the absurdity of this when Dissenters claim to be part of the Church. They take their stand on their Orders ; but Holy Scripture would seem to speak even more of the necessity of *jurisdiction* than of Orders. What authority can any Anglican quote for insisting on the latter and depreciating the former ? A Dissenter is more consistent in ignoring both than an Anglican in insisting only on one.

If the Church is visible, surely its unity must be visible. The Church is a body ; it cannot, then, be cut up into pieces. Can we imagine that our Lord would have founded a body which should become a mangled corpse, or a kingdom which should be divided against itself ? Could the Holy Spirit be said to abide in the Church always if it fell into such utter confusion ?

But you will say, "Many of us believe all Catholic doctrines, therefore we are Catholics ;" but, in spite of this, you are in visible communion with heretical bishops and priests : how can those be Catholic who communicate with heresy ? Others say, "We must have patience and wait ;" but what are they waiting for ? If they are in a state of schism they have no right to remain in it. Communion with the Holy See is either necessary or not. If it is necessary, every one who understands this should enter into communion at once, and not wait in a state of wilful schism under the plea of bringing others out of it later; if such communion is not necessary, then the whole Roman Catholic Church is wrong, and union is not to be desired. If both are wrong in some things, then our Lord's promises were vain, and the gates of hell have prevailed for centuries.

You say that in many Churches you have all that you need, all Catholic doctrines are preached and customs observed; but in how many Churches is this the case? Is this done with the approval of the authorities of the Anglican Church? If they do not forbid such, they do not encourage, and if in one Church the Bishop allows Catholic doctrines to be taught, he allows what you consider heresy to be taught in probably the next parish.

Can a Church be considered Catholic which, by its chief authorities, sends one man who teaches the Sacrifice of the Mass, Priestly Absolution, the Real Presence, and another who denies all these?

How can an Anglican know what to believe when he hears one doctrine in one pulpit, another doctrine in another, and sometimes even contradictory teaching in the same?

How can any one fancy that he is a Catholic when, if he believes aright himself, he is in communion with those who teach the most flagrant heresy, and all the Fathers taught that to be in communion with heresy was to incur the guilt of heresy?

This is what Newman, Faber, and others felt. You say

z

perhaps that, had they remained, things would have improved. It is far more likely that nothing of the kind would have happened because, had they remained, they would have been untrue to their convictions, and consequently in bad faith. God doubtless does bless the work done by many Anglican clergy, because they believe in their position; could we expect Him to do so in the case of any who should refuse the light, or who, by refusing to face the question, make for themselves a false conscience, and who, though doubtful themselves, should yet try to dispel the doubts of others?

If you consider what I have said, you will, I think, allow that logic is on my side; and even those who do not see their way to enter the Catholic Church will admit, that those who do so may be led by conviction rather than cowardice.

D. S. Y.

IT is difficult for one untrained in the art of committing self-analysis to paper to give an accurate account of the steps which led one from a home of deep Protestant piety to the Catholic Church.

I must begin by enrolling myself among the many who owe the grace of conversion, under God, to the example and writings of the late Cardinal Newman.

I can never remember having much difficulty in accepting any Catholic doctrine so soon as I found it could be held (as I thought) in the Church of England ; in fact, on understanding each and all, it was natural to me to accept them.

Hence, when at Oxford I began seriously to think, whenever a side was to be taken in a matter in dispute, *e.g.* the doctrine of the Blessed Sacrament, I always took the view held by Rome ; for here, at any rate, was an intelligible doctrine held on intelligible authority.

At the time of my ordination to a title, the appeal concerning Anglican Orders was being discussed, and I had hopes that ours would be recognized as valid. When the Bull actually appeared, hard work in an East London parish, and the absorbing needs of those living there, directed my mind from its importance.

But a change of life gave me more time for reading and reflection, and I gradually discovered that the arguments advanced against the claims of the Holy See might, with equal reason, be advanced against many doctrines I held already, and even against Christianity itself.

For instance, there is quite as much evidence in Scripture and in the Fathers for the Vatican teaching on the Chair of Peter as there is for the Divinity of the Holy Spirit, Grace, and Original Sin.

Again, the wars of Latitudinarian, Erastian, and Evangelical thought, which had passed over the Church of England since the Reformation, while they were unparalleled in her earlier history and in the rest of Catholic Christendom, made me wonder whether we of the " Catholic Party" were not also upon the crest of a wave, which before long might be succeeded by an abyss of proportionate magnitude.

The study of the history of the Reformation confirmed these ideas, and about the same time I learnt that Apostolic Succession was in itself no guarantee of orthodoxy, which brought me up to a most important point of view, namely, that the validity of Anglican Orders was not the central question. Nestorianism, Jansenism, and the Old Catholic Movements concreted this abstraction.

Before arriving at this I had often believed that doubts were a temptation, but now I saw that not only was investigation allowable, but it was a duty.

The absence of the Teaching Voice is got over on the High Anglican theory by an appeal to the living Church

in diffuso; whatever is taught by East and West together
is Catholic: " I disbelieve in the Papal claims for the same
reason as I believe in Purgatory, Invocation of Saints,
and Prayers for the Dead." But this canon broke down
over our Orders ; the East has done nothing to ratify
them ; the Western Patriarch had condemned them ; even
the Jansenists had refused to have anything to do with
them.

This enabled me to get over the greatest difficulty of
all: the denial of what had been the centre of one's
spiritual life—the Mass and the Confessional. It appeared
to me in this light: For the sake of your people whom
you love it would be better to undergo the risk of reordina-
tion, than to try and bring them to sacraments which are
unrecognized by your own standard of authority (viz. East
and West), and therefore extremely doubtful.

And yet other men held out—one's dearest friends,
and those to whom one had looked up for counsel. Some
of those who had submitted were not near to them in
sanctity ; it must therefore be fancy, scruples, etc., etc. So
I returned to hard work ; but not for long, for Newman's
words, which he put over his sermon " Ventures for Christ,"
were always with me—

> " Est alius locus, quo te transferam,
> Noli timere ne perdas :
> Dator ego eram, custos ego ero." [1]

So I made the venture, and found them true.

[1] " I have another place to which I would lead thee ;
Fear not any loss that this step may entail :
I gave thee all thou hast, and I will keep it for thee."

The Rev. BENEDICT ZIMMERMANN,

PRIEST OF THE ORDER OF OUR LADY OF MOUNT CARMEL, AND SUB-
PRIOR AT 47, CHURCH STREET, KENSINGTON.

BRIEFLY, I may say that I received an education which
was excellent in every respect, my father being a clergyman of the Swiss Church, and a dean. The Swiss Church,
though officially committed to the doctrines of Zwingli and
Calvin, was almost entirely in the hands of the Rational-
ists, and my father was the only clergyman of note in the
largest town of his country who upheld the belief in
the Blessed Trinity, the Divinity and Incarnation of Our
Lord, and the Inspiration of Holy Scripture. He fought
all his life for these fundamental dogmas, and suffered
severe persecution in their defence. It stands to reason
that his children could not remain ignorant of the discussion going on within the Church, and which for many
years formed the almost exclusive topic of conversation.
But a Church divided on points of such importance could
hardly be expected to command our love or respect.
Represented by a man of my father's piety and dignity,
it was worthy of sympathy; but, then, he was but one
against many of quite a different calibre.

In addition to the dogmatic indifference of the Church, its utter want of resource made a deep impression upon me. At an age when one requires help and encouragement, I found nothing of the sort. At school I sometimes got into trouble, but there was no one to whom I could have addressed myself for advice. My father often said to me afterwards, "Why did you not come to me, than whom you have no better friend upon earth?" But one feels sometimes shy in the presence of one's nearest and dearest friends. Moreover, I knew that he would have referred me to the Bible. Now, I felt already at that time, that we do not want the Church to tell us what is right and what is wrong, because our conscience tells us that clearly enough, but that we want her to stretch out her hand when we *are* wrong, and to help us up again. And in this the Swiss Church failed.

About this time, I began to take an interest in Catholic matters, such as the Liturgy, Monastic Orders, and, finally, Dogma. What struck me most was the promise made by our Lord to St. Peter, "Thou art Peter," etc., which puts the difference between the Catholic Church and the Protestant into the clearest possible light. Again, the Culturkampf, then raging in Germany and Switzerland, proved to me the justice of the Catholic cause and the palpable injustice of the Governments. Notwithstanding all this, I was not aware whither I was drifting (though I believe my parents were less shortsighted), until one day an intimate friend wrote to me: "You cannot imagine how glad I am to see that you have found that salvation is only to be obtained in the Catholic Church." This was a revelation to me, and came home like a shock; but it also taught me not to beat about the bush, but to pursue my aim steadily and systematically. Unable to bear the strain any longer, I was received, at the age of eighteen, unknown to my parents. This was a mistake, for not only did the fact become public property within a few weeks and give rise to recriminations in the daily papers, and, in short, cause no end of trouble, but it also put me into a false position which my extreme shyness prevented me from setting right.

Having spent some years in France, and afterwards filled a not unimportant office in my native country, I at last came to England, where I entered the Order to which I now have the honour of belonging.

A temporary estrangement between my family and myself, caused by my conversion and by my subsequent entrance into a Religious Order, disappeared entirely after a while, when it came to be better understood that such steps could not have been taken for any motive but the highest of all—the clear promptings of conscience.

THE END.

PRINTED BY WILLIAM CLOWES AND SONS, LIMITED, LONDON AND BECCLES.

Printed in the United Kingdom by
Lightning Source UK Ltd., Milton Keynes
142431UK00001B/11/A